Relax and Renew

With the
Kundalini Yoga and
Meditations of

YOGI BHAJAN

by

GURURATTAN KAUR KHALSA, Ph.D.

&

ANN MARIE MAXWELL

```
A COMPREHENSIVE SOURCE
OF STRESS RELEASE TECHNOLOGY
     Yoga Sets & Meditations for
          Neutralizing Tension
          Tranquilizing the Mind
          Balancing the Emotions
          Dealing with the Past
             Dispelling Fear
    Setting the Physical Plane in Order
      Healing Depression & Drug Abuse
           Restoration of Memory
            Banishing Negativity
             & Rejuvenating the
           Eyes, Nerves and Spine,
     Adrenals, Kidneys, Liver & Colon

       Plus a Handy Section for
         RELAXATION & RENEWAL
       IN A JIFFY (2-11 MINUTES)
```

CONCEPT, ORIGINAL TEXTS, EDITING, MARKETING
GURURATTAN KAUR KHALSA, Ph.D.

ILLUSTRATIONS, LAYOUT, COVER, RESEARCH, TRANSCRIBED TEXTS, EDITING
ANN MARIE MAXWELL

RELAX & RENEW 1-888029-04-8

Copyright December 1988
by Gururattan Kaur Khalsa, PhD
and Ann Marie Maxwell

The Yoga of Fullfillment

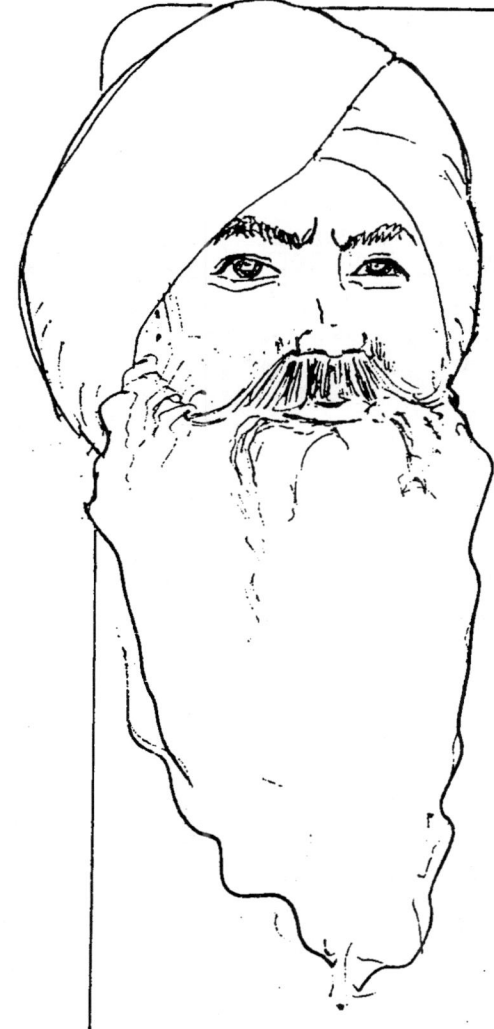

We are tapping, through consciousness, the supreme consciousness. It is not a subconscious process. There will be no miracles, tricks or denials, for this is the Yoga of Fulfillment.

The first qualification for Kundalini Yoga is that you seek that awareness. We will not get rid of the ego. For that matter we will not deny anything in us. We will expose the ego and make it universal!

We will not sit and beg softly that we may someday find God. We will make ourselves so strong and pure that God must come and look for us and look after us. God has got your number...let him look you up!

Yogi Bhajan
SIRI SINGH SAHIB BHAI SAHIB HARBHAJAN SINGH KHALSA YOGIJI
1971, Santa Cruz, California

Acknowledgements

We are grateful to Mark Lamm and Michael Turner for their graphic and detailed notes, and especially to Dyal Singh (Harvey) for his encouragement and support. A special thanks to Paula Stegen for typing, editing and a lot of hard work. And to all our brothers and sisters on the spiritual path, whose selfless dedication to sharing this truth makes such a book possible.

We are also indebted to The Kundalini Research Institute and the "3HO" Foundation, and to M.S.S. Vikram Kaur Khalsa for permission to use their previously published material.

May you all be blessed with the love, peace and prosperity of the Aquarian Age, and with happy, healthy and holy lives!

DISCLAIMER

The sets and meditations, with their titles, comments and claims, have been as accurately transcribed as possible from original class notes. They are not offered in substitution for medical advice or treatment. Best results will be obtained by exercising common sense and body awareness along with a proper diet and relaxation, in the practice of Kundalini Yoga, and supplementing it with a regular exercise program.

Additional copies of this manual can be obtained by writing to

YOGA TECHNOLOGY PRESS

Gururattan K. Khalsa
913 D Avenue
Coronado, CA 92118
(after August 1999 check address by phone or email)
(619) 435-3390   email: rattanak@concentric.net

Your comments and suggestions are welcome!

DEDICATION

To Yogi Bhajan,
Father of Kundalini Yoga in the West,

and to his students,
the teachers of Kundalini Yoga,

and to their students,
the future teachers.

TABLE OF CONTENTS

Forward	1
Stress Reduction & Inner Peace: Permanent Solutions	2
Creating a Balance & Strategies for Reducing Stress	6
Benefits of Kundalini Yoga & Meditation	8
Wholistic Effects of the sets and meditations in this Manual	10
Practicing Kundalini Yoga at Home (Tuning In, warming up, etc.)	13
Warm Up Exercise Set (NOTES)	14
Concluding a Set (NOTES)	15

YOGA SETS — 17

Wake Up Series (HEART)	19
Sun Salutations (NOTES)	20
15 Minute Morning Set (NOTES) Raises Kundalini Energy	21
Exercises for a Flexible Spine (NOTES - GSK)	22
Self-Adjustment of the Spine (SLIM)	28
Skull & Pelvic Bone Adjustment (NOTES) Set One	30
Skull & Pelvic Bone Adjustment (NOTES) Set Two	32
Exercise Series for Hips, Thighs & Legs (BEADS)	34
Spinal Set with Ardha-Matsyendrasana (NOTES) Excellent preparation for meditation - raises Kundalini Energy	35
Kriya for Regeneration (NOTES) "Those who master this will realize many benefits!"	36
Relaxation Series to Remove Negativity & Tension (NOTES)	38
Removing Tension & Negativity (NOTES)	39
Exercise Set for State of Mind & Paranoia (JOY) For paranoia, pituitary, abdomen, navel, youth, common cold, excess water.	40
Exercise Set for Relaxing & Releasing Fear (JOY) For fear, liver, kidneys, spleen, arthritis, tension, anger & ecstacy.	42
Meditation and Self-Reliance (MED) Works on fear, self-reliance, heart center, liver, sexual energy & courage.	44
Nerve Balance (NOTES - a slightly different version is in Survival Kit)	46
For Drug Damage (NOTES)	47
Memory Gland (#1) (NOTES)	47
For Memory Gland (NOTES)	48
For the Memory (NOTES) Raises Kundalini energy	49
Gheranda-Samhita - Head Set (NOTES) For the brain, intellect, mind, concentration, will-power, memory, throat, eyesight, teeth, facial muscles, halitosis, pimples & nervous strain!	50
For the Eyes (NOTES)	51
Personality, Nerves & Perception (NOTES - A variation of the set is in Kundalini Meditation Manual) For eyesight & foresight, physical & mental myopia, liver and kidneys.	52
Eye Set (NOTES)	53
Short Kriya to See Inner Beauty (MED)	55
Siam Kriya (NOTES) Ancient iniation kriya for meditation & sight	54
Anger Set (NOTES - GSK) Repairing damage to the system of anger	56
Stress Set for Adrenals and Kidneys (NOTES - GSK)	58
Exercise Set for the Kidneys (JOY)	60

Short Set for Kidneys (NOTES)	62
For Liver & Kidneys (NOTES)	62
Short Set for the Liver (NOTES)	62
Let the Liver Live (BEADS) "Whosoever will do this set will be set for life."	63
Purification of the Liver (NOTES)	64
Liver Set for Hepatitis (NOTES - A similar set appears in <u>Healing Through Kundalini - Specific Applications</u>)	65
Liver Set (NOTES)	66
Liver Lover (NOTES)	67
Exercise Set for the Liver, Colon & Stomach (JOY)	68
For Elimination (Set 1 - NOTES)	71
Elimination (Apana) Exercises (SADA) Enables one to completely master the digestive system	72
Navel Center & Elimination (MED) Good workout	74
Raise Kundalini in Quick Order (NOTES) Excellent preparation for deep meditation.	76
Opportunity & Green Energy Set (HEART, GSK) Attracts opportunities and prosperity by opening the Heart Center	78
Simple Exercise for Spiritual Healing (NOTES) Developing the power of the hands.	80

RELAX & RENEW IN 2-11 MINUTES

	81
Stress Reduction in 2-11 minutes	83
Reducing Stress through Proper Breathing - Breath of Fire, Long deep breathing, Right Nostril Breathing, Left Nostril Breathing Alternate Nostril Breathing explained.	84

PRANAYAMA

Breathing to Change Nostrils at Will & Alter Mental States (SURV, NOTES)	86
Basic Breath Series (SADA)	87
Anti-Hypertension Meditation (SURV)	88
Pikhana Bhakti Meditation (NOTES)	88
Anti-Stress Breathing (NOTES)	89
Energy & Relaxation for the Nerves (NOTES) Good for beginners.	89
Emotional Balance (SLIM)	90
Man Suhaave Mudra Kriya - To Tranquilize the Mind in 3 Minutes (SURV, NOTES)	91
Kriya to Balance & Recharge the Nervous & Immune Systems (NOTES)	92
The 4/4 Breath for Energy (SURV, NOTES)	93
Meditation for the Lower Triangle - To Repair Stress Damage and healing for the kidneys & adrenals (SADA)	94
Dhrib Dhristi Lochina Karma Kriya - Silent Meditation to Center & Balance (YOGA)	95
Vatsar Kriya - Cures body and elminiates acidity (NOTES)	96
For Self-Regeneration (NOTES)	97
Sitali Pranayam for regulating sexual and digestive energy, lowering fever, extending life span. (Many sources)	97

SHORT MEDITATIONS
- Long Sat Nams to Neutralize Tension (SURV) — 98
- For Concentration in Action & to Learn to Meditate (SURV) — 98
- 7 Wave "Sat Nam" Meditation (SADA) — 99
- Meditation for Powerful Energy (SURV) — 100
- Gyan Chand for Self-Healing, Tuning up Nervous System, & Disease Resistance (NOTES) — 101
- Ong in Virasan for Negativity (NOTES) — 101

EXERCISES
- Short Set to Remove Negativity (NOTES) Perfect for depression, anger, fatigue or stress (NOTES) — 102
- Strengthening the Nervous System (NOTES) — 103
- Quick Energizers (NOTES) — 104
- Quick Insomnia Relief (NOTES) — 105
- Quick Headache Relief (NOTES) — 105

Dealing with Crisis Situations — 106
Self Protection Tips — 107
Visualization & Problem Solving — 108
Meditation Facilitators - Single or short exercises to implement meditation when there isn't time for a set — 109
The Cosmic Teddy Bear - For after meditation — 112

MEDITATIONS — 113
Meditation in Kundalini Yoga — 115
- Shabd Kriya (MED) for deep sleep, radiance & patience — 118
- Meditation for the Central Nervous System (NOTES) — 119
- Rebirthing Meditation (NOTES) Burns away negativity — 120
- Natal Rebirthing Meditation (NOTES) — 121
- Meditation to Bring up the Past (NOTES) — 122
- Meditation for Surrender (NOTES) Establishes the appropriate relationship between the ego and the Infinite Self. — 123
- Seraba Sud Meditation (NOTES) For setting the physical plane in order — 124
- Ungali Pranayam - The Simram Pranayam gives you the power and authority to expand your consciousness (MED) — 125
- Sehaj Sukh Dihan with Mul Mantra (NOTES) Easy meditation to connect with the True Self — 126
- Laya Yoga #7 (NOTES) To raise kundalini and bliss out — 127
- Meditation for Inner & Outer Vision (MED) alters consciousness — 128
- Tratakam for the Eyes (NOTES) 3 exercises for vision — 129
- Maha Agni Pranayam to Reorganize Brain Secretions & Counteract the effects of marijuana (SADA, HEAL) Balances the hemispheres — 130
- Anti-Depression & Brain Synchrony Meditation - for former marijuana abusers (MED) Makes one positive & happy — 131
- To Break a Cocain Habit (NOTES) Balances Nervous System — 132
- For Emotional Balance & Repair of Damage Due to Cocaine Use with Kirtan Kriya (NOTES) — 133
- Medical Meditation for Habituation (NOTES) Activates Brain under stem of Pineal Gland, effective for addictions of all kinds — 134
- Moses Meditation for Memory (NOTES) — 135
- Meditation to Get out of Depresssion & for the Capacity to Deal with Life (NOTES, SURV) — 135
- Healing Meditation for Acute Depression (SURV) — 136

Breath Meditation to Strengthen the Mind & Immune System (NOTES)	137
Meditation to Perfect the Power of Prayer, Conquer Sickness and Become a Healer (NOTES) Too powerful to do it alone!	138
Rejuvenation Meditation (NOTES) Powerful & spacey	139
Maha Karma Shambhavi Kriya - For the Eyes and opening the energy centers. 'To harness the 3 powers of God!' (NOTES	139
Solam Pad Prana Kriya, Pt. 1 & 2 (NOTES) To transcend emotions	140
Adi Shakti Meditation - To magnify pranic potency (NOTES)	141
Mahan Kal Kriya (NOTES) For innocence & dispell fear	142
Shakti-Bhakti Meditation (NOTES) For physical euphoria, the 'great body' experience, helps relax for sleep	142
First Sodhung Mantra - Sunset Meditation for Harnessing ether (NOTES)	143
Tattva Siddhi Kriya - For Control of the Elements (NOTES)	143
Astral Projection (NOTES) Merging with light for elevation and relaxation	144
Arjuni Kriya (NOTES) Works powerfully on the glandular system - it can take you to the '3rd Blue Ether'!	145
Full Moon 'Such Such' Meditation (NOTES)	146
Chandra Kriya Mudra (NOTES) To be done on a full moon in a water sign - gives the 'great body' experience	146

APPENDIX   149

Supplementary Exercises for specific problems	151
Additional Exercises for the Nerves	151
Additional Exercises for Spinal Adjustment	153
Additional Exercises for the Eyes	156
Additional Exercises for the Adrenals & Kidneys	159
Additional Exercises for the Liver & Colon	161
The Spinal Nerves	164
Accupressure Points on the Spine & Back	164
The Eye Muscles	165
Digestive System	165
From Gururattan Kaur's Kitchen	167
Guidelines for a Stress Reducing Diet	168
Food Combining for Best Digestion	173
Gururattan's Guide to Grains & Legumes	174
Recipes	175
Mung Beans & Rice	175
Hummus	175
Cheddar Beets	175
Cottage Beets	176
Spinach-Watercress Salad	176
Tahini Salad Dressing	176
Breakfast Muesli	176
Earthy Red Nectar	177
Licorice-Sassafras Tea	177
Golden Milk	177
Yogi Tea	177
Healing Foods & Herbs for Stress-Related Problems	178
For Stress, Nerves, Kidneys & Adrenals, Liver & Eyes	
For Eyes, Elimination and Alcoholism	
Establishing a Personal Stress-Reduction Program	180

Fundamentals of Kundalini Yoga - Components 182
    Kundalini 182
    Prana & Apana 182
    Kriyas 183
    Asanas 183
    Mudras 184
    Bhandas 185
        Bhanda Exercise (MED) 185
    Chakras 186
    Mantras 188
    Pranayama 190
    Meditation 190
    Focus, Visualization & Projection 190
Bibliography 192
Authors 193

INDEX TO YOGIJI'S QUOTES

AGING & Youth	27
AM-PM	150
ANY ACT in the Name of God	148
ATTITUDE of Gratitude	18
AWAKENING the Chakras	18
BEAUTY	117
BEGINNING & Ending a Day	114
BHAGAUTI	141
A Clean BODY	148
BREATH	83
Opening the CHAKRAS	12, 18
DANCE of Shiva	191
DIVINE Light	114
DIVINITY	119
DOPE	134
DRUGS	132
EAT to Live	176
EVERYONE is Born a Saint	91
FAITH	48, 150
GOD Consciousness	45
Seek GOD Within	82
GODS or Demons	16
GRACE	117, 136
Attitude of GRATITUDE	82
Be GREAT	126
HAIR Antenna	29
Don't Just HANG Around...	180
HAPPINESS	150
HARMONY	147
HASSELS	93
HUMILITY	103
I AM	148
IMPROVE	148
LAUGHING	118
LEAN, Thin & Skinny	166
LET GO & Flow	148
LIFE IS NOT AN EXPERIMENT	148
LIVE LIFE	123
Self LOVE	82, 191
Trust and LOVE	82
MARTIAL ARTS	107
MEDITATION	114, 150, 191
NEGATIVITY	16, 96
NOW	27
ONG SOHUNG	100
OVEREATING	166
PURITY	180
PURPOSE	99
ROAD TO RIGHTEOUSNESS	18
SEEK God Within	82
On SELF-BLESSING	112
SELF Control	18
SELF Esteem & Grace	136
SELF IMPROVEMENT	180
SELF LOVE	82, 191
SELF RESPECT	27
SELF SURRENDER	123
SERMON on 2 Cushions	117
SHIVA	191
SICKNESS	96
SIKH DHARMA	16
SPIRITUALITY	16
SUBCONSCIOUS	120, 122
SURPASS your Teacher	180
SUGAR	166
TRUST & Love	82
VEGETARIANISM	166
YOGA	18
YOGA of Fulfillment	iii
YOU ARE THE UNIVERSE	117
YOU ARE INCARNATION OF GOD	119
YOUTHFULNESS	29

FORWORD

We live in a period of rapid change. The stress that most of us experience relates to how to handle the pressures of this change, which comes from two sources: (1) keeping up with the pace, including information and energy overload, and (2) frustration from the resistance to change, within ourselves and in society as a whole.

The techniques offered in this manual help us function in harmony with the new realities and energies and enable us to reduce our resistance. They empower us to effect personal change and to act in the world. For the world we live in requires individuals who are not only healthy, emotionally stable and spiritually balanced, it demands that we be capable of actively and creatively participating in making the earth a better place to live. We need to practice techniques that help us achieve inner peace while maintaining our feet solidly on the ground. Techniques that give us boundless energy, drive and resources to forge a world of love, kindness and hope.

The stress reduction techniques offered in this manual will enable you to improve and maintain your physical and mental well-being, reduce daily stress, and deal more calmly with crisis situations. The emphasis is on short, powerful techniques that produce the quickest results. Use these techniques and watch the results for yourself.

The Kundalini Yoga exercises and meditations offered were brought to the West by Yogi Bhajan, who studied and traveled in India for over 30 years. Yogi Bhajan has lived in the United States since 1969 and has dedicated his life to sharing ancient technologies that can help modern men and women live in happy, healthy consciousness.

Until this time, these techniques were taught only to an elite group and were unpublished. These techniques are compiled from thousands of years of teachings. They belong to no group, but are the heritage of humankind everywhere. It is the birthright of every human to have access to them. Let us share with others as we learn.

There is no way to express the joy, peace and strength I have experienced from practicing this technology. The only way to express my gratitude is to share these teachings with others, so that they too may experience health, happiness, inner joy and in turn, help others on the planet.

In gratitude.

Humbly,

Gururattan Kaur Khalsa

STRESS REDUCTION & INNER PEACE: PERMANENT SOLUTIONS

STRESS REDUCTION THERAPIES

Stress is the number one killer in the Western world, according to medical studies, for it is the cause of heart failure, and contributes to many other diseases, including drug abuse, a problem of grave national concern.

The most common remedy for stress is to treat the symptoms, by taking tranquilizers, alcohol or tobacco, or hide them in chronic television viewing or overeating. Stimulation is then required, like coffee and speed, to replace the depleted or drugged energy, which is like driving a car with one foot on the accelerator and the other on the brakes, comparing the engine to the heart and adrenals.

Another approach to stress reduction is offered by professional therapists, and counselors. While most of these techniques do provide temporary relief they always fail to provide a long-term cure, because they do not deal with the total human being - specifically with the human spiritual nature.

KUNDALINI YOGA & STRESS RELEASE

A permanent and successful treatment for stress must operate in a metaphysical framework, for it is only in the realization of our unlimited and divine identities that we can begin to enjoy inner peace and happiness.

Such a therapy is offered by Kundalini Yoga, which recognizes the true, spiritual nature of the human being, and offers proven, scientific and ancient technology for attaining his potential.

Kundalini Yoga and Meditation addresses the issues that produce stress, providing the body with the muscular and nerve strength and flexibility to handle stress and to excell in the material world.

Moreover, it provides the mind with powerful techniques to identify itself with Divinity, kindle creativity, attain serenity, and enjoy life. As the body becomes strong, capable, graceful and flexible, so does the mind.

THE QUEST FOR SECURITY

All of us seek the eternal, unchanging reality to be found only in the spiritual world. Any effort to attain stability or security in the physical realm is doomed because flux and change (very often unpredictable and sudden) is the very nature of physical existence!

It is this futile effort to control the world, and resist or deny change that causes tension, frustration, insecurity and depression. Nevertheless, this search for security is a manifestation of the very deep, real desire in each of us to find that eternal, infinite and universal aspect of ourselves - our very soul and consciousness.

This deep human longing for changeless reality is only to be resolved by going within and finding, there, that place of peace that connects us to the rest of the universe. There, in that vast space of peace and ecstacy, we are released from the pressures of everyday life and its accompanying stress.

TRANSCENDING THE POLARITIES OF THE MIND

Through meditation we can learn who we really are and of our divine purpose on earth. By transcending the mind and its world of duality (the world perceived as I - others, like - dislike, good - bad, pleasure - pain, white - black, yin -yang, allies - enemies, victory - defeat, etc.), we can elevate consciousness to its true nature.

The play between the polarities of the mind yields doubt, insecurity, distrust, judgements, pain and attachment. Even when the mind is shifted to the experience of pleasure, we know it won't last, and in this tiresome duality we are always subject to pain and conflict.

The mind has three capacities:

1. The <u>negative mind</u> calculates, judges, thinks defensively, but predicts failure.

2. The <u>positive mind</u> sees opportunities, is benevolent, thinks optimistically, and expects success.

3. The <u>neutral, conscious mind</u> sees the highest good for all concerned (win-win!), and is aligned with the Universal Mind, accepting all that life delivers.

The positive and negative minds operate in duality, with egotism and insecurity, attempting to control, resisting submission to circumstances and authority, and seeking to fulfill desires.

The neutral mind, however, is guided by intelligence, consciousness and selflessness. It is characterized by identification with Divine Will, and produces effortles, hassleless, positive achievement.

Yogi Bhajan says: "There are two ways of living in this world - the way of worry, and the way of relaxation. If you worry, you have to concentrate to imagine a result, but if you tune your mind to the Universal Mind, then things will come to you."

ATTITUDES OF THE NEUTRAL MIND

Cultivation of the following attitudes will help transcend duality and the accompanying stress, conflict and pain.

TRUST: Believe in a power beyond yourself, and identify with it. (Then you aren't responsible for the world!) Allow your will to align itself with Universal Will (following your heart), and go beyond beliefs and doubts to trust yourself and God.

ACCEPTANCE: Life is in balance - accept it all. Nothing is good or bad but thinking makes it so. It is the nature of the universe to establish balance; thus, trying to prevent perceived bad will also block desired good. Instead, welcome challenge and difficulty, enjoying the indicated activity, and growing in each situation.

GRATITUDE: The attitude of gratitude for all that is, all that happens, for the very air we breathe and the wonderful bodies we live in attracts blessings and produces a state of grace and joy. Enjoy who you are, what you have and what you are doing in each and every moment.

COMPASSIONATE DETACHMENT: Clinging to certain persons, situations or the past is spinning in non-reality. No moment, person or circumstance in the physical world can be caught and held. Instead, practice compassionate detachment, helping when possible, but remaining uninvolved, and knowing that we attract the events and people we need at the appropriate time in life, and then allow them to go, at the appropriate time.

NON-JUDGEMENT: By evaluating, classifying and determining the rank and use of everything, we assume power over life and inflate our egos. Giving up judgements reduces stress and promotes humility.

UNCONDITIONAL LOVE: See yourself and everything and everybody as God's Divine Creation, and treat yourself and everything and everybody accordingly. Unconditional love includes love of self, love of life, and love of others. It is a state of being, and not directed exclusively at specific persons or things.

ACQUIRING THE NEUTRAL MIND

Meditate and trust the messages that come during meditation and relaxation. This is the neutral mind and the higher consciousness speaking. Be willing not to have to "figure it all out" in the positive-negative mind mode. Be still and know!

Listen for the spaces in the mind instead of its thoughts. Include spaces and silence in your communications with others. Listen for Infinity and be open to receive the universal sound current and knowledge. Give your inner peace a chance.

Open the Heart Center. Fear, anger, attachment, hate and greed may have closed our heart centers, which can be opened by unconditional love. (See Transitions to a Heart-Centered World for exercises and meditations to open the heart center.) Give with compassion and kindness (to yourself, too!). Open up, relax, and dissolve obstructions.

Observe without reacting. Feel and experience each situation without becoming emotionally and judgementally involved in it.

Express emotions spontaneously, and let them go! Allow yourself to feel emotions without reacting to them, judging or repressing them. Be innocent and don't fear or judge your spontaneous self. Feeling and emotion move the world, revealing potential, freedom and creativity that we may have otherwise never suspected. Repressed emotion (for fear of rejection, or disapproval) is stored in the muscles and organs, obstructing circulation and causing pain or disease. Experience the emotion without identifying with it. Say "I feel angry, rather than, "I am angry. This allows us to feel and release the emotion without becoming stuck in it. Notice which feelings liberate and enliven us and which ones control and confuse us, causing stress. Change the thought patterns that produce the latter. It is also important, in expressing our feelings, to identify and claim our feelings as our own, without projecting them and blaming others.

Be aware of and responsive to the body down to the cellular level. Unexpressed emotions, stored stress and unresolved memories block cellular communication and vitality. Pay attention to the needs of the body. Learn to pulsate with the universal pulsation and feel it at the heart center, and at the 3rd eye. Perceive your connection with the universal flow and be willing to open up and transcend blocks.

Exercise and move all parts of the body. Stimulate the organs and glands and circulation with regular exercise. Our bodies require it. We can either exercise and enjoy it, or allow the mind to provide exercise in tension, stress and nervousness.

EMPOWERING PRINCIPLES

EXERCISING CHOICE: Realize that we can choose between defeating, frustrating, negative attitudes or reactions, and empowering, liberating joyeous ones. The energy generated in exercise, pranayama and meditation is neutral, but how we use it - for the attainment of our truest desires, or for futile, busy, unsuccessful activity is up to use. We may not be able to control events, but we may control how we react. That choice is called free will.

INTEGRATION: Feeling integrated with the environment and others, rather than alienated or threatened, is the first step in feeling connected with the universe. Concluding a meditation is a good time to experience this feeling.

SELF-ACCEPTANCE: Accepting ourselves and our own issues is relaxing in itself. This is a product of unconditional love.

DEFINING RESPONSIBILITY: Choose not to feel responsible and guilty for events and circumstances we have not created. This includes choosing not to notice and react to minor irritations, thus attracting them! Don't borrow problems. This doesn't preclude feelding compassion, and giving aid when possible - just don't put oneself at the center of the trouble, as its cause or savior.

TAKING RESPONSIBILITY: On the other hand, take responsibility for oneself and ones own issues. Stop "scapegoating" (blaming circumstances, others, the status quo, genes, the government, early environment, parents fate, or "Murphy's Law" for our own condition. They may have influenced us, but the way we deal with issues is our own choice. By accepting responsibility for the present situation, we empower ourselves to effect change, and take control over our own lives.

CHANGING OURSELVES: Rather than try to change the world and others, let's change ourselves. The world changes all the time without our permission, anyway. Lets not cling to an obsolete version of ourselves like a parental role, the stance we assumed in school, helpless victem, or debauched bon vivant. As we drop defeatist, negative and depressed points of view, it will be a different world and we will attract what we truly desire and expect.

SEEING OPPORTUNITY: Turn apparent failure into opportunity. Each failure is a chance to learn and change. Be spontaneous enough to see the opportunities in every situation and go with the flow. A positive attitude keeps us growing and helps solve issues so we can move on. We are meant to succeed! Otherwise there would be no cosmic play!

PRACTICE

Attitudes like acceptance, lack of judgement, non-attachment, unprejudiced receptivity, trust, unconditional love and gratitude attract desireable events, conditions and relationships. This is a relaxing, pleasant and effective way of life. As daily practice, choose one of the above attitudes and integrate it into your life for a week or a month. Then choose another Gradually, they become 2nd nature, helping to sustain the peace of ind and relaxation sustained in yog exercise and meditation. Without them, the ego flips back into the same old destructive games.

GROUP MEDITATION

Group meditation is vital because meditative energy increases dramatically in a group. This high vibrational energy creates speedy and powerful changes in the mental, emotional and subtle body which effects the physical body down to the cellular level. The group creates a powerful connection of universal and unconditional love which is experienced as oneness. Group consciousness is the beginning of Universal Consciousness, so group meditation "soups up" spiritual progress.

CREATING A BALANCE
STRATEGIES FOR REDUCING STRESS

Creating balance in life is one of the keys to stress reduction, and essential for health, happiness and serenity. Balance also facilitates the ability to serve and help others. Balance is physical, mental, spiritual and practical.

PHYSICAL BALANCE

For a healthy body and the elimination of tension and disease, we must exercise every part of the body, strengthing the immune and nervous systems. The same energy can be used for work and play, or for stress and tension.

Physical vitality adds another dimension to the joy and peace that can be experienced in worldly life. With a vital body, we can experience states of awareness and connectedness to the self and the universe not available through the mind alone.

A New Age goal is to bring heaven down to earth, so we don't have to escape into other realms. Part of the preparation for that is being grounded and centered so that we can pull in new knowledge and manifest it on the planet. Taking care of the body creates a solid foundation.

MENTAL BALANCE

Mental balance helps us to be consistent, one-pointed, clear and peaceful. Modern technological society is a root cause of mental imbalance. It is based on and rewards, almost exclusively non-verbal, goal-oriented, linear and action-oriented left brain activities. The intuitive, poetic, sensitive, flowing and spiritual right brain activities are often undervalued or altogether absent. Techniques in this manual heal the left/right brain split and correct the imbalance in our consciousness, healing the mind by stimulating the intetrative mechanisms.

SPIRITUAL BALANCE

A major source of stress and frustration is alienation from our inner selves. We are often completely unaware of its very existence, even denying it or associating it with negative conceptions. The techniques offered here allow us to experience the peace and strength within. This allows us to know ourselves and our potentials. Gradually, meaning and stability are realized through the harmony between the conscious and unconscious selves and between the ego and the soul.

This technology changes our perception of problems. Ultimately, stress is not created by factors and situations from without, but by our attitudes and reactions to them. The basic problem is the lack of a sense of individual meaning and value. Kundalini yoga and meditation help us regain and re-affirm this meaning and value.

PRACTICAL BALANCE

"Tension is good if followed by relaxation" says Yogi Bhajan. Tension is simply the magnetic attraction between an intension and its realization. Like an invisable line it stretches between the present and a proposed future goal, or between the inception of an old desire and the present. Such tension works in our favor to focus attention (energy) on fulfilling values and achieving goals.

Simple tension is enhanced by harmonious multiple goals. (A desire to be an emminent concert pianist, for example, could be implemented by desires to lead an unconventional life, to see the world, or to live in luxury.)

But stress ensues from holding conflicting intensions (such as the would-be virtuoso also desiring to be a prize fighter). We sometimes allow parents, friends or society to establish our goals, often in opposition to our own heart's desires. Young women often experience conflict between wanting to pursue a career and the desire to marry and raise a family A family man may feel he must work hard and earn more monmey to 'enjoy life' but then finds he has neither the time nor the energy to enjoy regular recreational activity, take a vacation, or even relax.

STRESS-PROOF YOUR MIND-SET: Our deepest desires, even if they are consciously unknown to us, will manifest! And they will persistently nag until they are recognized or actualized, causing vague feelings of uneasiness. Meditation and relaxation will reveal these "soul priorities" and enable us to harmonize our conscious lives and goals with them.

Setting clear and uncluttered goals, establishing priorities and perimeters, eliminating unproductive activity and reserving time and space for ONESELF is good stress reduction strategy. We must give ourselves permission to turn off the phone, lock the door, cancel stress-producing plans and appointments, and say "no". We must each stand at the center of our own life, fulfilling our own goals before entertaining alternatives.

STRESS-PROOF YOUR BODY: A relaxed, and well-aligned body is necessary to exercise with ease and meditate effectively. Spinal misalignment is a common effect of stress and also contributes to it by blocking energy to the brain and other parts of the body. Exercising, especially those sets and exercises that adjust the spine and neck, can be enhanced by an occasional or regular massage and visits to a holistic chiropractor. Other ways of releasing tension are soaking in a hot tub or jacuzzi, running or walking barefooted on grass or sand, listening to beautiful music, and simply playing.

STRESS-PROOF YOUR ENVIRONMENT: Get rid of irritating, disturbing, demanding noise, dissonant music, TV war-movie soundtracks, fighting, yelling and high-pressure commercials. Allow only one primary sound at a time and turn down the radio or TV to take a phone call or visit with guests Modulating your own voice will influence others to do the same.

Even if you aren't consciously aware of the effects of air pollutants, your body is, and it reacts with stress. Breathing smoke is harmful to the heart and lungs. Some artificial fibers emit toxic fums that irritate the eyes and the mucous lines. Smog is another stresser. Avoid such pollutants as much as possible and cleanse and recharge yourself in nature and healthy environments on a regular basis.

Avoid participation in rush hour scenes. Try to change your hours, by alternating early and late shifts with another employee. If you must drive or commute in rush hour traffic, equip yourself to listen to beautiful, serene music, or read inspirational material. You can also transform the immediate environment on a bus or train, by silently blessing the neighboring passengers and engaging them in positive telepathic or vocal conversation.

BENEFITS OF KUNDALINI YOGA AND MEDITATION

The meditations and yoga exercises in this manual present an opportunity to acquire the mental, physical and spiritual capacity to enjoy life to the fullest. Instead of becomming stressed from the intensifying energy and rapid changes occuring on the planet today, we will be able to "get high" from the transition to the New Age. Practiced, these techniques will "tune us in". Kundalini Yoga is a powerful scientific technology, developed over thousands of years, to access higher light energy and produce a conscious mode of living, implementing creativity and productivity - fast! We can expect the following results.

PROBLEM SOLVING: We can't always avoid problems, but we can be more effective in handling them. By changing perspectives, being less emotional and uninvolved, we can raise our consciousness to attract or provide solutions, thereby rising to a position of power, able to effect change rather than helplessly stand by playing the victem.

CLEANSING: Yoga and meditation powerfully cleanses us of physical, mental and emotional obstructions, worn-out attitudes and beliefs, leaving us space to acquire beneficial and useful new ones, and opening us to access higher knowledge and our own inner selves.

A BETTER WAY OF LIVING: There are three levels of being -

1. Life is a series of problems to be solved, and the best we can hope for is to find solutions, or that the problem will just go away.

2. Life is a series of opportunities, and problems can be turned into opportunities for lessons and growth.

3. Life is a miracle, a series of synchronistic events unfolding at the right time and place, in a constant flow. As we raise our vibrational frequency, we move into miraculous living.

OPPORUNITIES & VALUE FULFILLMENT: The ability to manifest our deepest desires reveals itself, and we can perceive and draw opportunities to us. We no longer have to go out and manipulate or fight for what we want.

CONTROL: As we gain more control over our lives, we have less need to exercise control, because we are in the process of discovering and accepting life as it unfolds, and we feel more secure and trusting.

DIVINE ATTITUDES: As we transcend the mind's duality, new attitudes about life, ourselves and others appear like acceptance, trust, gratitude and non-attachment, and we live with fewer expectations or judgements.

CHARACTER: Greater mental clarity and focus is achieved, and it is easier to act consistently, to finish tasks, be truthful, fair and honest.

HEALING: Our healing powers manifest and our presence, touch, words or smile heals.

HEALTH: The immune system is strengthened and we enjoy vibrant health and abundant energy.

PRESENCE: With the development of the electro-magnetic field (aura), not only is our health improved, but we become more poised and effective human beings.

PURE KNOWING: With meditation comes intuition - knowing and feeling what is right and best, and no longer having to reason through the pro's and con's of each situation.

PROTECTION: Intuitive powers alert us to dangers, and we do not attract negative forces. Sometimes the univverse changes our plans so that we don't get on the plane that crashes!

PRAYER POWER: Clarity, humility and devotion clear the channels for our prayers to be heard and answered.

JOYFUL LIVING: Life becomes relaxed and fun. We feel taken care of, become "unreasonably happy" and EXPERIENCE THE COSMIC TEDDY BEAR!

HIGHER AWARENESS: Through meditation we establish an intimate relationship with ourselves and the God within. This relationship opens us up to higher level relationships with others

THE UNIVERSAL CONNECTION: The congruent alignment of body, mind and spirit opens channels to other dimensions of existence and the universe unfolds within our minds.

IMPACTING WORLD PEACE AND BECOMMING A FORCE FOR GOOD: The more we elevate consciousness and the quality of our internal being, the more positively we affect the world and those around us. Inner peace becomes outer peace.

A DRUGLESS HIGH: The use of drugs fulfills many purposes - 'uppers' for mental and physical energy, 'downers' for relaxation and sleep, halucinogens for entertainment and escape. Much drug use results from the deep longing for spiritual revalations, and the sensual delights, euphoria and pleasures they offer. These altered states of consciousness allow us to talk with God, transcend time and space, experience sights and sounds cellularly, and perceive the world as pure sensation without meaning or morality, and ourselves as simple 'sensers' devoid of character, self-interest, purpose or ego. (And other drugs magnify the ego, diminish sensitivity and sensory awareness, but seem to sharpen the rational achievement-oriented mind.) In any case, the price is high - loss of freedom, self-respect, dignity, family friends and mental and physical health

In Kundalini Yoga, one can experience the same effects without loss of character, ego or values. Furthermore, we are enabled to apply the insights gained to the material world, as well as satisfy the deep craving for spiritual meaning. Kundalini Yogs is eminently healthy and perfectle legal (if not conventional), and it allows us to exercise more control over our lives (rather than relinquish it). Moreover, we are encouraged to live in the world, enjoying it without judgements, successfully meeting its demands and challenges.

Along with the exercises and meditations to break addiction and repair the damages of drug abuse, this manual offers some that quickly and rather easily alter consciousness - (try 'Astral Projection' & 'Pushma Kriya' for tripping, 'Shakti-Bhakti Meditation' for physical euphoria, 'Meditation for Inner & Outer Vision' for extra-normal sight, and for a 'lift' try 'Meditation for Powerful Energy'). Extraordinary effects can be obtained from many sets and meditations but some must be practiced for 40 days to be fully experienced.

With this in mind, we are pushing Kundalini Yoga for drug abusers. With our feet on the ground, couched in present time and place, earthly identity intact, voluntarily relinquishing the ration mind's monopoly on focus, we will experience the same or better highs in meditation.

WHOLISTIC EFFECTS OF THE SETS & MEDITATIONS IN THIS MANUAL

This manual address all aspects of stress reduction. Such seemingly diverse sets as those for the eyes, the colon, and for prosperity are all related to the topic and to each other.

In the sets and meditations in this manual, various parts of the body and mind are exercised and stimulated to produce specific and far reaching effects. The interrelationship between all parts of the body, and between the mind and the body, and between the subtle body, its centers and the physical organism is inseparable.

Stress exhausts the adrenal glands, and overeating and drug abuse overloads the liver. The eyes are affected by liver and kidney malfunction, and a malfunctioning liver contriutes to constipation, which causes (and is also caused by) stress! Displacements of the spine contribute to disease in all parts of the body and to stress, (which also displaces the spine). Etc., etc.! Included here are sets and meditations for the spine, nerves, eyes, adrenals and kidneys, the liver, colon and for general healing and rejuvenation.

CHAKRAS
THE SUBTLE ENERGY CENTERS
AND PHYSICAL, EMOTIONAL COUNTERPARTS

The chakras are subtle energy centers perceived as situated along the spine (and not on the front of the body, as they are often pictured). They are numbered from #1 at the anus, to #7 at the top of the head, and energy is thought to move up the spine and through them, transforming to higher frequencies as it moves up. (See appendix.)

The <u>First Chakra</u>, at the anus, is associated with elimination and the eliminating organs. When properly functioning, a person is well-grounded and securely comfortable with earthly existence, but a blocked first chakra indicates hidden fear, instability, insecurity, possessiveness and the inability to let go, attitudes that certainly interfere with the functions of the colon.

Creative, sexual energy is generated in the <u>Second Chakra</u>, the powerful center that produces life, healing energy and all forms of creativity when it is in balance. An imbalance leads to obsessive sexuality and tendencies to jealousy and revenge.

Power and vitality are seated at <u>the 3rd, the Navel Chakra</u>, at the navel (the Japanese "Hara"), which is said to be the center of physical energy, strength and well-being. When it is strong we enjoy robust health and the ability to commit, persevere, sustain intensions, break or make habits, and "the steam" to make a difference. If it is misaligned or weak we may be susceptible to illness, without character, and lacking in nerve strength. (It may be well-developed but blocked, so that energy cannot ascend to the heart center, and that will can result in greed, selfishness, egotism, power-seeking and possessiveness.) The adrenals and kidneys are associated with the navel center which give us energy and the reserves to act quickly under fear or stress, and to overcome fatigue. The navel chakra is also closely associated with the organs of digestion, and a well-developed navel area aids the best function of those organs.

The seat of true love, compassion and our relations with others is at the Fourth Chakra, the Heart Center which is associated with the Thymus Gland. This is the first really 'human' chakra. A strong Heart Center enables one to be compassionate but unattached, and able to act for the higher good of all. An awakened Heart Chakra also allows us to love ourselves without egotism or selfishness. The power of wish-fulfillment (symbolized by the 'Wishing Tree' in the smaller lotus below) is a quality of the awakened heart chakra, but then the person's wish will be granted for good or evil, making it important to maintain an optimistic attitude to prevent idle, negative, or depressed thoughts from materializing. A strong immune system and healing abilities are also attributed to the Heart Chakra and the Thymus Gland. A blocked or undeveloped heart center may result in selfish attitudes and emotional, inharmonious relationships. Opening and healing the heart transforms existence. The energy from the earth and the wisdom of the ethers meet at the heart to manifest heaven on earth. We can relax and attract opportunities and live in abundance and prosperity, with the power to heal ourselves and others, and experience unconditional love of ourselves, God and others. (Please see Transitions to a Heart-Centered World for sets and meditations especially for the Navel and Heart Chakras.)

The Throat Chakra, when opened and developed, bestows truthful speech and intuitive powers. It is associated with the Thyroid Gland which controls metabolism in the physical body. Stimulation of the 5th Chakra and the thyroid gland can reduce body weight, and has a beneficial effect on the nervous system.

The Brow Chakra, or 3rd Eye between the eyebrows, is associated with the Pituitary Gland, which regulates the entire endocrine gland system. The opened 6th Chakra gives us the comfortable feeling that we dwell in an inner community as well as an outer one, with which we inter-communicate our thoughts, emotions and dreams, enriching our lives with intuition, and spiritual love.

The Crown Chakra on top of the head is associated with the Pineal Gland. Science is now beginning to recognize the Pineal Gland as a super-normal link between the physical and inner worlds. The 7th Chakra is our univsal connection, our channel to Cosmic Consciousness. At least 50% of all Kundalini Yoga sets and meditations open the "1000 petaled lotus".

The chakras do not necessarily awaken and function in order. There are many happy, healthy active people with well-developed lower chakras who are completely unaware of the upper ones. Conversely, there are some talented healers, metaphysicians and channels whose upper chakras are strong and active, but whose bodies may be weak, suseptible to disease, and unattractive due to weak lower chakras. Yogi Bhajan's sets and meditations awaken all the chakras at once, maintaining a healthy physical and spiritual balance.

SPINAL FLEXIBILITY & ALIGNMENT

To remain youthful, reduce tension and prevent backache, stay flexible! When all of the 26 vertebrae are stimulated, spinal fluid circulates contributing to mental clarity and good memory. Each of the energy centers of the subtle body (chakras) receives an infusion of energy resulting in physical balance and general well-being. Displacement and misalignment of the spine and pelvis obstructs the flow of energy and causes discomfort in exercise, distraction in meditation and general ill health as well as discomfort. We have included sets to adjust the spine as well as stimulate and exercise it.

NERVOUS SYSTEM STRENGTH

Techniques to strengthen the nervous system implement the transition from emotional existence to sensitive awareness, allowing us to experience life at higher energy and consciousness levels. A strengthened nervous system dramatically reduces stress, and yields inner calm, mental clarity, and physical strength and endurance. A healthy nervous system also bestows the sensitivity to exercise intuitive and meditative capacities, and is essential to successfully meet the challanges and opportunities of daily life. Exercises in this manual repair nerve damage, strengthen and regenerate the nervous system.

BRAIN BALANCE

The postures, mudras, mantras and angles assumed in these exercises and meditations exert pressures that reflex to the brain to alter thought patterns, (as well as to other parts of the body). The right and left hemispheres are thereby balanced and integrated, permitting access to previously unused parts. This regenerates, awakens and strengthens the brain, developing intellect, memory, creativity and foresight. Some exercises break addiction and repeair the damages of drug abuse. Others restore memory, relieve depression, reverse negativity and promote relaxation. Still others specifically balance the hemispheres of the brain, and some simply get us high!

ADDITIONAL MATERIAL

Because so much stress is felt from financial pressures, we have included the powerful and popular "Opportunity and Green Energy Set", from <u>Transitions to a Heart-Centered World</u> (which also contains many meditations just for attracting opportunities, abundance and prosperity.) And because raising Kundalini energy is central to the practice of Kundalini Yoga, we have also included "Raise Kundalini Energy in Quick Order", another extremely effective set.

It is our hope that this manual provides you with everything you need to Relax and Renew.

OPENING THE CHAKRAS: If we go from center to center, powers will come and bring madness. Therefore, we open them all simultaneously. We want to develop intuition, not psychic power.

March 8, 1970

PRACTICING KUNDALINI YOGA AT HOME

TUNING IN

Before beginning Kundalini Yoga practice, always "tune in" by chanting the ADI MANTRA as follows:

Sit in meditation posture with a straight spine and center yourself with long, deep breathing. Then place the palms together in Prayer Mudra at the Heart Center, fingers pointed up at 60°, base of thumbs pressing against the sternum.

Inhale, focussing at the 3rd Eye Point and chant,

　　Ong na mo

("I call on Infinite Creative Consciousness") while exhaling and extending the sound, vibrating it in the cranium. Take a sip of air and resume

　　Guru dev namo　("I call on Divine Wisdom".)

Inhale and repeat 2 more times. This chant rprotects and connects us with our higher selves. Properly done, it stimulates the pituitary and automatically tunes us in to higher consciousness.

WARMING UP

The effects of the sets and meditations is enhanced by thoroughly warming up the spine and stretching before practice (see following page).

DURING EACH EXERCISE

During each exercise, focus at the 3rd eye (brow) point unless otherwise specified, without blocking out other awareness (breath, posture, etc.)

CONCLUDING AN EXERCISE

Unless otherwise directed, inhale, and hold the breath (still maintaining the posture) and apply "Mul Bhand" (root lock - see appendix) either with the breath held in or out.

BETWEEN EXERCISES

Relax a moment afterwards, and go deep within to observe the effects of each exercise (making each exercise a mini-meditation).

PROCEDURE

If you are unable to do the exercise for the specified time, cut them all proportionately (ie. in half) and then repeat the set if possible. Always follow directions as precisely as possible. Neither omit nor add an exercise, and don't skip around, but do them in order, without interuption for maximum benefits.

CONCLUDING A SET

Conclude each set with adequate relaxation followed by "grounding exercises" (see "Concluding a Set").

WARM-UP EXERCISE SET
September 7, 1974

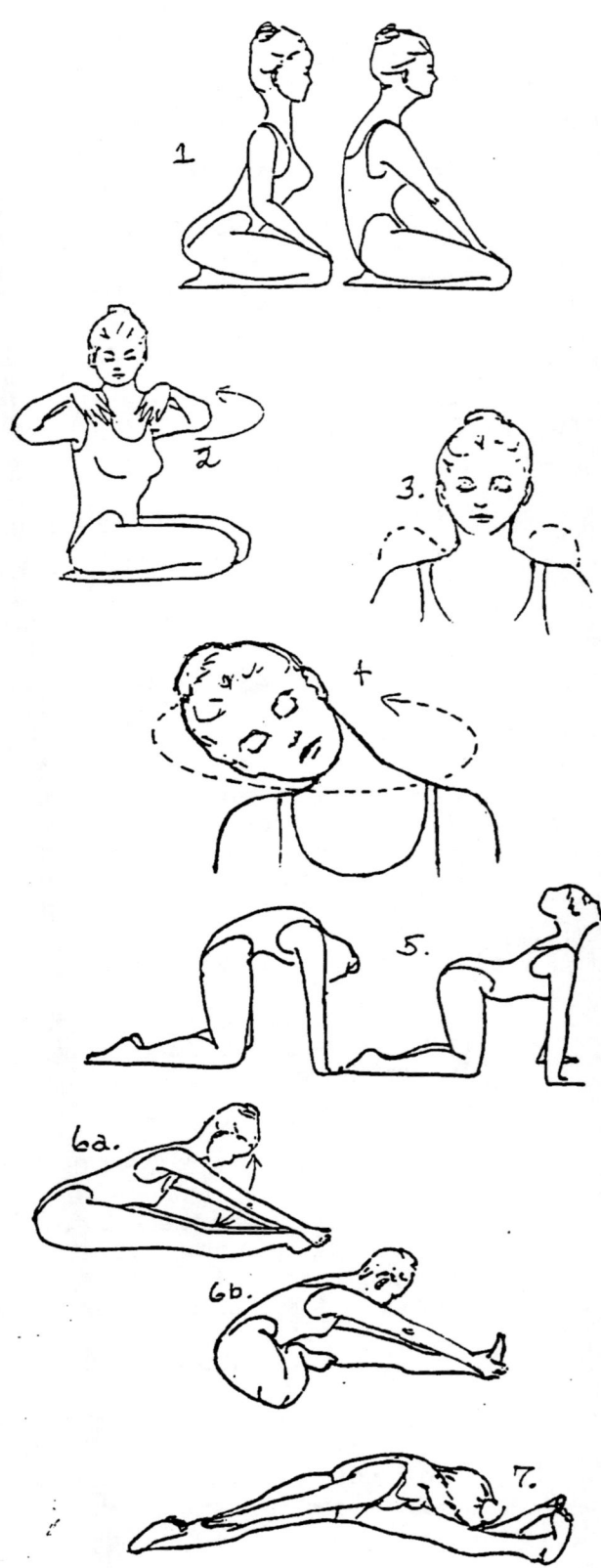

1. CAMEL RIDE: Sitting on heels, flex the spine back and forth, inhaling as it arches forward, exhaling as it contracts back, for 2-3 minutes. (Also known as SPINAL FLEXES)

2. TWIST: Sitting on heels, with hands on shoulders, fingers in front and thumbs in back, twist spine back and forth for 2-3 minutes.

3. Relax hands down on knees, and inhale raising shoulders to ears, exhale relaxing them down again and repeat for 2-3 minutes

4. NECK ROLLS: Place chin on chest, and then circle the head right, so that the right ear touches the right shoulder, then circle back, arching the neck, then to the left (left ear to left shoulder), and then forward again. Continue making slow, smooth circles, ironing out any kinks as you go, and reverse directions for 2-3 minutes.

5. CAT-COW: On all "4"s, with thighs directly under hips, arms directly under shoulders, thighs and arms parallel to each other, arch the back up with the exhale, lowering the head to the chest. On the inhale, press the tummy towards the floor as the neck arches back, and continue, increasing speed as you go for 2-3 minutes.

6. LIFE NERVE STRETCH:
A. Both legs stretched out in front, bend at the hips and grab toes, and exhaling pull the head down to the knees, allowing it to rise on the inhale, for 1-2 minutes.
B. Place left heel in right thigh and repeat, pulling head to right knee on the exhale for 1-2 minutes. Switch legs and repeat.

7. Spread legs wide apart, grabbing onto to toes, and inhale, exhale head down to alternate knees for 1-2 minutes. (Times added by G.K.)

CONCLUDING A SET

After a long relaxation, particularly one that follows a series of exercises, you will find that doing the concluding exercises below helps to ground you and bring you back to reality:

1) On your back, begin rotating your feet and hands in small circles. Continue in one direction for 30 seconds, then in the other direction for another 30 seconds.

2) Cat Stretch: Keeping both shoulders and the left leg flat on the ground, bring the right arm back behind the head and the right knee over the left leg till it touches the floor on the far side of the body. Switch legs and arms and repeat the exercise.

3) Still on your back, bring the knees up and to the sides, and rub the soles of the feet and the palms of the hands together briskly, creating a sensation of heat. Continue for 1 minute.

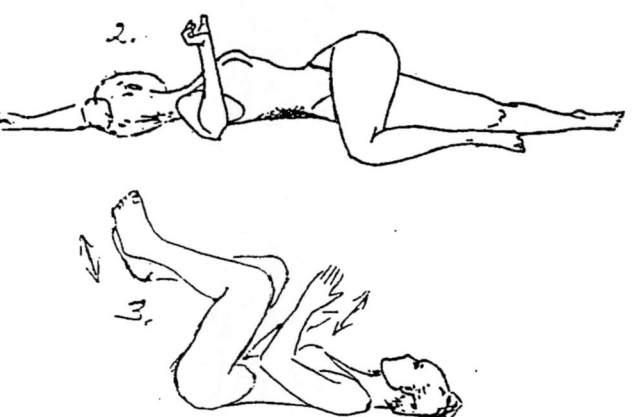

4) Clasping knees to chest with both hands, begin rolling on the spine. Roll all the way back till the feet touch the ground behind the head, and all the way forward till you're sitting up. Do this 3 or 4 times at least.

(5) Sit up in easy pose, palms together in prayer mudra at the heart center. Eyes are closed. Inhale completely and say a prayer of thanks. Exhale and let the thought go.

(6) A happy conclusion is to sing this song: <u>May the long time sun shine upon you, all love surround you, and the pure light within you, guide your way on. Repeat.</u>

NEGATIVITY: Fight your own negativity. Don't let negativity enter your ears or your eyes, or confusion results. If we conquer this, we conquer the world.

                              Undated

GODS & DEMONS: It takes the same energy to become a god as it does to become a demon!

                         June 24, 1972

SPIRITUALITY: Being spiritual is, without reservation, to wish good to all. Without reservation!!!

THE FOUNDATION OF SIKH DHARMA: "Nanak Nam Cherdi Kalaa Tere Bhaane Sarbaat Ka Bhalaa" - Nanak, through the grace of Thy Holy Nam, let everybody be exalted! Through Thy Grace, through Thy Will, let everybody be good, happy and prosperous!!!

                                    March 11, 1985
                        Beads of Truth, Summer '85

Yoga Sets

THE ROAD OF RIGHTEOUSNESS: There is one road which takes you to the destination, and all others mess you up. It is the Road of Righteousness. In this journey you have to believe that you are a complete, total, perfect self.

You know when you are ... the conscious mind must cross through the subconscious and dwell in the neutral mind. Then the Supreme will show up.

June 19, 1972

WE ARE TO AWAKEN OUR CONTROL CENTERS. This Kundalini Yoga is a process by which man unfolds the shakti in him to expand his awareness. It will transform the infinite personality of God into a finite consciousness in you.

1971 (Santa Cruz)

SELF CONTROL: If you can't control the self, you can't control the Kundalini energy. This is the basis of yoga.

June 15, 1970

YOGA: The whole body has been made to adjust to all the complication of postures and positions which can activate the brain's thoughts, extensions and performance so that man can experience what he wants to know - and that is the UNKNOWN of HIMSELF.

May 1, 1975

WAKE UP SERIES

Yogi Bhajan recommends the following series, every morning upon (or even before) arising. They can be done while still in bed.

1. **Stretch Pose:** Lying on back, arms and legs kept straig. raise feet head and hands 6" off the ground and hold with Breath of Fire from minutes or as long as possible. Eyes should look at big toes, and hands point towards feet. If the waist comes up, place hands beneath hips for support. If held less than a minute, rest and repeat pose, increasing time daily. Sets the navel.

2. **Nose to Knees:** Bend the knees and clasp legs with arms, raising head so that nose comes between knees and hold with Breath of Fire for 2 minutes. Combines Prana with Apana.

3. **Spinal Rock:** In same position, rock back and forth on the spine from neck to tailbone for 1 minute. Distributes pranic energy and relaxes spine.

4. **Ego-Eradicator:** Sit in Easy Pose and raise arms to 60° out to the sides, fingertips on pads of fingers, thumbs extended straight up and hold with Breath of Fire for 2 minutes. Then deeply inhale and VERY SLOWLY raise arms until thumbtips touch overhead, flatten hands and slowly arc them down, sweeping the aura with the palms, collecting any darkness, negativity or sickness, and press and release it into the earth, to clean and energize the aura. Feel light around you and meditate on that light.

SUN SALUTATIONS

The familiar Salute to the Sun is usually done at sunrise and sunset, (12 rounds each). Yogis consider it indespensible to lifelong health and fitness, and claim it moves every section of the spine backwards and foreards. It is performed in conjunction with de breathing, in a slow, steady continuous rhythm, facing the rising or setting sun.

Hands and feet remain in place throughout (except of course when the feet move back, or when standing). STRETCH to full extension in each pose, holding for as long as the breath can be held in or out. Visualize the posture before doing it, and be sure that the vertebrae are perfectly aligned.

If you are familiar with them, try to do them excellently, with heels kept together, weight evenly on hands and feet, and move with even grace and elegance. Beginners start with six rounds, and work up to twelve.

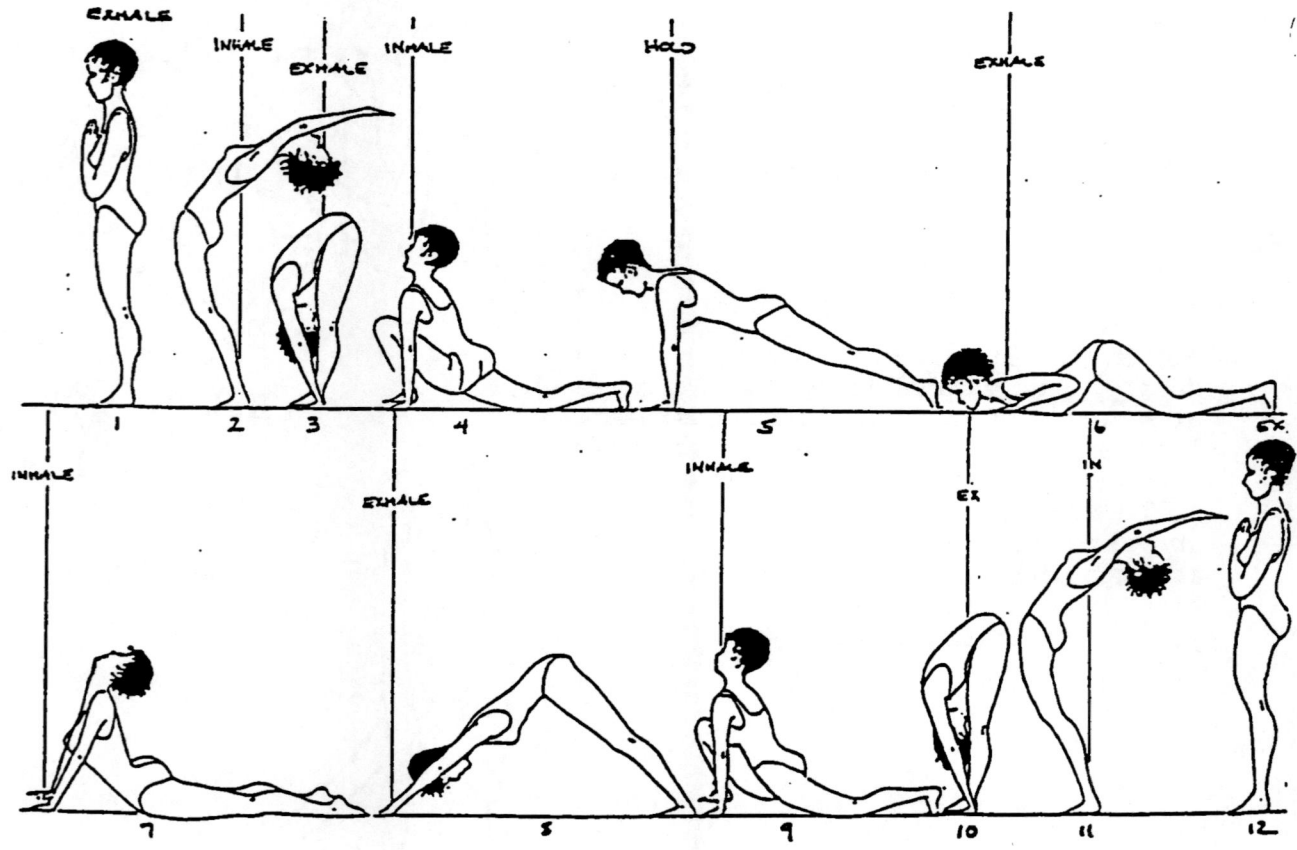

15 MINUTE MORNING SET
April 9, 1970

1. Stand and extend arms straight out and slightly pressed back, pointing thumbs straight up. Hold with Breath of Fire for 2 minutes. Then inhale deeply, slowly raising arms overhead 'til thumbs meet, arch back, and exhaling, slowly bend forward to touch toes. Charges electro-magnetic field.

2. Sit, spreading legs wide apart. Grab left foot and lower head to left knee, with Breath of Fire for 2 mins. To end, deeply inhale, completely exhale and pull Mulbhand, holding as long as possible. Relax and repeat on right side.

3. Locust Pose: On stomach, place hands palms down under thighs (beginners use fists) and inhale as you raise the straight legs as high as possible. Exhale and apply Mulbhand, holding as long as possible. Repeat and continue for 3 minutes, relax 2.

4. Cobra Pose: Concentrating at the 3rd eye, arch torso up in Cobra. Inhale, exhale and pull Mulbhand, holding as long as possible. Repeating as long as possible. Repeat and continue for 3 minutes. Relax 2 mins.

5. Shoulderstand: On back, raise legs and hips perpendicular to the floor, supporting them with the hands, weight on shoulders, neck and upper arms. Take 3 deep breaths, and on 3rd exhale apply Mulbhand, kicking buttocks rapidly with alternate heels for as long as possible. Inhale, repeat and continue for 3 minutes, resting 2 minutes

6. Sit in Easy Pose, and lie back down, hands folded in Venus Lock on the stomach. Meditate at 3rd eye.

COMMENTS: This powerful set raises Kundalini energy and is excellent preparation for meditation. (#3-6 were designated "15 Minute Morning Set" - #1 & 2 increase the time.).G.K.

EXERCISES FOR MAINTAINING A FLEXIBLE SPINE

Low back pain is one of the most common health complaints of adults and one of the most common causes of absenteeism. A quick fix for a back ache is not as easy as a quick energy pick up. The best way to avoid back aches is to do preventive exercises.

This series of exercises works systematically from the base of the spine to the top. All 26 vertebrae receive stimulation and all the energy centers receive a burst of energy. There is increased circulation to the spinal fluid which contributes to greater mental clarity. This series will give increased vitality, help prevent backaches, reduce tension, and keep you young by increasing the flexibility of the spine.

This can be done in the morning as a way to give you added energy for the day. It can also be done in the evening before dinner to revitalize you after a busy day and give you energy for the evening.

Rotate the Pelvis

Sit in easy pose. Place the hands on the knees. Deeply roll the pelvis around in a grinding motion. Do 26 rotations in each direction.

This exercise starts opening up the energy in the lower spine and aids in digestion.

Spinal Flex

Sit in easy pose, grab the ankles. As you inhale, flex the spine forward, keeping the shoulders relaxed and the head straight. Do not move the head up and down. Exhale and relax the spine back. Continue rhythmically with deep breaths for 1-3 minutes or up to 108 times. As you inhale feel the energy go down the spine and as you exhale feel it come back up to the third eye. Bring SAT down and NAM back up the spine. To end, inhale deep, hold it, apply rootlock, exhale and relax. Feel the energy circulate.

This exercise stimulates and stretches the lower spine.

Spinal Flex On Heels

Sit on the heels, place the hands flat on the thighs. Continue spinal flex as above.

This exercise works higher up on the spine.

Neck Rolls

Roll the neck slowly in one direction and then in the other. Continue for at least one minute in each direction. Do this very methodically so that you do not skip, but work out areas of tension.

This exercise removes tension in the neck and stimulates the thyroids.

Shoulder Stand & Plow

On the back, raise legs and torso above the head, supporting the body with the hands at the waist and extending the legs and hips into a straight line, with long, deep breathing for 1 to 2 minutes. Then drop the feet back over head into Plow Pose, resting arms on the ground. Rest there a minute before slowly lowering hips onto floor, vertebra by vertebra.

This exercise bends and stretches the entire spine, especially the neck and thoracic vertebrae. It stimulates the thyroid and the throat chakra, and relaxes and energizes the spine.

Fish Pose

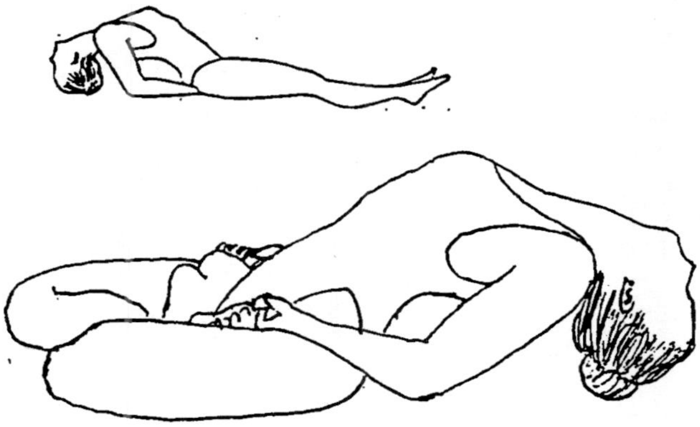

Sit in Lotus Pose, or with legs outstretched, and lie back on the elbows, arching the sternum up, with the weight on the top of the head and the hips. Grab big toes with opposite fingers and do Breath of Fire or long deep breathing for 1 to 2 minutes. (With legs stretched out in front, rest on hips, elbows and top of head.)

Fish Pose is the counter-pose for Plow and Shoulder Stand. It prevents or corrects rounded shoulders and jutting neck. It also stimulates the thyroid and the throat chakra.

Side Twists

Sit on the heels, place the hands on the shoulders, fingers in front and thumbs in back. Inhale, twist to the left, exhale, twist to the right. Twist your head to each side as well. Gradually feel an increased rotation in your spine. Keep elbows parallel to the ground. <u>To end</u>: inhale center, hold the breath, apply rootlock, exhale, relax and feel the energy circulate. Continue 1-2 minutes or 26 times. This exercise can be done standing up, allowing the arms to swing freely with the body.

This exercise opens up the heart center and stimulates the upper spine.

Side Bends

In Easy Pose, clasp hands behind neck in Venus Lock and bend straight sideways at the waist to touch elbow on the floor beside the hip, and then reverse. Inhale as you bend left, exhale right. Don't arch or contract the back but bend sideways only. Do 1-2 minutes or 26 times. This exercise can be done standing, allowing the arms to swing freely.

Side bends are good for the liver and colon and for spinal flexibility.

Shoulder Shrugs

Still on the heels or in easy pose shrug both shoulders up with the inhale and down with the exhale. Inhale up, hold, apply rootlock, relax. Do for less than 2 minutes.

This exercise loosens up the tension in the shoulders.

Cobra

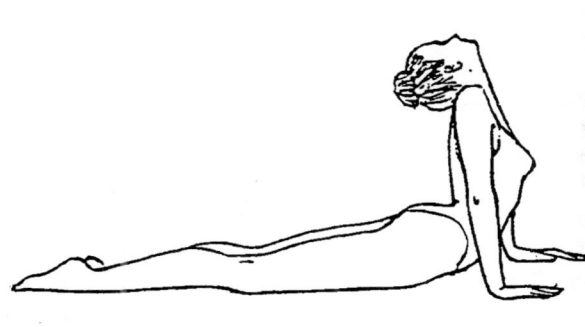

Lie on the floor with the palms on the floor under the shoulders. As you inhale, slowly arch the spine up, leading with the nose, then chin, then pushing off with your hands vertebra by vertebra, until you are arched back as far as possible with no strain in the lower back, concentrating on a good stretch from the heart center up. Breath long and deep or do breath of fire. To end, inhale, hold, pull the energy up the spine and exhale, <u>very slowly, one vertebra at a time</u> come down. Relax. 1-3 minutes.

This exercise strengthens the lower back. removes tension in the back and balances the flow of sexual energy with navel energy.

Rock and Roll on the Spine

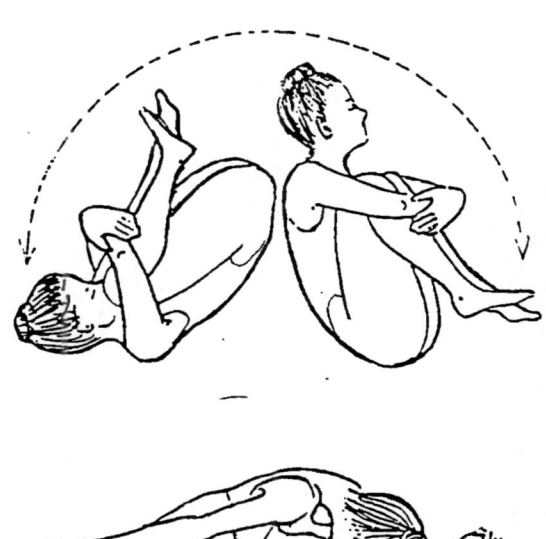

Bring your knees to your chest, grab them with the arms, and rock back and forth on the spine, massaging it gently from the neck to the base of the spine. 1-2 minutes.

This exercise circulates energy and relaxes the spine.

Alternate Leg Stretches

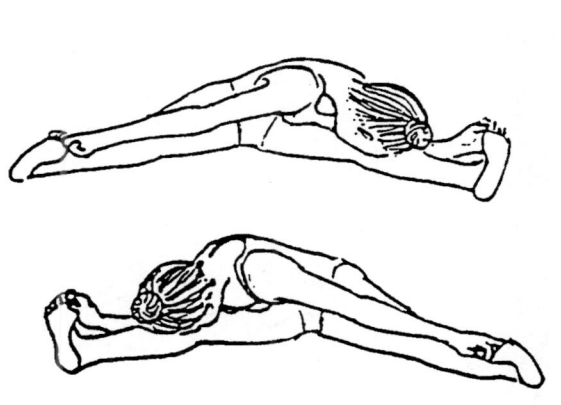

Spread the legs wide apart, grasping the toes or any other place on the legs where it is possible to keep the knees straight. Inhale center and exhale down to the left leg, inhale center and exhale down to the right leg. Continue with powerful breathing. Inhale center, hold the breath, apply root lock and then relax. Bring the legs together and bounce them up and down a few times to relax the muscles and massage them. Loosen up the muscles, but do not strain them. Bend from the lower back and get a good stretch in the back. 1-2 minutes.

Life Nerve Stretch

Legs outstretched, bring right foot into left thigh, and slowly bend over the left leg to grab the foot or ankle (or wherever it is comfortable), keeping the leg flat on the ground. Breathe long and deep or do Breath of Fire for 1-2 minutes. Inhale deeply and slowly come up. Bounce the legs and massage them. Switch sides and repeat. This exercise stretches leg muscles and lower back.

Cat Cow

Come on the knees and the hands, inhale as you flex your spine down and bring your head up. Exhale as you flex your spine up in an arched position with the head down to the neck. Keep the arms straight. Continue rhythmically with powerful breathing, gradually increasing the speed as your spine becomes more and more flexible. Inhale in saggy cow, hold, pull the energy up the spine, exhale and relax on the heels. Sit and slow down the breath and feel the energy circulate. Concentrate at the third eye. 1-3 minutes.

This exercise is known as the self chiropractor. Done regularly it loosens up and adjusts the spine.

Pick Me Up Exercise

Lie down on your back and just relax for a moment. Then bend your knees and draw the heels up towards the buttocks, keeping the feet flat on the floor. Grab your ankles and holding on to them, slowly raise the hips up, arching the lower spine and lifting the navel towards the sky. As you lift up, slowly inhale the breath through your nose. Hold the breath as you gently stretch up, lifting as high as is comfortable, then slowly relax down again as you breathe out through the nose.

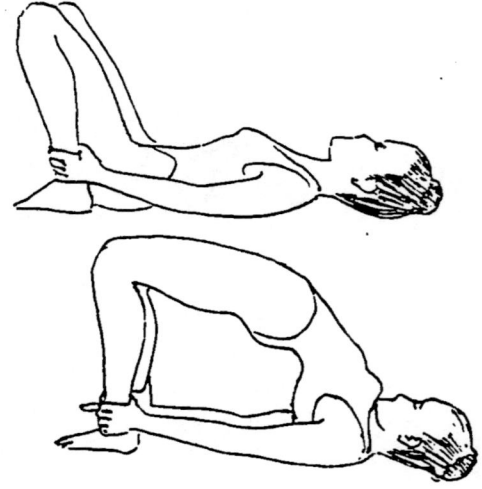

Slowly repeat this lifting up and down movement a minimum of twelve times, synchronizing the breathing with the movement of the hips, and a maximum of 26 lifts. To go from the minimum number of 12, to the maximum number 26, increase your total 1-2 lifts per day. To end, inhale up, hold the breath for ten seconds, then relax down, stretching the legs out. Relax and feel the energizing effect of the exercise.

Exercise Tips: If you can't grab your ankles, let the arms be at your side and lift up using the arms to help push you up. People with any history of lower back pain should check with their doctor before beginning. Try to let your breathing do the work--inhale the hips up and exhale them down. This exercise will automatically get you to breathe deeply. Keep the eyes closed throughout this and other exercises so that you can feel your body move rhythmically, without visual distractions. Rest on your back for two minutes after the exercise and just enjoy its vitalizing effect!

This exercise releases abdominal stress! It gives you an immediate boost of energy throughout your body that lasts well into the day. It also stimulates your thyroid. It allows you to breathe deeper and adds to your energy level. It moves the energy from the lower spine to the upper spine.

Relaxation

Deeply relax your back, hands to the side, palms facing up.

> SELF RESPECT: The moment you value yourself, the whole world values you!
>
> March 3, 1970
>
> NOW: Tomorrow will take care of itself, and yesterday has already gone. The time is now! There is no initiation, no one to carry you across; you must stand on your own two lotus feet.
>
> June 19, 1972

SELF ADJUSTMENT OF THE SPINE

1. Stand with the palms together at heart center. Raise the left leg and place the sole of the foot on the inside of the right thigh, so that the heel touches the groin, or place the foot <u>on</u> the thigh in Lotus Pose, in Tree Posture, breathing long and deep, palms together in Prayer Pose, and breath long and deep for 2 minutes.

Then bring the palms overhead stretching the arms up and keeping the elbows straight, palms together for 2 more minutes.

Switch legs and repeat for 2 more minutes in each position.

COMMENTS: Ideally the heel of the raised foot should be resting <u>on</u> the pelvic bone. The body should be balanced with the spine firm. There will be pressure at the base of the spine and all the vertebrae will automatically be adjusted. Especially effective for women, and good for menstrual problems.

2. Stand straight with heels together, toes pointing out at 60° to each other. Interlace fingers and place palms on top of the head. Bend knees and squat all the way down, keeping heels on the ground (buttocks 2-3 inches above the ground). Spine should be kept straight but the lower back will bend slightly in order to balance the body. Eyes look straight ahead to balance, inhale down, and exhale up taking 5 seconds to arise, and 5 seconds to descend. 21 repetitions.

COMMENTS: The angle of the back will allow the discs of the lower spine to adjust and balance themselves.

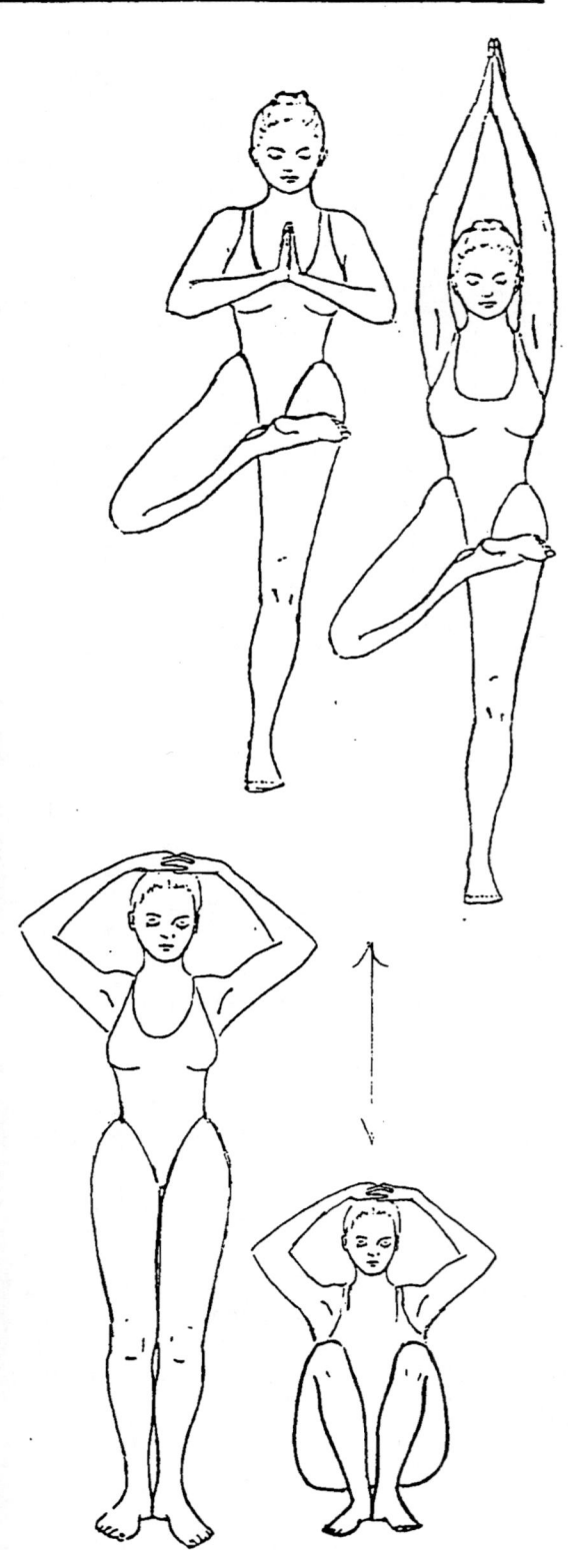

3. Stand and spread the legs as wide as possible. Bend forward from the waist and grasp toes, keeping the knees outside of the arms. Bring the back parallel to the ground and keep the head up in Table Pose. Then bounce the lower back and buttocks up and down 11 times, inhaling up and exhaling down, head remaining in place throughout. Stand and breathe normally for 5 seconds, and then repeat bouncing 11 more times, 11 bounces per 7-8 seconds. Continue for 3 mins.

COMMENTS: This exercise corrects the sciatic erve in the thighs. There is no other system which can make this correction as well. The sciatic nerve only hurts if it is out of place. This exercise will relieve any pain.

4. Standing, spread the legs as far apart as possible. Stretch sideways to the right, bringing the left arm up and over the head, and stretch the right arm down to the right foot, both arms straight. Hold for 10 seconds and slowly switch sides, stretching to the left foot and holding for 10 seconds. Continue without pause for 2-3 minutes.

COMMENTS: Very helpful in correcting the balance of the musculo-skeletal systems of the back.

HAIR ANTENNA: Tie your hair up on the solar centers for 6 months without cutting or trimming it. Hair pulls in solar energy to the "ojas" like antennas. Then the antenna will be clear.

October 16, 1971

YOUTHFULNESS: A man can be young as long as he wants to.

March 22, 1974

SKULL & PELVIC BONE ADJUSTMENT
January 1, 1982

These challenging sets adjust all the skull bones through the pelvic bone system, where the breath of life is triggered anwhere the breathing power of the pranic body is located. The lungs are cleansing processors, the diaphram is a help and it is through the spinal column that energy flows.

Set One

1. On stomach, place hands beneath shoulders and push up into Cobra Pose with arms straight, spine fully arched, and head dropped back. Kick the buttocks with alternate heels even faster than you think you can for 1 minute. Relax for 1 minute.

2. Squat into Frog Pose, heels raised and touching each other, arms between legs directly under shoulders, fingertips on floor. Do not alter position of arms during exercise. Inhale into standing position, hands coming off the floor, the straight, tight arms maintaining the same angle with the body, and exhale as you squat down. Continue at a constant constant, strong pace for 2-3 minutes and proceed immediately to next exercise. (For digestion

3. Continue as in #2 but with the arms crossed over the chest, Indian Chief style, for 2-3 minutes (for sexual energy), and proceed immediately to the next exercise.

4. Continue as above, but with the hands in Venus Lock (fingers interlocked, palms facing down) on top of head, for 2-3 more minutes (for the nervous system) and proceed, without pause, to the next exercise.

5. Standing straight, feet a few inches apart, extend both arms out to the sides and angled slightly forward. The left hand is held just below shoulder level and the right is just above shoulder level and a little farther from the body than the left. Relax the hands and let the balance come, feeling poised and strong. Raise onto the

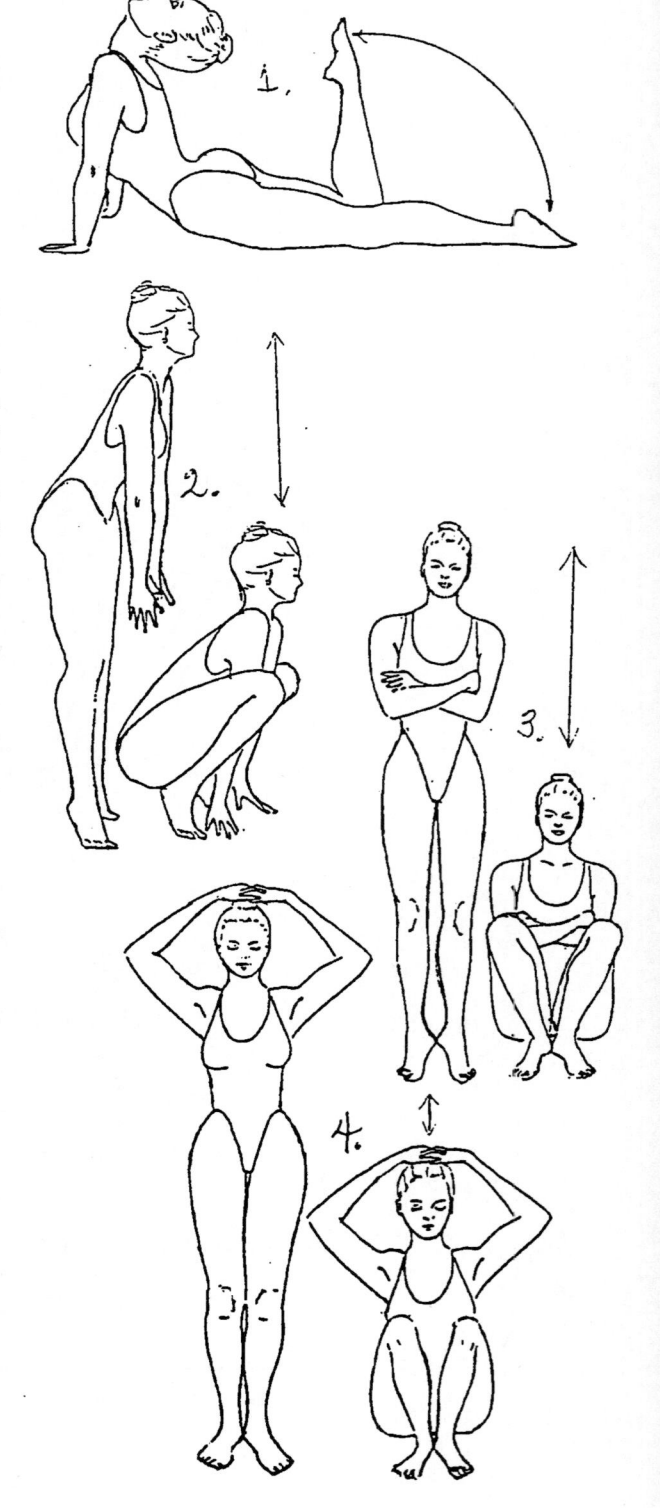

balls of the feet and keeping them in place, pivot 1/5 turn to the right (twisting from the waist) and lower heels to floor. Repeat 4 more times to face front again. Reverse the twist/pivot 5 times to the left to face original position again and continue making another circuit in the same direction. Repeat from beginning keeping the magnetic balance of the hands, moving slowly with control and a meditative mind as a worship that becomes a dance, going from side to side with the eyes closed for 4-5 minutes.

6. Squat with feet 2-3 feet apart, so that thighs are about parallel to the ground, as if you are seated in a chair. Bending forward from the waist slightly, extend arms down and out at the same angle as the legs, elbows above knees, forearms 120° to upper arms, with palms facing down. Begin bouncing up and down from the knees as you twist from the waist, side to side, taking several bounces to twist to each side, arms moving along with upper body, with eyes focused at 3rd eye for 2-3 minutes. It is like blessing the earth, a basic movement of an Indian dance.

7. Stand on left foot, without bending either knee, extend the right leg straight out in front, parallel to the floor, holding on to the right ankle with both hands by bending forward a little from the waist, but keeping the spine straight, and try to hold it for 2-3 minutes concentrating at the 3rd Eye point. This is called Kundalini Praan Dandh.

8. Feet 3 feet apart, clasp hands in Venus Lock, stretch arms up to the right and swing them down powerfully as if swinging an ax, and follow thru stretching the arms up to the left and down. Continue swinging and striking with force on alternate sides for 2-3 minutes. Then relax 10-15 minutes in Corpse Pose or Easy Pose.

Set Two

1. In Easy Pose, place right hand over left, fingers of both hands pointing away from body, with both palms facing down. Then pass right fingers between left fingers and press pads into the left palm, locking left fingers over them. (Similar to Venus Lock except palms both face down.) Stretch arms up to the right, keeping elbows straight, and swing them down to the right, return them up, right again and continue swinging for 1 minute. Rev3rse hand position, and with left hand on top, repeat on the left side for 1 minute. Change sides again and continue 1½ minutes, and again for another minute. Move from the base of the spine and move like mad!, using the weight of the hands like a hammer.

2. Regular Frog Pose, keeping fingertips on the floor, arms straight between legs, and raise buttocks, dropping head, and repeat, with the heels raised and touching each other. Be quick, but don't be crazy. 1½ minutes.

3. Lie on back, feet flat on the floor close to buttocks and catch ankles and raise hips in Inverted Bow. Lower and raise the hips very fast with Breath of Fire, and this time, go crazy! (Go all the way up.) Continue for 3 minutes.

4. Lie down on back and lock hands under head with heels close together. Sit up and touch nose to knees, quickly and return to original position for 2 minutes.

5. Still on back, raise legs to 60°, and alternately open and close them with a criss-crossing motion for 30-60 seconds, separating them wide apart. Without a breake, incorporate the arms, raising them straight up when the legs are apart, and bringing them down to the floor behind the head as the legs cross for 3 more minutes.

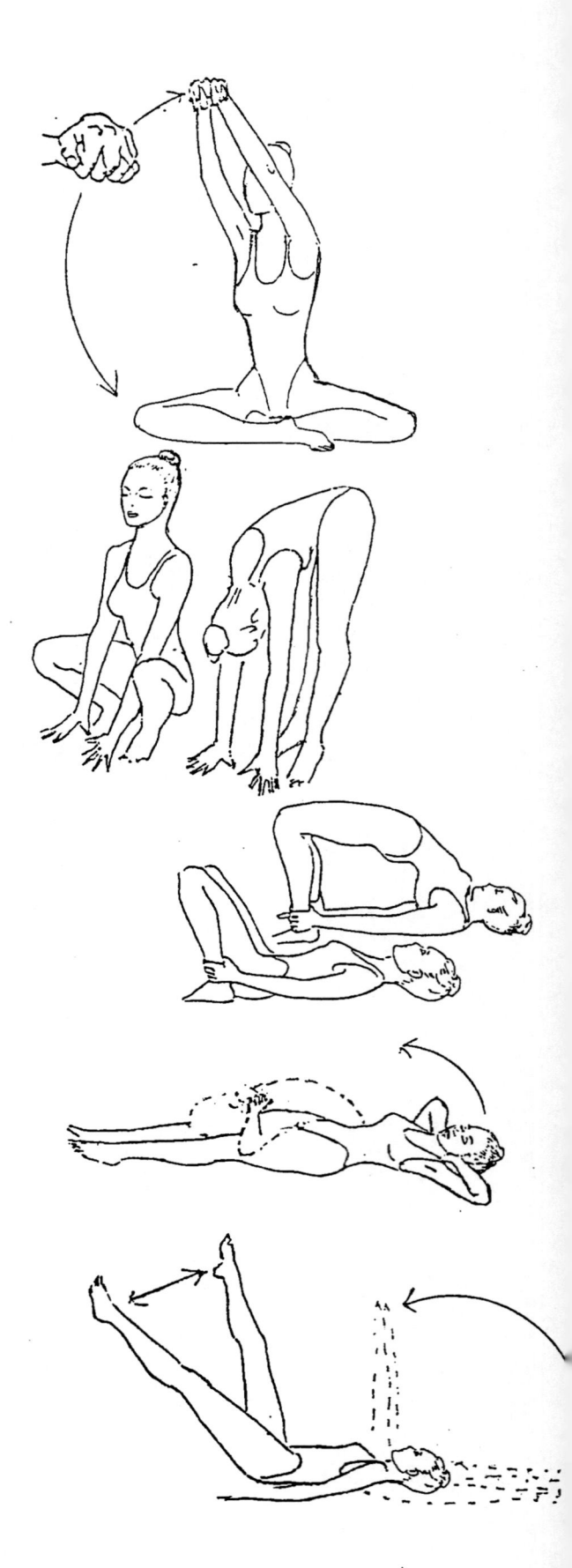

6. 52 Frogs, again, and immediately proceed to next exercise.

7. Assume Cobra Pose and come up into Platform Pose on knees (with body straight from head to knees), inhaling. From Platform on knees, exhale into Lady's Pushup (bending elbows and keeping the body straight, bring the nose to the floor). Alternate platform and pushup position 52 times.

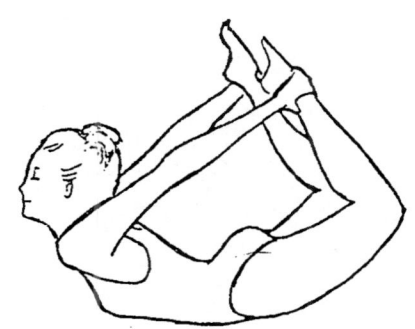

8. Bow Pose. Lie on stomach, catch ankles arching the spine and raising hands and feet as if trying to bring the toes to the head. Rock back and forth like a rocking chair, using the breath to rock you. "Whoever shall rock like this for 15-20 minutes will never see old age!" Keep up for 2 minutes.

9. In Easy Pose, absolutely straight like a Yogi, hands in Guyan Mudra, chant the Ardas Bhaee Mantra for 3 minutes.

```
Ardas Bhae
Amar Das Guru
Amar Das Guru,
Ardas Bhae

Ram Das Guru,
Ram Das Guru
Ram Das Guru,
Sache, Sahee
```

EXERCISE SERIES FOR HIPS, THIGHS & LEGS

When the hips, bones and other joints in the hip area aren't adjusted and set properly, the spine is affected, also. It will be off just enough to cause backaches and also the body will be off balance. Yogiji has given this set of exercises specifically to get the whole area stretched out, set in place and strengthened so that our spines and our beings will function properly. It is an excellent series for overcoming sciatic nerve pain and keeps that nerve in condition.

1. Lie down on back with legs wide apart, feet raised 2 feet off the floor, legs straight. Alternately, in time with the breath, inhale as left heel comes in, and exhale as right comes in and left goes out, bring each heel as close to the groin as possible, maintaining the 2 foot elevation, for 1 minute. Relax.

2. Sit up with legs stretched as wide as possible. Catch the right big toe with both hands and bounce up and down, bringing the head to the knee, inhaling up and exhaling down, 20 times. Repeat on the left leg.

3. In same posture, holding onto right toe with right hand and left toe with left hand, exhale down to the right leg and inhale up, exhale down to the left leg and inhale up, continuing 20 times.

4. In the same posture, holding toes with hands as before, pull head down to the center to floor, inhaling up and exhaling as you bounce down, rapidly with Breath of Fire, 20 times. Relax

5. Sit on heels and place palms on floor in front of knees, so that you are leaning forward slightly (buttocks remaining on heels). Flex the spine, inhaling as you arch back, exhaling as you slump forward, stretching the upper spine for 3 minutes. Relax.

SPINAL SET WITH ARDHA-MATSYENDRASANA
August 18, 1969

1. Ardha-Matsyendrasana (Spinal Twist): Seated in Easy Pose, cross the right leg over the left knee. Left arm reaches around the outside of the right leg, and grabs the right foot or ankle, twisting the spine and neck to look over the right shoulder. Sit evenly on both buttocks, not on the heel, and keep the spine perfectly straight. Hold the pose with Breath of Fire for 6 minutes. Inhale, hold, pull Mulbhand and relax. Reverse arms and legs and repeat. Then relax with long, deep breathing for 2-3 minutes. (The longer you remain in the pose, the easier it is to maintain.)

2. In Easy Pose, extend arms straight out to the sides, hands in Guyan Mudra. With Breath of Fire, raise and lower alternate arms slowly (8-12 breaths per stroke) for 6 minutes.

3. Yoga Mudra: Sit in Lotus Pose or Siddhasana, and lower the head to the ground, clasping the hands in Venus Lock on the back. Chant

Ek Ong Kar
Sat Nam
Siri Wha Guru

for 5-11 minutes, pulling the locks and spinning energy up the spine - (see Laya Yoga #7).

COMMENTS: This is an excellent preparation for meditation, because it increases spinal circulation and raises Kundalini energy. Spinal twist is practiced for obtaining Siddhis (super-natural powers), and it is a good way to release the spine. The 2nd exercise opens the Heart Chakra, and the third brings Kundalini energy up the spine. G.K.

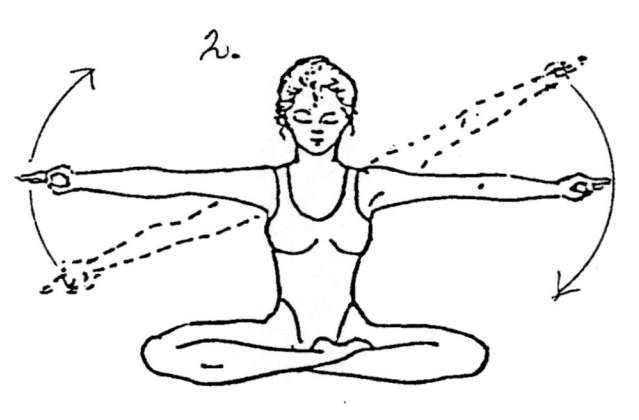

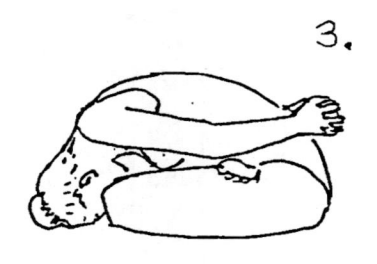

KRIYA FOR REGENERATION

Given by Singh Sahib (Yogi Bhajan)
December 27, 1982

1. In Celebate Pose (sitting between heels), arms level with shoulders, thumbs on Mercury mounds, inhale and criss-cross arms in front, still at shoulder level, and back out to sides. Keep elbows straight and arms high, and swing powerfully. Balances the sinuses and effects pituitary. (7 minutes.)

2. Still in Celebate Pose (or on heels, in Rock Pose), rotate fists and forearms around each other, keeping thumbs on Mercury mounds. Circle away from the body, at heart center. Fast! Look at hands and concentrate on them. For the Pineal gland and sinuses. This is "Drishti Tratka Kriya". (7 minutes)

3. Stand on one leg, extending the other straight up and back, parallel to the ground, with hands at knee cap to maintain balance. Change legs. Takes away old age, wrinkles, all mental, physical and spiritual deteriorations. The best thing for the spine. (3½ minutes each side)

4.(A) In Shoulder Stand, bend the knees, straining them to the sky, bringing the heels down as far as you can, weight on hands. This is "Bapareet Karnee". (3½ minutes)

4.(B) Still in Shoulder Stand, inhale and lift the legs, exhale, making the sound "hum" as they come down and kick buttocks. Repeat. (The "hum" is not spoken in the normal way, and is made with the back of the nostrils, and very nasal.) To stop aging and grey hair. (3½ minutes)

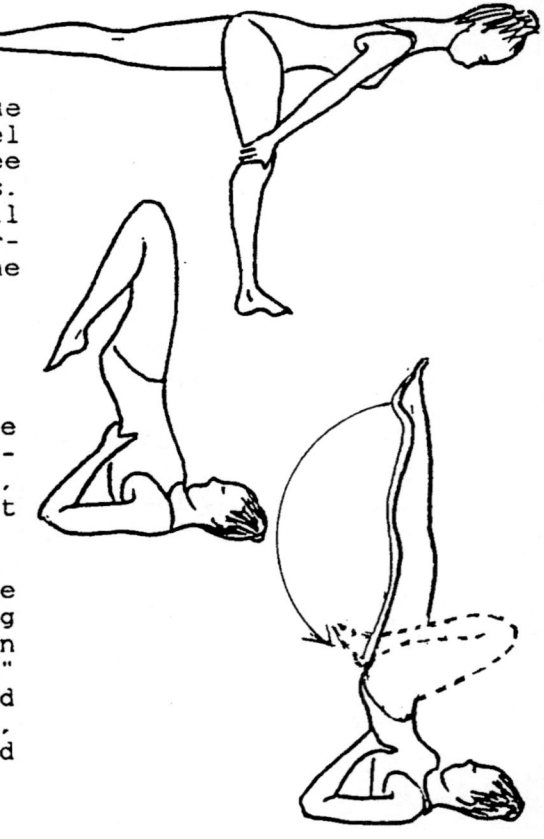

37

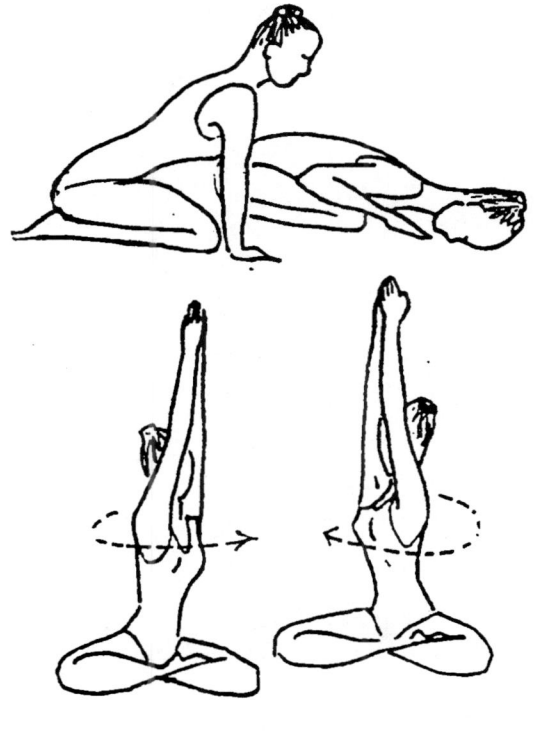

5. Sit on heels (Vajrasan or Rock Pose), and put palms on ground before you. Exhale and touch forehead to the ground before knees & hands, and inhale up. Hands stay in place. This is "Chinese Pranayam" - the best exercise for the neck. (7 minutes)

6. In Easy Pose, place palms together overhead, arms straight, and twist torso left and right. Keep neck in line with the spine and move from the hips. (3½ minutes)

7. In the same position, bend side to side, breathing long and deep, inhaling to the left, exhaling to the right. Swing from the hips like a tree, and bend as far as you can. This is "Pinjanee". Best exercise for the liver (and waistline). (3½ minutes)

8. Stretch right leg out, sitting on left heel. Grab toes an push spine totally straight, breathing long and deep through the mouth, powerfully. This is "Shakti Chaloni Chosh". (7 minutes)

As originally given this set is to be done three times for the full seven minutes each exercise. To begin with, cut times in half, working up to full time. Repeat once or twice at short or long times.

COMMENT: Those who master this will realize many!!! benefits

RELAXATION SERIES TO TO REMOVE NEGATIVITY & TENSION

February 15, 1972

1. In Easy Pose, inhale for 5 seconds, exhale for 5 seconds, and pump stomach for 5 seconds. Continue for 5 minutes.

2. Lying on back, raise hips ONLY off the ground, without using hands, keeping legs and back on the ground. Hold with long, deep breathing for 1-3 mins. (For youthfulness.)

3. On back, raise both legs 4-6 inches and hold with long, deep breathing for 1-3 minutes. "The whole body will salute you and you can digest anything." All toxins will come out and it is good for the heart.

4. Raise left leg up to 90°, keeping the rest of the body relaxed with long, deep breathing for 3 minutes. Cleans toxins and renews vigor.

5. Raise head only, keeping the rest of the body relaxed, with long deep breathing for 3 minutes. Good for headaches.

6. Make a pillow of the right arm and relax on the right side, raising the left leg as high as possible and hold with relaxed body for 3 minutes.

7. Relax on the stomach for 1 minute. Good for the colon and eliminates toxins

8. Catch heels with hands and pull into buttocks without raising the body and hold with long, deep breathing 3 minutes

9. Raise upper body in Cobra with the support of the hands and hold with long, deep breathing for 3 minutes or as long as possible.

10. In meditation pose, chant

    Ad Gurey Name,
    Jugad Gurey Name,
    Sat Gurey Name,
    Siri Guru Devi Name

for 5 minutes. Set takes 26-31 minutes. You'll come out of it as fresh as from a sleep. Tension is good if followed by relaxation.

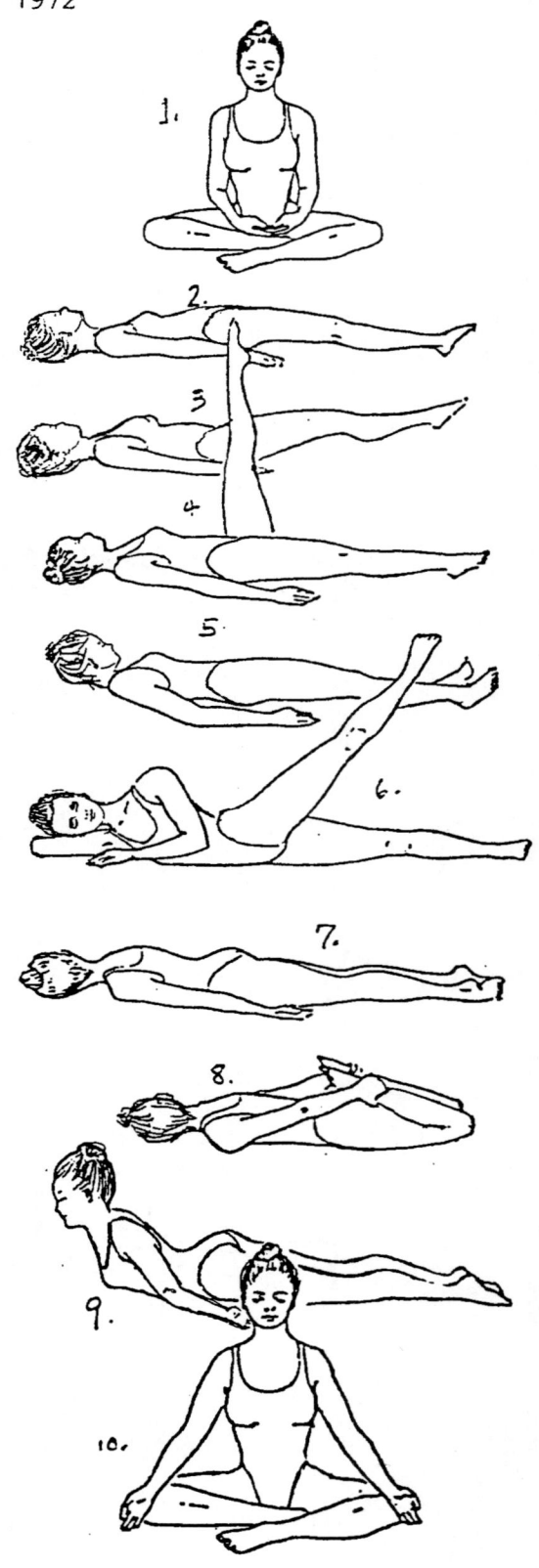

REMOVING TENSION & NEGATIVITY
Exercises for tension & periodic headache

1. Apply thumbs to cheeks, below eyes and massage in a circular motion for 3 minutes. Releases tension.

2. Right hand flat, place base of palm on center of forehead just above the nose. Vibrate hand 3/4" up and down, twice a second, meditating on the brow point for 3 minutes. For eye tension and mind focus.

3. Center of right palm on center of skull. Look up through top of head and massage in small circular motion for 3 minutes. Aids memory.

4. With hands in Venus Lock behind neck, lean back 60°, and raise legs to 60° and hold for 3-10 minutes. Can be done in the morning to balance the Electro-Magnetic Field.

5. On back with legs up to 90° and spread apart 60°, hold on to toes with long, deep breathing for 3 minutes.

6. Seated in Easy Pose, roll head on neck easily for 2 minutes.

7. In Cobra Pose, walk your hands forward lightly dragging the body for 5 minutes.

8. In Easy Pose, silently meditate on
    Sa-Ta-Na-Ma
for 5 minutes.

For tension and periodic headache.

SET FOR STATE OF MIND AND PARANOIA

1. In Easy Pose, extend arms straight out to the sides and close the fingertips to the base of the palms, pointing the thumbs straight up. Apply chin lock and rotate the hands at the wrists so that thumbs point back, then up, straight ahead, down and back, continuing with powerful breathing for 7-8 minutes. This works on the pituitary and breaks through paranoia.

2. Bend elbows and arc the hands up to almost touch thumbs to shoulders on the inhale, and straight out again on the exhale, one cycle per second, with powerful breathing for 2 minutes to stimulate the pituitary gland.

3. Spinal flex in Easy Pose. Inhale arching the spine (belly & chest forward), and pull the neck tucked tightly in and up, then exhale, contracting the back, pushing the chin out slightly, slowly (1-2 seconds per cycle) for 4 minutes. Stimulates thyroid/parathyroid balance and promotes weight loss. Done correctly it will keep one looking young.

4. Still in Easy Pose, extend hands out to the sides again, palms facing up, and on the exhale bring the hands to the shoulders. Inhale and lift the elbows up as far as possible, lifting the shoulders and the entire spine. Exhale and lower elbows, inhale, extend hands out to sides, etc. One cycle takes 2 seconds. Continue for 3-4 minutes, mentally chanting (and coordinating) with powerful breathing:

Har,   Har,   Har,

5. Lie flat on back with arms relaxed at the sides. Heels together, raise them 6 inches off the floor, keeping the knees straight and toes forward, and begin long, deep and powerful breathing from the navel point for 2-3 minutes. Works on lower abdomen and navel.

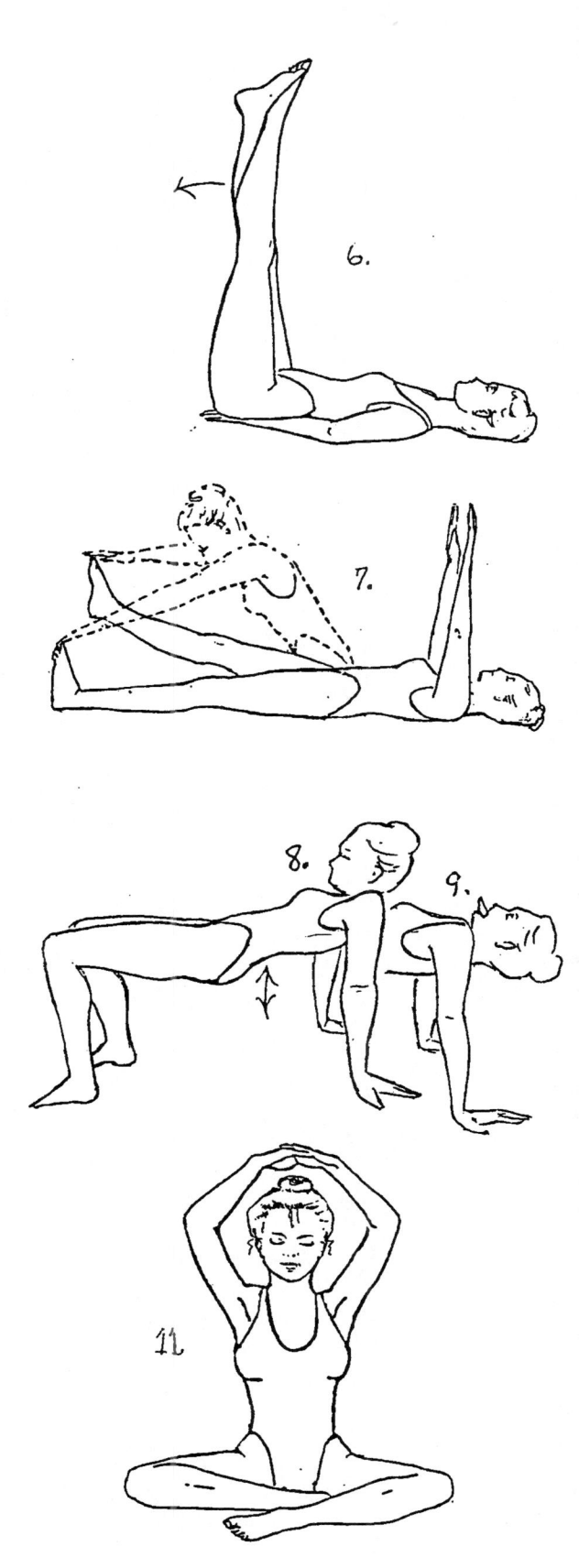

6. Still on back, place hands under buttocks, palms down, and cross legs at the ankles, keeping them straight. Inhale and raise legs up to 90°, exhale and lower them, rythmically with powerful breathing for 3 minutes, reversing the cross of the ankles as needed. Removes excess water from the body.

7. Lying flat, spread legs apart and raise both arms to 90°. palms facing the feet. Inhale and sit up touching the toes with the hands, as you exhale. Then inhale and lie down again, coordinating the movement with the breath for 6 minutes. This works on the pelvic bone and removes feelings of paranoia.

8. Bridge Pose. Sit up, hands beside hips, fingers towards feet, elbows locked, and bend knees drawing the feet in to the buttocks, and raise torso so that the body from the knees to shoulders forms a straight line parallel to the ground, with the arms and lower legs at right angles. With the chin tucked into the chest, move the body up and down for 3-4 minutes. Works on buttocks and hips and keeps you young.

9. Same posture as above, but with the head back and parallel to the rest of the body. Open the mouth and stick the tongue out with heavy breathing. This is Reverse Lion Pose. Continue for 1-2 minutes. Then begin purring like a lion, allowing the back of the tongue to vibrate as though gargling. Continue powerfully for 1 minute as a preventative against the common cold.

10. In Easy Pose, sing "Nobility" for 4-5 minutes or breathe long and gently for the same period.

11. Interlace fingers into open Venus Lock with thumb tips touching and pointing back, and raise arms over the head forming a halo with your hands. Focus eyes at the tip of the nose and breathe through the navel point. Listen to the "Jaap Sahib" tape and sing along, copying the sound exactly, or breathe long, deep and gently for 9 minutes.

EXERCISE SET FOR RELAXATION & RELEASING FEAR

1. Stand and bend forward from the waist, keeping the back parallel to the ground. Reach behind you and hold on to your calves to maintain balance, and flex the spine as in Cat/Cow. Inhale and flex the spine down as if someone were sitting on the back, neck arching up, and exhale arching spine up, tucking chin to chest. Use hands, knees and feet as a firm base of support, legs remaining straight. Rhythmically coordinate movement with breath for 7 minutes. Works on kidneys & liver.

2. Still standing place hands on hips and rapidly rotate torso from the waist in large circles, powerfully for 9 minutes. Rejuvenates spleen & liver. (You may feel nauseous as liver releases toxins.)

3. In Easy Pose, make fists of hands and place them in front of you as if grasping a steering wheel, and twist the body from side to side to the maximum, keeping elbows and allowing the neck to move, for 4 minutes. Works on the kidneys. The neck must move to release blood to the brain.

4. In Easy Pose, extend arms up at 60°, palms facing up, fingers straight, thumbs extended. Rapidly open & close hands bringing fingertips to base of palms for 7 minutes. Breaks up deposits in fingers & prevents/removes arthritis.

5. In Easy Pose, extend arms out to the sides parallel to ground and make sides parallel to ground and make fists with thumbs tucked inside on the mounds of little fingers. Inhale through the mouth and flex elbows bringing fists to shoulders, and exhale thru the mouth as arms are straightened out to the sides, moving rapidly and breathing powerfully coordinating movement with breath for 6 minutes. Removes tension from neck and purifies blood. Fears will leave when you powerfully project out on exhale.

6. Same hand position as #5, palm side of fist facing down, stretch arms straight out in front and rotate fists in small circles, left fist counter-clockwise, right, clockwise, at heart level, elbows straight, fists tight, moving shoulder blades and muscles under shoulders for 2 minutes. Adjusts muscles under breasts - if they are tight, you are uptight.

7. Crow Squatts with straight spine, feet flat on floor, fists with thumbs out at neck level, inhale up and exhale down for 3 minutes.

8. Sitali Pranayam: In Easy Pose, hands on knees, spine straight, curl the tongue protruding it slightly past lips. Inhale smoothly and deeply thru mouth, exhale thru nose for 4-5 minutes Then play 'Dukh Bhanjan' tape, if available, and meditate on the healing vibrations of the Golden Temple and the sound current of the shabad (words), coordinating breath to music for 2 more minutes. Effective against anger, bad moods and temperament.

9. Continue listening to the tape as you raise and curve the arms upwards. Close the eyes and rhythmically move your body to the music, with feeling. Stop thinking and move with the beat. If you can bring your body into exact rhythm with the music, you can go into a state of ecstacy. Continue 10 mins.

10. In Rock Pose, place hands on thighs and listen to 'Jaap Sahib' tape, bowing the forehead to the floor to the Namastang rhythm, bowing on 4 counts & resting on 1. (Without music move as follows to 10 beats: down on 1, up on 2 down on 3, up on 4, down on 5, up on 6, down on 7, and up on 8, 9, & 10.) Continue for 8 minutes. This exercise has been known to heal any rock formations in the body such as kidney and gall-bladder stones.

11. In meditative pose, calm and collect yourself and feel that you are going to realize God's light in you. Totally remove all difference between yourself and Him. Lock hands behind the head, elbows out to the sides and apply pressure, keeping spine straight. Close the eyes and chant aloud with the 'Jaap Sahib' tape, copying the very essence of it, feeling the vibrations go through your hands to the back of your head. (Without the tape, breathe long and gently in that position.) Continue for 8 minutes and relax.

MEDITATION & SELF RELIANCE
March 3, 1972

1. (A) Sit with erect spine and legs extended straight out, arms parallel to the ground and fingers pointed forward.
(B) Inhale and lean back 60°, hold, raise the legs as high as possible, and hold the position and the breath as long as possible. Exhale and lower legs.
(C) Bend forward grasping the toes and pulling firmly on them with normal breath for 11 minutes.
(D) Take several deep breaths, inhale and repeat parts (A) & (B), 3 or 4 times. (Sets the balance in the aura between North & South. Puts pressure on the liver to clean the body and increase courage.

2. Sit on heels with palms on thighs flexing the spine forward and powerfully whispering

    Sat,

and backwards, powerfully whispering

    Nam,

sounding like a snake. Contonue the spinal flex at a medium pace for 8 minutes. Then deeply inhale and exhale 4 times and relax.

3. Sit straight and press palms together, locking thumbs, (Pranam Mudra) at heart center. Press firmly on the palms and apply pressure to the center of the chest. With the entire weight of the upper body on the hands, concentrate all the mental energy at the root of the nose, and meditate in this pose for 10 minutes.

4. In Easy Pose, spine stretched erect, move the waist side to side in a regular rhythm for 3 minutes. Works on the liver.

5. Spinal Flex in Easy Pose, holding on to the ankles, rapidly and accenting the forward motion so there is a slight pulling pressure on the sex organs. Continue for 3 minutes and then relax completely.

6. Sit erect with hands in Guyan Mudra and concentrate on the root of the nose, chanting

    Sat Nam.

as you turn the head to the right shoulder, and

    Wha Guru.

as you turn the head to the left shoulder. Continue in a steady rhythm for 11 minutes.

COMMENTS: Personal radiance is blocked by fears. Fear comes with dependence. The only acceptable dependence is on the Guru and Wisdom for that will lead to self-reliance, and banish all fear. If self-reliance is strong, you are protected and those with you are protected.

This series promotes self-reliance and energizes several physical areas of the body. 1 & 4 work on the liver, 2 & 3 open the heart center of compassion and surrender, the finite identity to Infinite Wisdom. 5 works on sexual energy. 6 is a meditation that can be extended to 31 minutes When turning left, your reliance is focused on the Infinite Wisdom. Reliance in "Wha Guru" gives self-reliance as a unit in "Sat Nam".

GOD CONSCIOUSNESS is the freedom that you get from getting out of your fear complex. When your fear complex leaves you, you are God.

    Yogi Bhajan

NERVE BALANCE

1. (A) On back, raise left leg and right arm each up to 60° and hold for 1 minute, breathing through the left nostril.

   (B) Switch legs and arms and continue with left nostril breathing for 30 seconds.

   (C) Inhale deeply, exhale completely and pinch both nostrils holding the breath out for 30 seconds.

   (D) Relax on the back for 5 minutes.

2. On back, raise right foot and right arm 6" and hold with long, deep breathing for 2½ minutes. Inhale, hold 10 seconds exhale and hold out for 3 seconds Relax for 3 minutes.

3. On back, raise both feet, legs straight, toes pointed forward 2-3 feet with hands behind neck in Venus Lock, elbows on the ground with long, deep breathing for 2 minutes.

4. Back Platform on elbows. Raise left leg up to 60° and hold with navel breathing for 1 minute Relax 2 minutes.

5. Walk around on the knees, only (without touching feet to the ground) with arms out to the sides at 60° for 2 minutes Relax. (For 4th vertebrae.)

6. Jump up and down on the toes for 2 minutes.

7. TIRKUTI KRIYA: Soles of feet together, clasp feet with the hands and raise them 6 inches off the ground. Inhale, exhale and pull the head down to the left knee, inhale up, and exhale down to the right knee for 2-3 minutes. (Variation, lower head to center.)

(Some times added by G.K.)

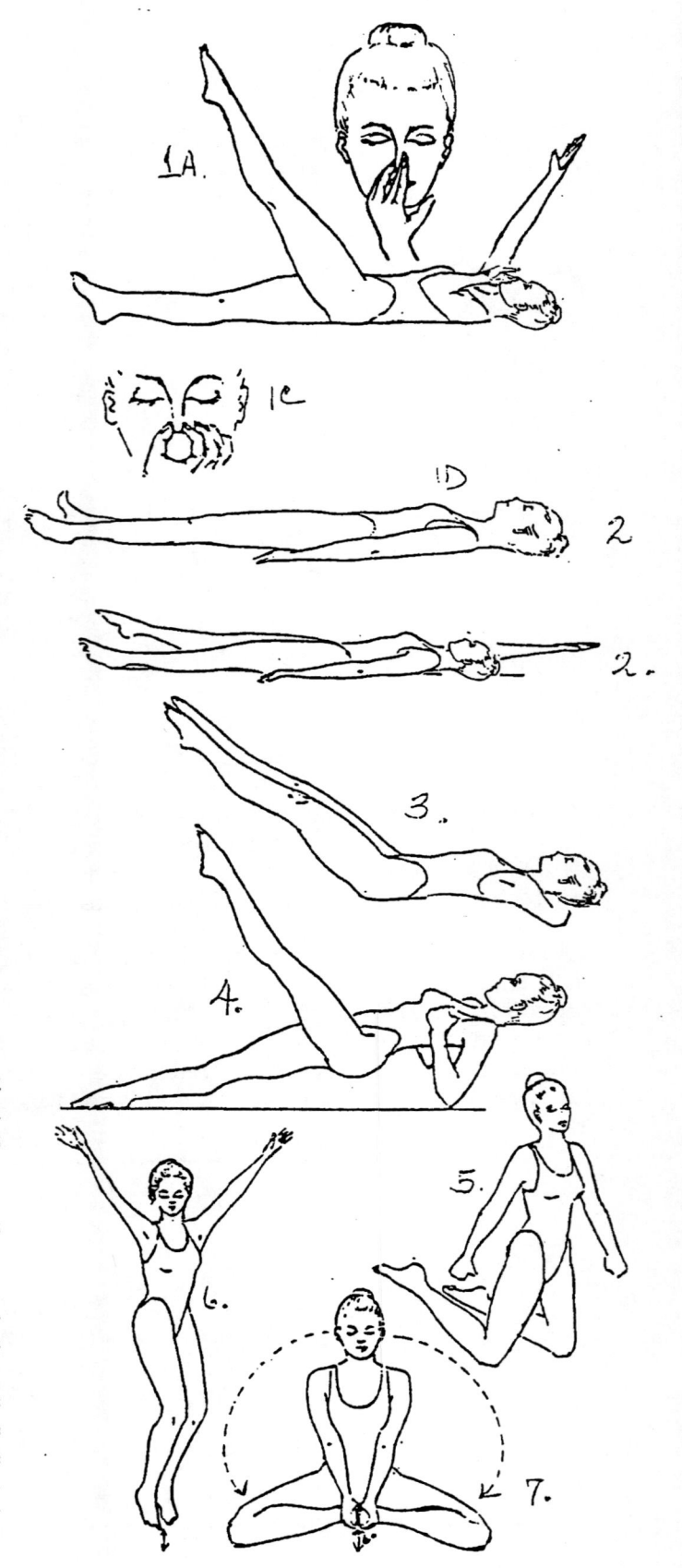

FOR DRUG DAMAGE

1. On back, with hands in Venus Lock behind the neck, raise (straight) legs to 24" and hold with long, deep breathing for 3 minutes.

2. Still on back, raise legs to 90°, inhale and spread them wide, exhale and bring them together. Repeat and continue for 3 minutes.

3. Bring knees to chest, wrap arms around legs and roll back and forth on the spine for 3 minutes.

4. In Rock Pose, place hands 8" before knees, inhale, exhale and bend forward placing forehead on the floor. Inhale up and exhale down for 3 minutes.

5. Still in Rock Pose, place hands in Venus Lock above the head and chant

   Hum, hum, hum

   for 3-11 minutes. ("Hum" means "We the total Universe")

6. Relax in Corpse Pose on the back.

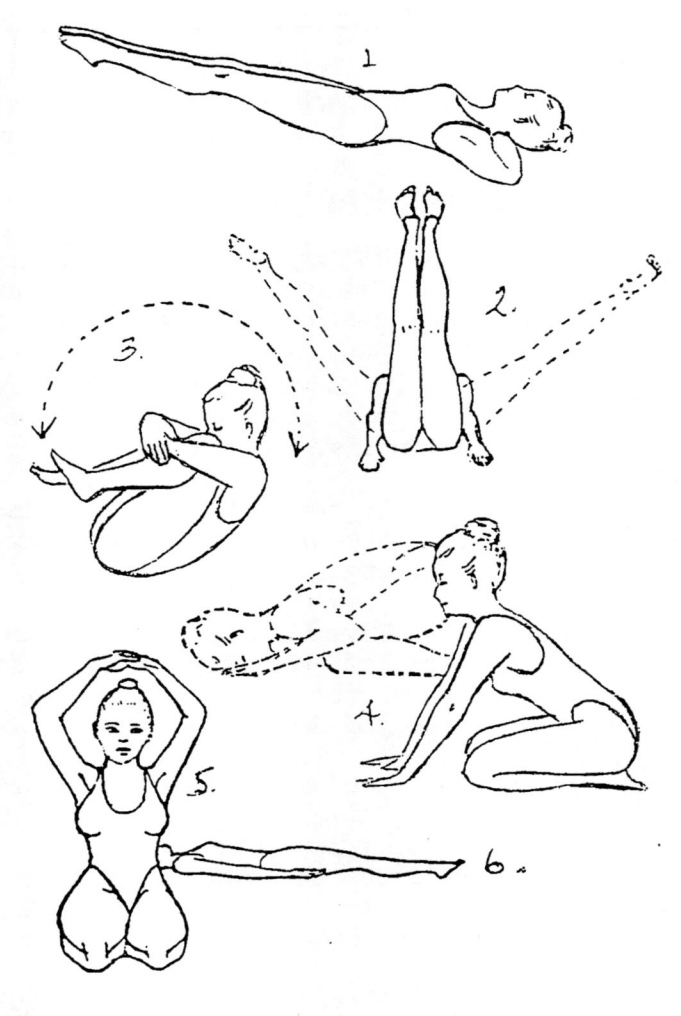

MEMORY GLAND

1. In Easy Pose, hands in Venus Lock behind back, inhale, apply pressure where skull and spine meet, exhale hold the breath out and lower forehead to the ground. Repeat 3 more times,

2. In Rock Pose, hands interlocked in Venus Lock behind neck, inhale and incline torso back to 60°, slowly, and exhale back up to 90°, slowly, repeat and continue for 1-3 minutes.

3. In Rock Pose, stretch arms back, straight and parallel to the ground, hands in Guyan Mudra, palms up, drop head back with Breath of Fire and hold for 1-3 minutes. Inhale, hold the breath, exhale and relax.

FOR MEMORY GLAND

1. On back, hands in Venus Lock behind neck, raise legs up to 60° and raise the head, with long, deep breathing for 3 minutes.

2. Sit up, placing hands behind hips and lean back to 60°. Exhale inhale and straighten arms, lifting body in a modified Platform Pose. Exhale and resume seated posture. Repeat and continue for 3 minutes.

3. In the same seated posture, meditate at the brow point for 3 minutes.

4. Visualize your eyes in the back of the head and meditate there for 3 minutes (in Easy Pose and Guyan Mudra).

5. Sit on 1 heel and stretch the other leg straight back, arms also stretched back and meditate at Brow Point with long, deep breathing for 3 minutes. Switch sides and repeat.

6. Alternately shrug shoulders for 3 minutes.

7. Stand, bend over and walk with the hands grasping the ankles for 3 minutes.

8. In meditation posture, chant the Guru Gaitri mantra for as long as you wish.

Gobinde, Mukunde,
Udare, Apare,
Haring, Karing,
Nirname, Akame.

NOTE: The Memory Gland is located ½ inch under the skull, in line with the 3rd Eye.

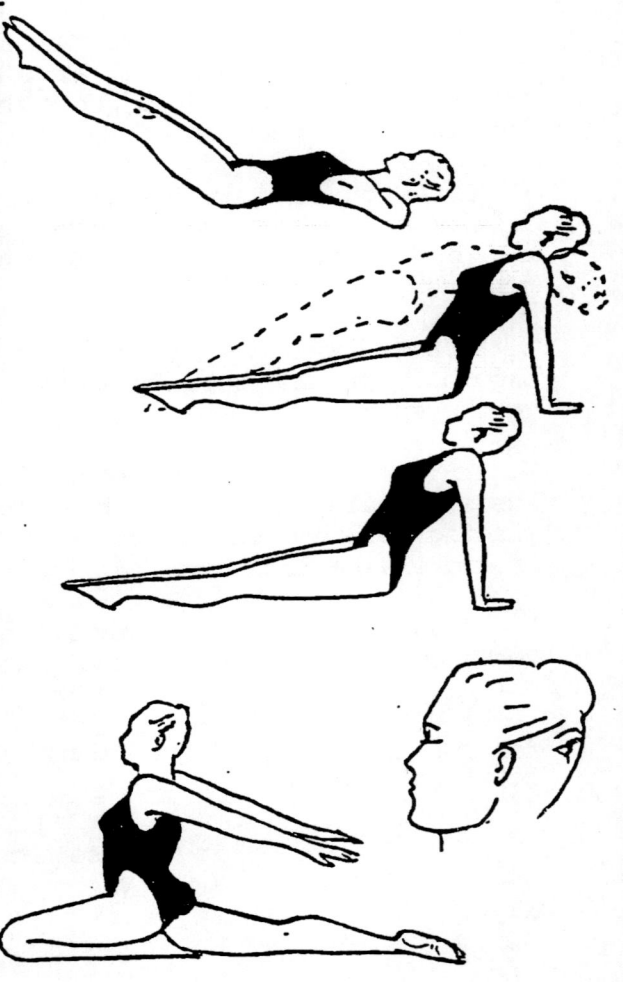

FOR THE MEMORY
December 30, 1969

1. Do regular pushups, supporting the weight on the big toenails. Inhale up, and exhale down for 2-3 minutes.

2. Bow Pose with Breath of Fire for 2-3 minutes.

3. Cobra Pose with long, deep breathing or Breath of Fire for 2-3 minutes.

4. Body Drops in Lotus Pose. Lift body off the ground and drop it down, repeating for 1-2 minutes.

5. Stretch legs out in front with the feet 1½ feet apart. Bend down and grab ankles, exhaling down and inhaling up, using the elbows to draw the head to the knees. Then inhale, exhale, hold the breath out and apply Mulbhand.

6. Back Platform - on back, raise body to hands and feet, arms and legs, and body straight. Inhale and turn chin to left shoulder, exhale and turn to right shoulder for 1-2 minutes. Repeat the exercise with the left leg raised up parallel to the ground. Then repeat, raising the right leg, 1 minute each.

7. Sat Kriya for 3-5 minutes. Seated on heels, raise arms overhead pressing palms together, keeping elbows straight and hugging ears. Inhale and pull the navel point & chant
    Sat
exhale, and relaxing the navel, chant
    Nam

8. In Easy Pose, breathe long and deep for 3 minutes relaxing the mind. Then, deeply inhale, hold the breath and apply Maha Bandha: Pull all three locks (Mulbhand, Diaphragm Lock and Neck Lock - see appendix) at once and meditate.

COMMENTS: Meditate in Maha Bandha - it is the most powerful yogic kriya. You are one breath away from God and He is in your circumvent force!

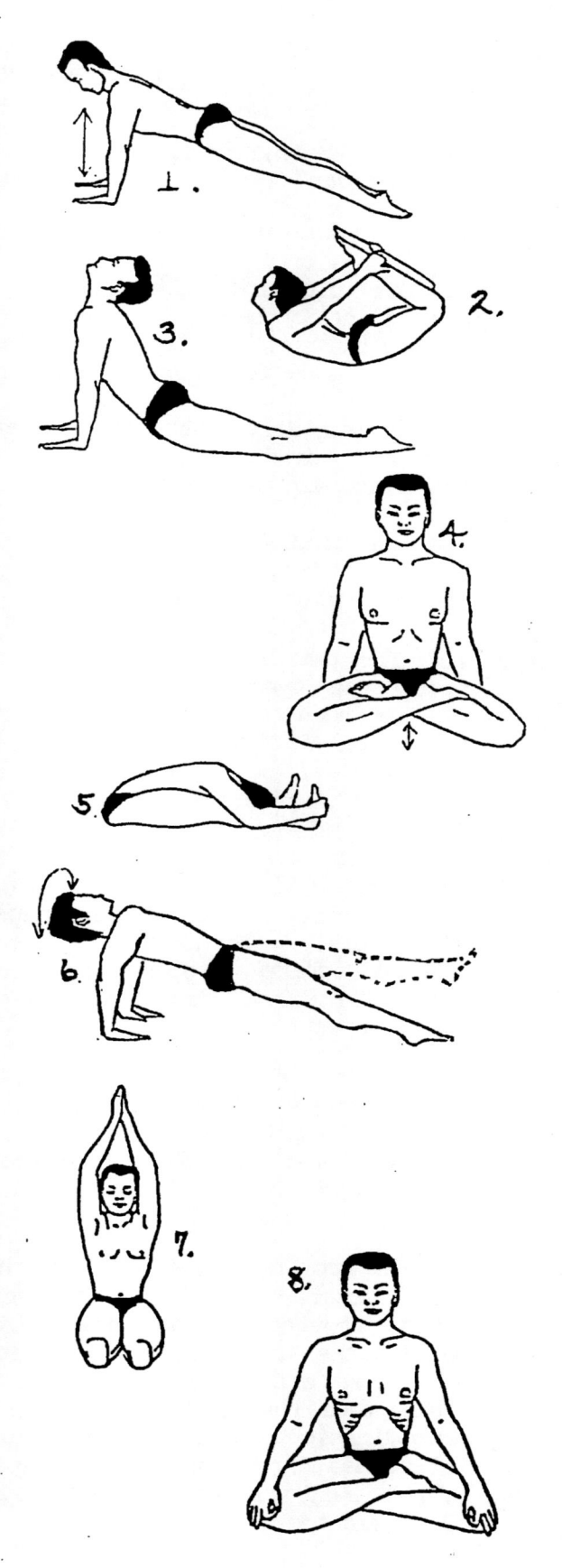

GHERANDA-SAMHITA
Head Set

For the brain, mind, intellect, concentration, will-power, memory, throat, eyesight, teeth, facial muscles, halitosis, pimples, & nervous strain

All exercises are done standing up.

1. For clearing the Pharynx: Tilt the head slightly back, keeping the eyes open and hold with gentle breathing. Clears phlegm. Good for singers. 2-3 minutes.

2. Prayer Pose with long, deep breathing for 2-3 minutes. Sublimates the sexual drive and aids concentration.

3. For mind & will power: Feet together, tilt the head way back with eyes open, and do Breath of Fire for 2-3 minutes.

4. For developing memory: Stand up and focus the eyes on a spot 5 feet ahead of the toes, with Breath of Fire. Good for mental fatigue and improves the memory. 2-3 minutes.

5. For developing the intellect: Press chin into the notch in the sternum and do Breath of Fire. "By doing Jalandhara Bhanda, the nectar that drips from the 1000 petaled lotus is not burnt up in the digestive system, and it controls the life force, kindling the Kundalini". 2-3 minutes.

COMMENTS: #1 thru 5 are effective in curing states of mental and nervous strain, causing nutrition to flow to the brain tissues and glands. Bending the neck interrupts venous return and stretches the spinal cord and the peripheral nerves.

6. Improving eyesight: With all your will, stare at a spot between eyebrows, feet together, and head tilted back. Stimulates the junction of nerves between the eyes and ears, and aids the muscles that move the eyeball, the iris, and the coordination of those muscles. Prevents blindness and cures all eye diseases. Throw away glasses in 40 days practice! 2-11 minutes.

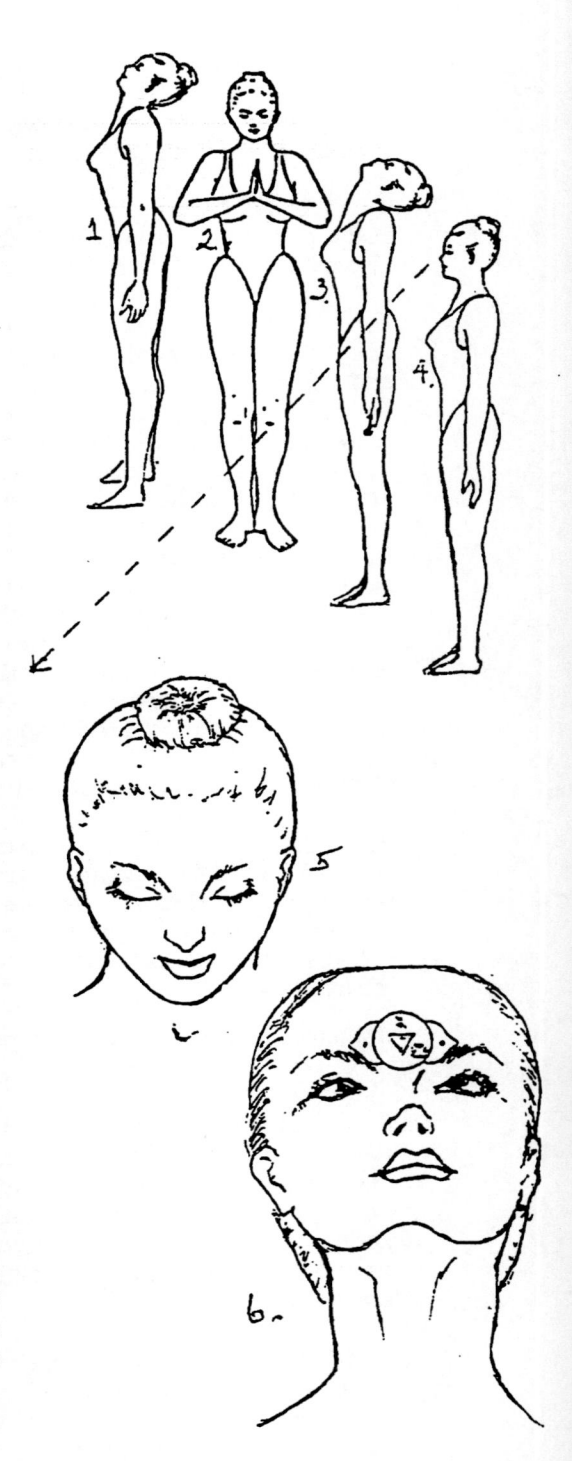

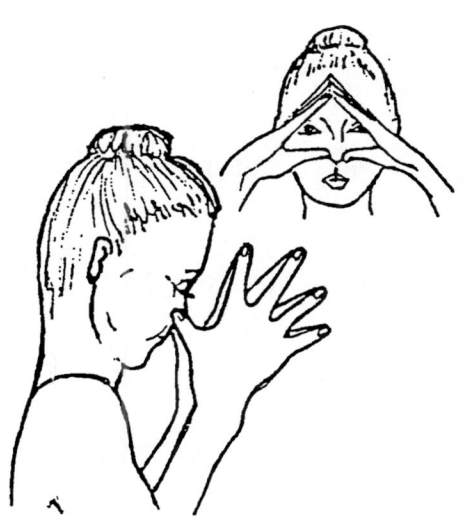

7. Rejuvenating the cheeks: Join fingertips and close nostrils with thumbs. With eyes open, inhale through "crow beak" (puckered lips), hold the breath and close the eyes, dropping the chin into the sternal notch, and puffing cheeks out with the breath. Hold as long as possible, then return head to normal, open eyes, and exhale SLOWLY through the nose. This aerates the oral cavity, bringing fresh air where germs breed. Good for facial muscles, strengthens teeth, cures pyorrehea caries, halitosis and pimples!!! This practice makes a man free of old age symptoms and gives the longevity of a camel. Repeat several times.

NOTE: Times were unspecified and have been added by G.K.

FOR THE EYES
1970

1. Stretch legs out in front, and bend over, grasping and pulling on big toes. Roll eyes to the 3rd Eye, and hold until pain comes. Prevents blindness.

2. Seated in Easy Pose, hands in Venus Lock in the lap, look to 3rd Eye, sending energy and white light to the eyes for 3 minutes.

3. In Easy Pose, look out the back of the head for 1-3 minutes. Inhale, exhale, and pull Mulbhand, holding for 30 seconds.

4. In Easy Pose, close eyes and roll them in a circle for 3 minutes. Inhale, pull Mulbhand, and continue to circle the eyes for another 30 seconds.

PERSONALITY, NERVES & PERCEPTION

1. In Rock Pose, stretch arms straight out in front, parallel to the ground and lean back 30° from vertical fixing eyes on a point straight ahead without blinking for 3 or more minutes. Keep body still. This exercise can be increased, slowly, to 31 minutes.

2. Stretch legs out in front, bend the left knee up to the chest and lift the right leg up to 60°, wrapping arms around legs, hands together in Venus Lock. Fix the eyes on the raised toes and hold the position for 2 minutes, breathing long and deep, keeping legs as straight as possible. Inhale, hold and relax. Switch legs and repeat. Then repeat the entire exercise again.

3. In meditation pose and chin lock, breathe through the left nostril, staring at the 10th gate (Crown Chakra) for 1½ minutes. Relax. Repeat 3 times. On last inhale, apply Mulbhand and hold for as long as possible, exhale and relax.

4. Maha Karma Shambhavi Mudra: In Lotus or Easy Pose, hands in Guyan Mudra, apply Chin Lock (Jalandhara Bhanda) and concentrate at the 3rd eye as you roll the tongue back and suck on it with long, deep breathing. As you inhale, apply Mulbhand, visualizing "Sat" rising up the spine, and as you exhale, visualize "Nam" going out the top of the head for from 3-31 minutes. This is good for pain in the eyes and the optic nerve, opens the chakras, and allows one to 'harness the 3 powers of God'.

COMMENTS: This set works on physical and mental myopia, the liver and kidneys, eyesight and foresight.

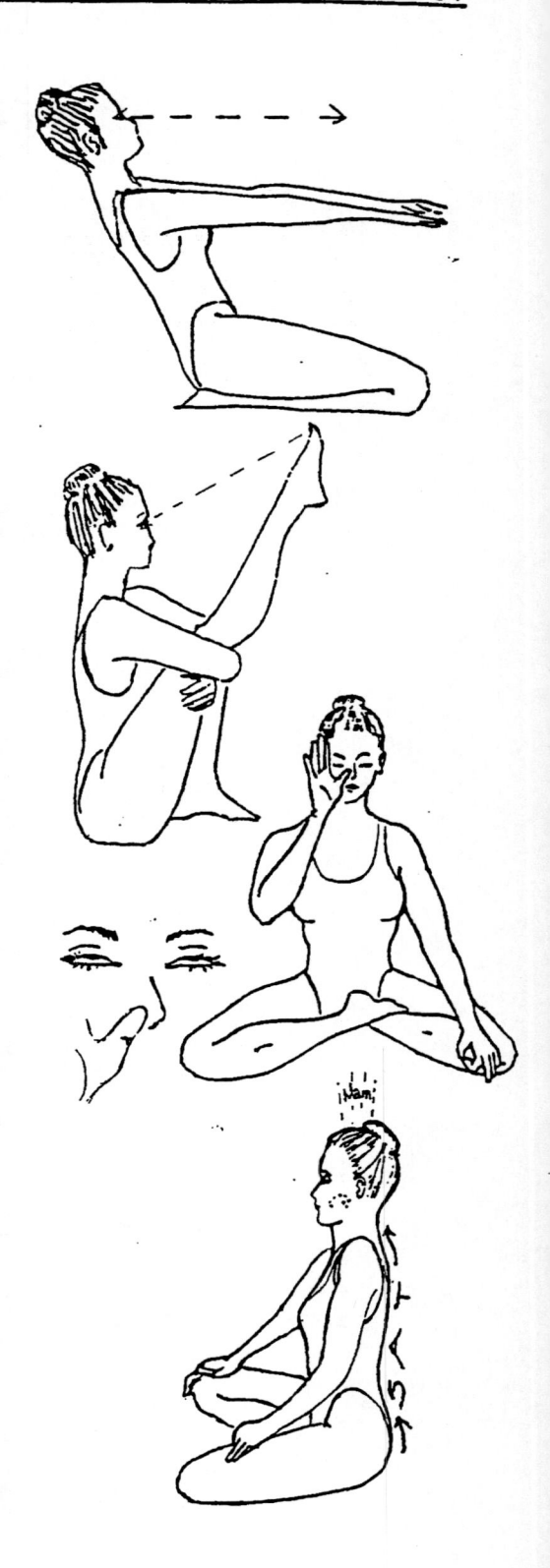

EYE SET

1. Stare at nose without blinking for 2 minutes.

2. Stare at one object with one eye, only, for 2 minutes. Repeat with the other eye.

3. Inhale and roll eyes in one direction 10 times. Exhale and roll them in the other direction, 10 times.

4. Move eyes rapidly, focussing on one object after another, alternating distant and near objects, for 5 minutes.

5. Inhale and look to extreme upper left corner. Exhale and look to extreme lower right. Repeat 10 times.

6. Stick out the tongue as far as possible while rolling the eyes. (This is good in Cobra Pose.) 2 mins.

7. In Rock Pose or Easy Pose, lean back 60° and stare at a point on the ceiling without blinking. Allow the eyes to water and continue for 2-3 minutes.

8. Make a "U" of the thumbs and forefingers, and place them around the eyes, pointing in the direction of sight, with Breath of Fire for 2-3 minutes. (Concentrates electro-magnetic field around the eyes.)

9. Two leg life nerve stretch: Stretch legs out in front, bend over and grab toes. Roll eyes back until they hurt and hold with long, deep breathing for 5 minutes.

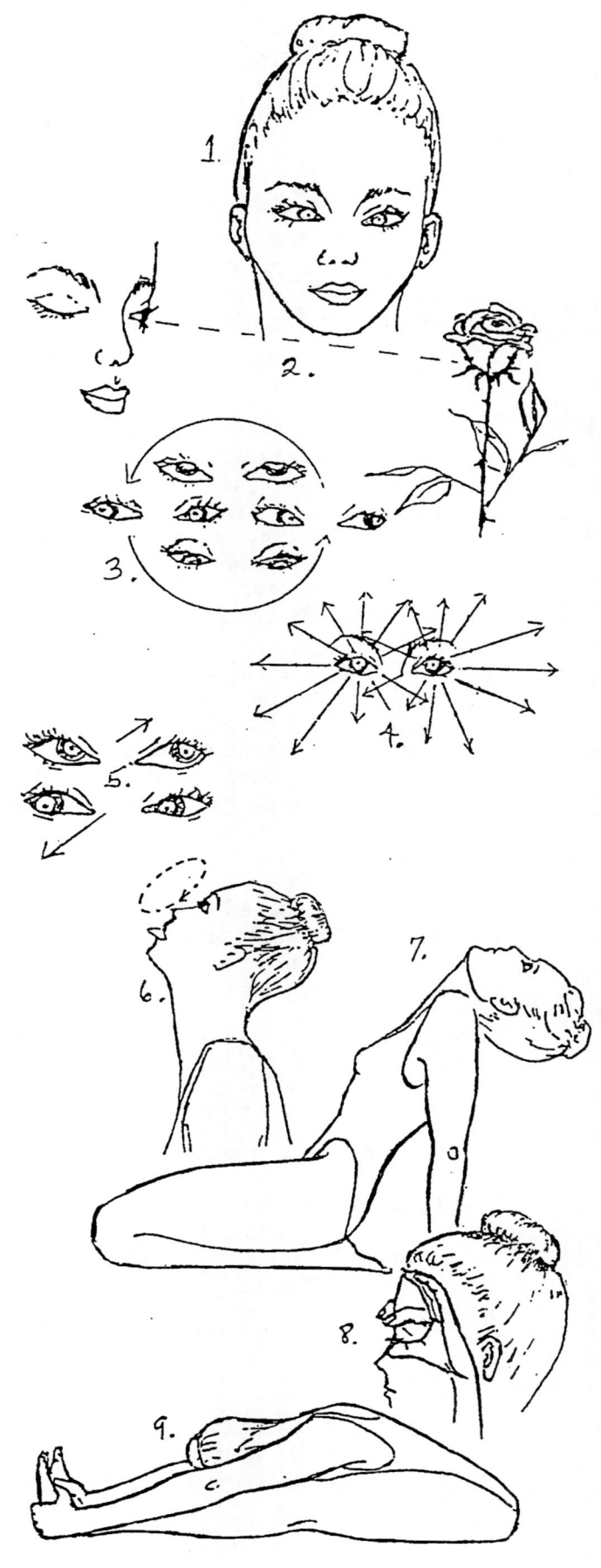

SIAM KRIYA
November 13, 1973
For Eyes & Parathyroid

1. Squat and extend left leg straight back, tops of toes on the ground in ½ Cobra, ½ Crow. (Right knee is raised.) Gazing at tip of nose, inhale

               Ra

and exhale   Ma

for 11 minutes. Then inhale, sit down and relax. Your thighs will tell the story. It is an old Siamese initiation Kriya, taught by an Indian Rishi, Siama. Siam then consisted of India, and Siam (Thailand) and was called Siamdesh. They found the secret of nothingness and everything.

2. Legs stretched straight ahead, bend forward, grab toes, and arch head back, fixing eyes up without blinking. Think of God for 11 minutes. The parathyroid must be stretched - no other way! You will feel something abnormal, but keep up. Entire electro-charge of the body will change. This exercise can save you from blindness, doing it honestly. Look up: there is a God sitting up there, hanging upside down. A MUST preparation for serious meditation.

3. In Easy or Lotus Pose, focus on top of head and silently put

     Ra Ma

on brain for 5 minutes.

4. Aloud, chant

    Ra Ra Ra Ra
    Ma Ma Ma Ma
    Sa Ta Na Ma
    Sa Ta Na Ma

for 11 minutes.

Enjoy the heritage of knowledge. Learn to subject yourself to an infinite object so there will be no objection.

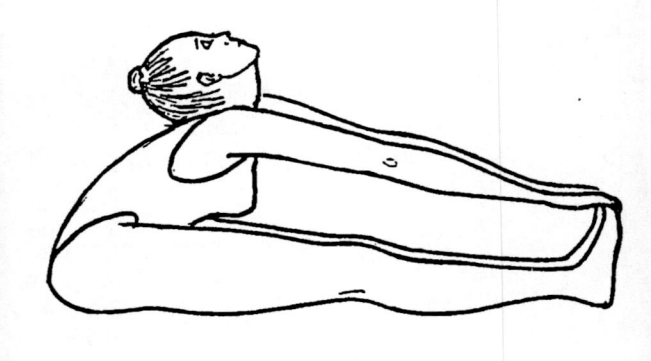

SHORT KRIYA TO SEE THE INNER BEAUTY
February 9, 1970

A. Sit in Easy Pose with a straight spine in Prayer Mudra and apply chin lock, looking at thumbs without bending the neck. Breathe long and deep for 6 minutes and gradually build to 11 minutes.

B. Sit in Celibate Pose, knees spread with buttocks on floor between heels, hands grasping knees firmly with straight elbows. Vibrate the lower spine so the buttocks rock back and forth on the ground as rapidly as possible with grace for 3 minutes. Inhale deeply and mentally circulate the energy throughout the body.

C. Stretch legs out in front and bend forward, grasping toes. Completely relax, letting all outside vibrations go, and merging into the infinite peace and light within. Continue for 5 minutes.

D. Sitting in Easy Pose again, chant to the infinite ecstasy using any mantra that stirs your heart.

COMMENTS: In Kundalini Yoga there are many practices which produce a state of union or ecstasy by combining the energies of prana and apana and raising the energy through the pineal gland. On the physical level, one drop of distilled semen is pulled from the base of the spine up the central channel of the spinal cord and injected near the pineal gland. This activates the radiance of the pineal gland which then interconnects the secretions of the pituitary and pineal glands and, in turn, opens man's brain potential.

The first exercise opens the higher centers. As you breath deeply, you will feel a tingling at the forehead if the posture and concentration are correct. This reflexes into the pituitary gland, and all eye problems are prevented or improved by regular practice, gradually building time.

The second exercise opens the lower spine and stimulates the transfer of ojas to the higher centers. Though enjoyable, it must create a sweat.

The third exercise opens the spine, and in the relaxation that follows, all tension and blocks are removed, allowing one to sample the inner joy. "It is He who is sitting in you. It is you who is watching Him in you. You and He are one. Relax into the Universal Spirit, and feel the flow pervading you."

ANGER SET
Repairing damage to the system of ill-placed anger

This set helps deal with major stress on the glands, brain & pituitary. It adjusts the glandular system.

1. Press the nerve in the middle finger of the left hand above the knuckle with the right thumb, and hold for 3 minutes.

2. Arms parallel to the ground, hands in fists with thumbs pointing up, press arms back, chin tucked in, and do Breath of Fire for 3 minutes.

3. Roll shoulders for 1 minute.

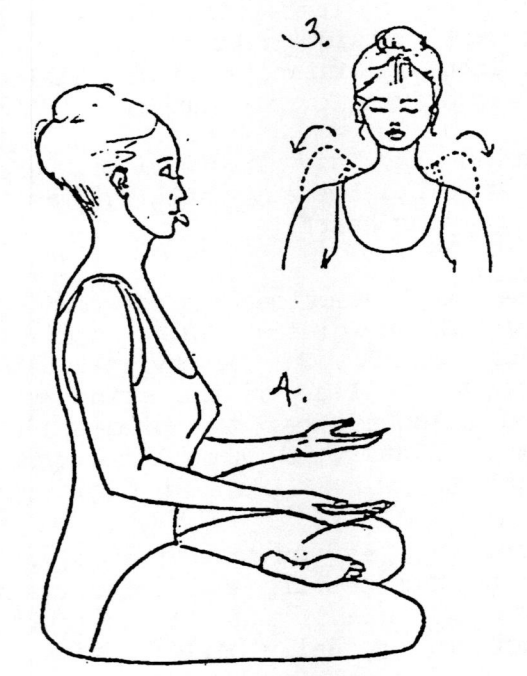

4. Forearms parallel to the ground, and out at 45°, palms up, stick the tongue out as far as possible and pant from upper chest. After anger this adjusts the nervous system. 3-5 minutes. To end, inhale and exhale deeply several times.

5. Press palms together at heart center. Breathe long and deep from the navel for 6 minutes. To end, inhale, press palms hard and pull in the navel.

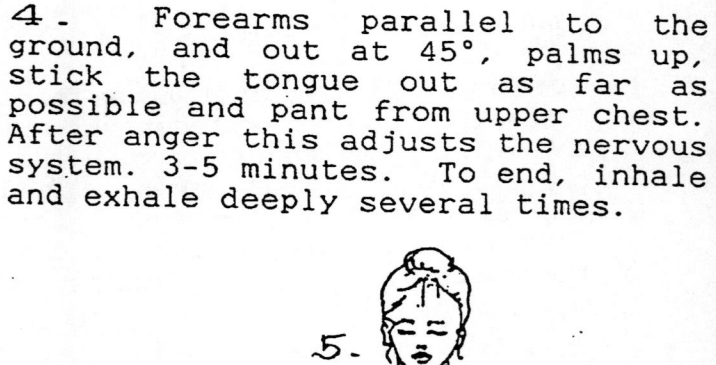

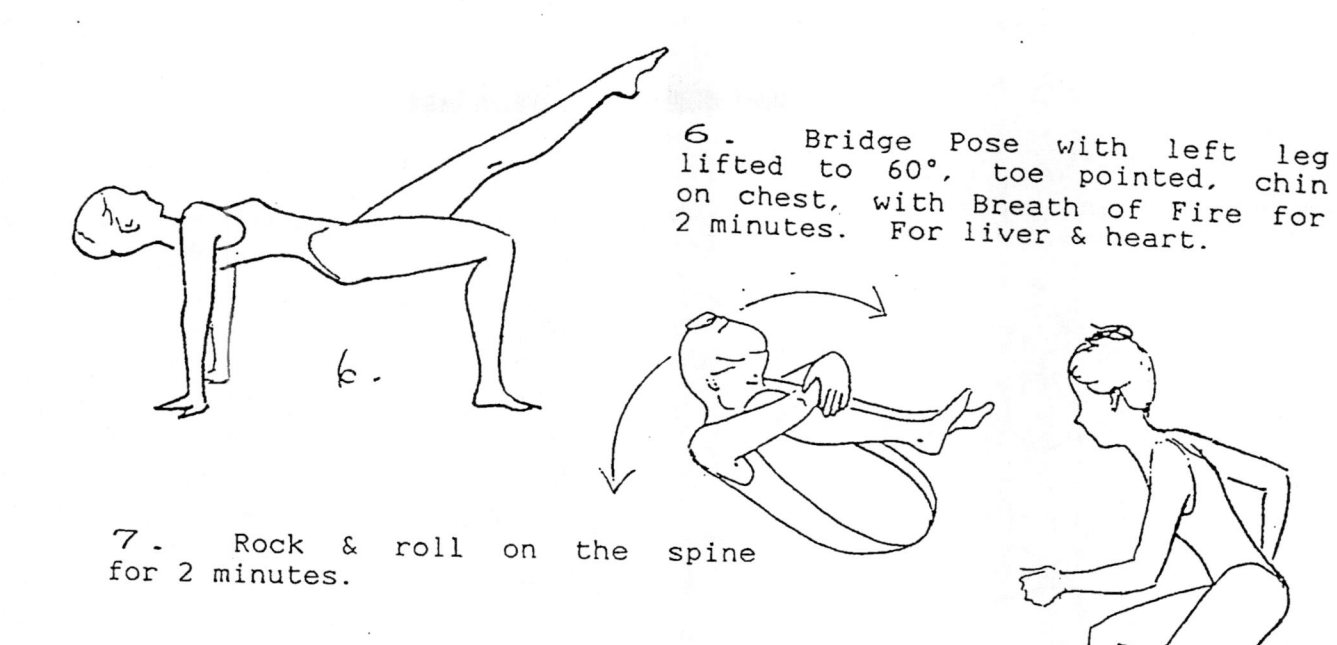

6. Bridge Pose with left leg lifted to 60°, toe pointed, chin on chest, with Breath of Fire for 2 minutes. For liver & heart.

7. Rock & roll on the spine for 2 minutes.

8. Run in place with Breath of Fire for 3-5 minutes.

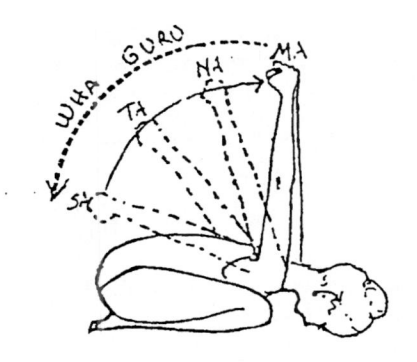

9. Sit on heels, bring forehead to the floor, hands behind back in Venus Lock. Inhale, lifting hands ¼ up with each ¼ breath, and exhale smoothly down. This breaks the aura and strengthens the adrenals, and gets someone off your back. 3-11 minutes.

10. Inhale, and sit up, and exhale into Easy Pose. Block alternate nostrils with left thumb and ring finger. Inhale right, exhale left, for 11 minutes.

11. Inhale, stretch, and open and close the fists.

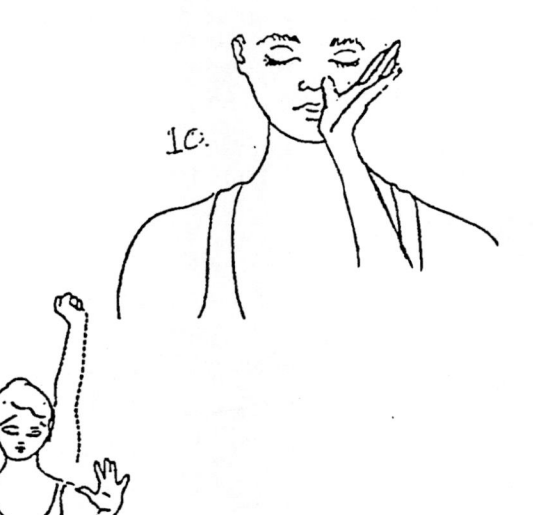

STRESS SET FOR ADRENALS & KIDNEYS

1. In Easy pose, rub palms together, and inhale stretching arms out to the sides, parrallel to the ground, palms facing out. exhale and bring hands together, hitting the bases together, fingers stretched in Lotus Mudra. To end, inhale with hands together.

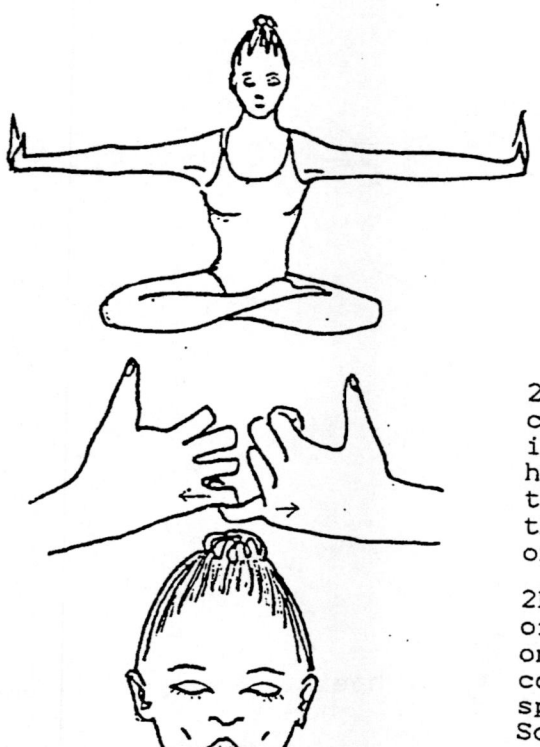

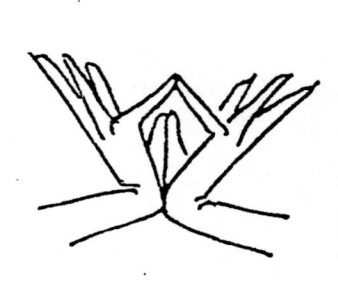

2A. Interlace pinkies in front of heart center & pull, curling the other fingers into pads, thumbs sticking up. Lower the hands to solar plexus and feel a pull across the back, with Breath of Fire from below the navel. This generates heat and works on one side of the adrenals.

2B. Inhale, pucker mouth and begin Breath of Fire through puckered mouth, working on the other side of the adrenals, and cooling (still in Easy Pose with straight spine.) Inhale and concentrate at the Solar Plexis.

3. In Easy Pose, left hand on back at bottom rib, palm out, right arm straight out, palm forward and up and 60°. Keeping spine straight, stretch from shoulder. With eyes wide open, chant Hara, hara, hara, powerfully from the navel.

4. In Lotus, do body drops, inhaling up and exhaling down.

5. In Easy Pose, hands in front of solar Plexis, left hand facing body, right hand pressing left wrist with the base of palm. Look down with powerful, long, deep breathing. The power of the breath is the depth to which you will cleanse.

6. Sit with legs stretched out in front, arms out front parallel to the ground, hands in fists, thumbs pointing up. Inhale stretching forward, exhale leaning back. Powerful breath. Keep arms parallel to ground.

7. On back, bring heels to buttocks, grab ankles and inhale up, exhale down.

8. In cat-cow position, exhale as you bring left knee to forehead, and inhale as you stretch leg out in back. Do not overextend. Switch legs.

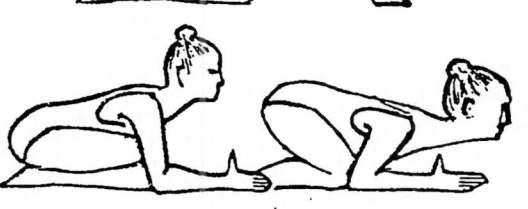

9. Sit on heels, bring forearms to the ground in front of knees, palms together, thumbs pointing up. Inhale as you stretch over the palms, and exhale back. Keep chin up to create pressure in the lower back.

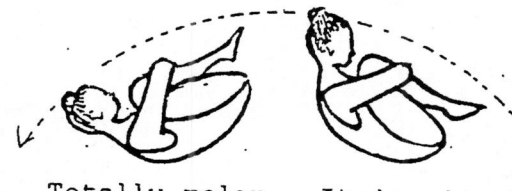

10. Bring knees to chest, nose between the knees, breathing normally, and roll back and forth on the spine.

Totally relax. It is nice to relax for an hour afterward. Have a glass of water. This set is done with very little pause between the exercises.

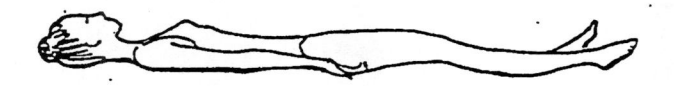

COMMENTS: Do we have a reserve capacity to get to our destination despite the snowstorm? Our energy can be flowing, we can be eating well, sleeping enough, but if our adrenals fail, it is hard to keep up. We get tired and snappy. Glandular balance, and in particular, strong adrenals and kidneys are important to have that extra edge, to control anger and hypoglycimia. Without strong adrenals and kidneys, the heart can't function well either.

EXERCISE SET FOR KIDNEYS

1. Sit, extenting arms and legs straight out in front. Tightly fold fingers onto the pads and point the thumbs up. Inhale, exhale and bend forward from the hips keeping arms parallel to the floor, with heavy, powerful breath becomming heavier as you continue. 2 bends every 5 seconds for 5-6 minutes.

2. On back, bend knees and grasp ankles and raise buttocks, pressing the navel up as you inhale, and exhale back down. Feet, neck and arms remain on the ground. This exercise works on the neck, kidneys, urinary tract, and is helpful for hernia. The heavy breath stimulates the pituitary gland.

3. On hands and knees, arms and legs straight and about shoulder and hip width apart, begin Cat/Cow with heavy breath, inhaling as the spine flexes down and head arches up, and exhaling as the spine curves up for 2 minutes. (B) Remain in Cow Pose and stretch the left leg back and up holding for 30 seconds. Then switch to the right leg for 30 seconds. (C) Changing legs again, kick the left buttocks with the left heel for 1 minute. Reverse legs and repeat. This exercise works on the kidneys.

4. Lie on back, wrapping arms around legs and hugging knees to chest. Tuck nose up between knees and hold it, relaxing in his position for 1-2 minutes. Remain in Nose to Knee Pose singing or breathing long and deap for 7-9 minutes. (Songs suggested are "Nobility" and "All Things Come from God").

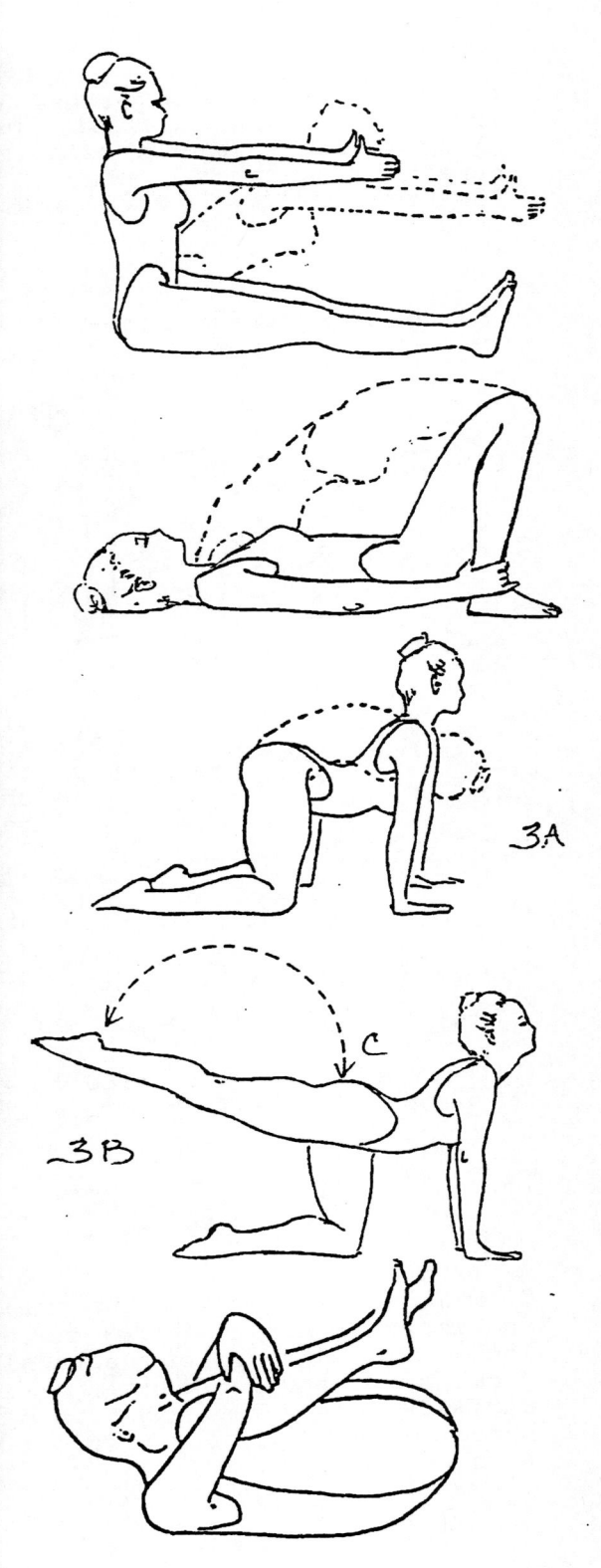

5. In Crow Pose, crouch with knees drawn into chest, soles of feet flat on floor, and stretch arms straight out in front, parallel to the ground, balancing there for 1 minute. Then begin continuously chanting

Har Har Har . . .

with the tip of the tongue hitting the upper palate with each repetition. Feel the connection between the tip of the tongue and the navel, and chant for 2-3 minutes. Then inhale deeply, tighten the lips and mouth and balance the entire body with the breath, holding the breath for 20 seconds, feeling that you are in complete contro. Then exhale, inhale and tighten again, balancing the body under your control for 3 seconds, and exhale and relax. This exercise stimulates the kidneys and urinary tract. If you feel dizzy during the exercise it indicates that you need to drink more water.

6. Sit in Easy Pose, with both hands in Guyan Mudra. Hold left forearm parallel to the ground in front of the chest, palm facing down. The right forearm is near the side, perpendicular to the ground, the right palm bent back and facing the ceiling beside the ear, stretching back at the wrist as far as possible. Stretch the spine up, pulling on the muscles of the buttocks, hips and sides, lifting the upper structure until there is no weight on the buttocks. Pull in the abdomen and lift ribs and diaphragm up, chest out, chin in. Hold for 30 seconds and then release tension. Repeat and continue for 5 minutes, then relax. (B) Maintaining the strong upward pull, with the tip of the tongue chant

Wahe Guru Wahe Guru
Wahe Guru Wahe Jeeo

keeping the waist area drawn up. The eyes will feel heavy and the breath will become very light. Accuracy of the mudra essential. Continue for 5 minutes and relax.

This is called KUNCHUN MUDRA. It is very powerful and purifying, enabling total relaxation of the body. When the posture is very accurate, it is equal to exercising 48 hours straight! There is no limit to the length of time you can practice this mudra but make sure to build the time slowly.

SHORT SET FOR KIDNEYS

1. DRink lots of water and pump belly for 1-2 minutes.

2. On back, lift legs up to 60° and hold with long, deep breathing 1-2 minutes.

3. Legs up to 60°, scissors kick for 1-2 minutes.

FOR LIVER & KIDNEYS

1. Lie on back in Lotus Pose for 1-2 minutes.

2. Cat stretch, pressing right knee to the left side of left knee with shoulders on floor. Hold and reverse

3. Inverted Camel, grasping ankles and lifting buttocks, holding for 5 minutes. (For liver.)

4. On back raise arms and legs 2 feet off floor, and spread them wide apart. Hold until you shake.

5. Bundle Roll: Keep arms straight and tightly at sides, and roll the body over and over across the floor and come back again.

SHORT SET FOR THE LIVER

1. Cobra Pose with long, deep breathing for 1-3 minutes. Inhale, hold and pull Mulbhand, relax.

2. Platform Pose. In raised pushup position, keep body and arms perfectly straight. Inhale, pull Mul Bhand, exhale, pull Mulbhand. (Poisens go to the liver).

3. Lie back on heels, arms straight up, and pump stomach for 2-3 minutes.

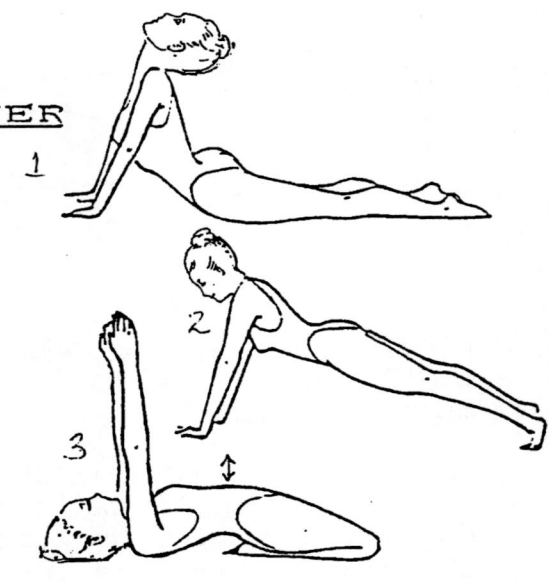

LET THE LIVER LIVE
January 30 & February 18, 1985

1. Lie on the left side resting the head on the hand, and raise the right leg straight up holding the toe with the right hand (both legs straight), with Breath of Fire for 4 minutes.

2. Arch up into Half Wheel ose hands & feet flat on floor. Breathe in and out through the nose, then in and out thru the mouth, alternating in complete breaths for 4 minutes.

3. On left side, repeat *1 with Breath of Fire for 2 minutes.

4. Stand with legs 18-24" apart bend forward and reaching as far back as possible, stretch hands thru the legs to touch floor, holding for 1 minute. Then do Breath of Fire through a rolled tongue for 3 minutes in same position.

5. Repeat exercise *1 with "Cannon Breath" (powerful, explosive breath through the mouth) for 30 seconds.

6. In Easy Pose, stand up and sit down again without using the hands, 52 times.

7. Still standing, hands on hips, roll upper torso in large circles for 2 minutes. "Anyone who shall do this exercise for 11 minutes morning and night will have no problem with Mr. Liver."

8. Relax.

COMMENTS: "When you do not consciously relate to your body, your mind does not relate consciously to you. - Whosoever will do this set will be set for life". YB (This set is available on tape from Golden Temple Recording.)

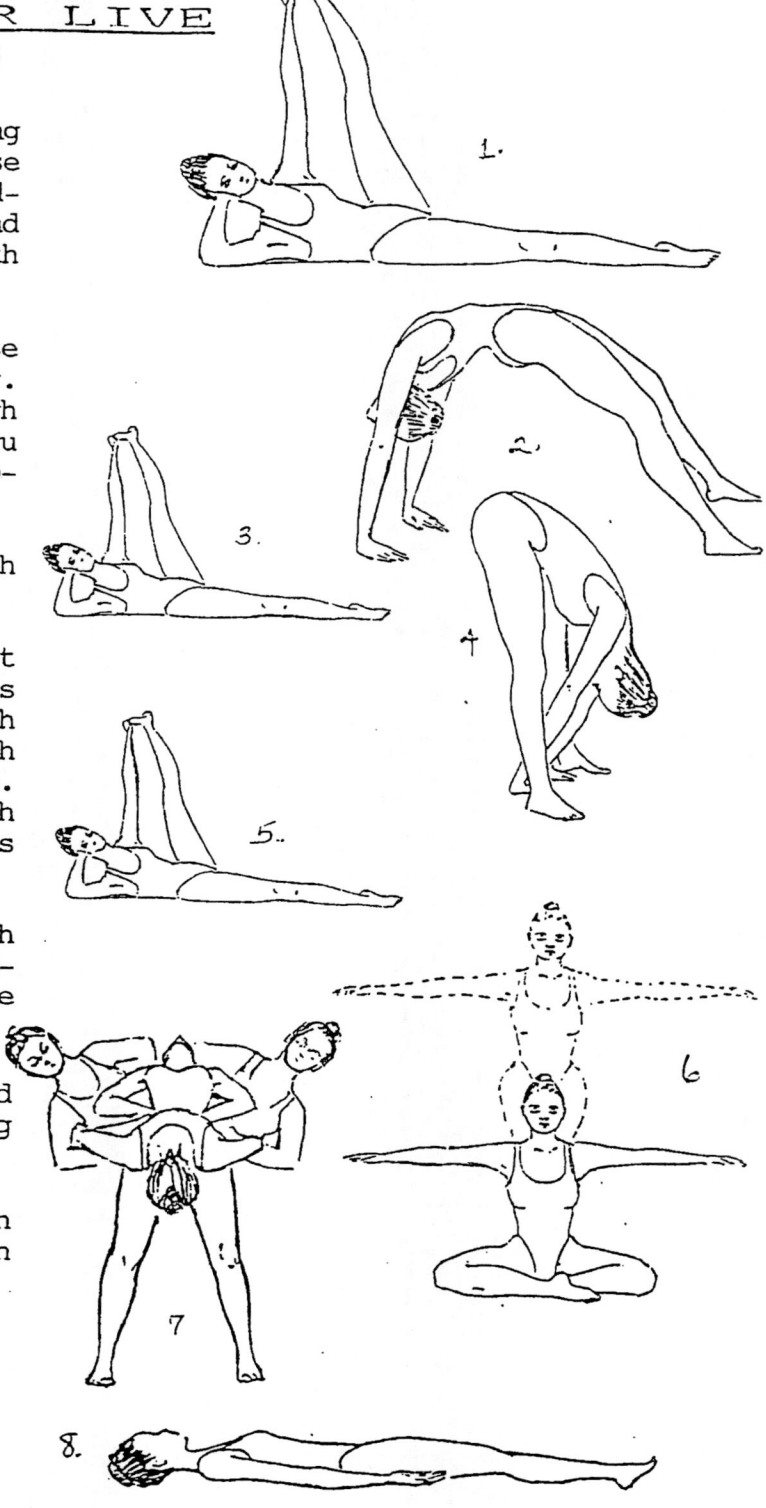

PURIFICATION OF THE LIVER
August 22, 1980

The liver is one of the most important organs of the body, filtering a huge volume of blood every few minutes. Its function can be impaired by the prolonged intake of sugar, becoming a source of disease in many. To help correct this, Yogiji gave us this set.

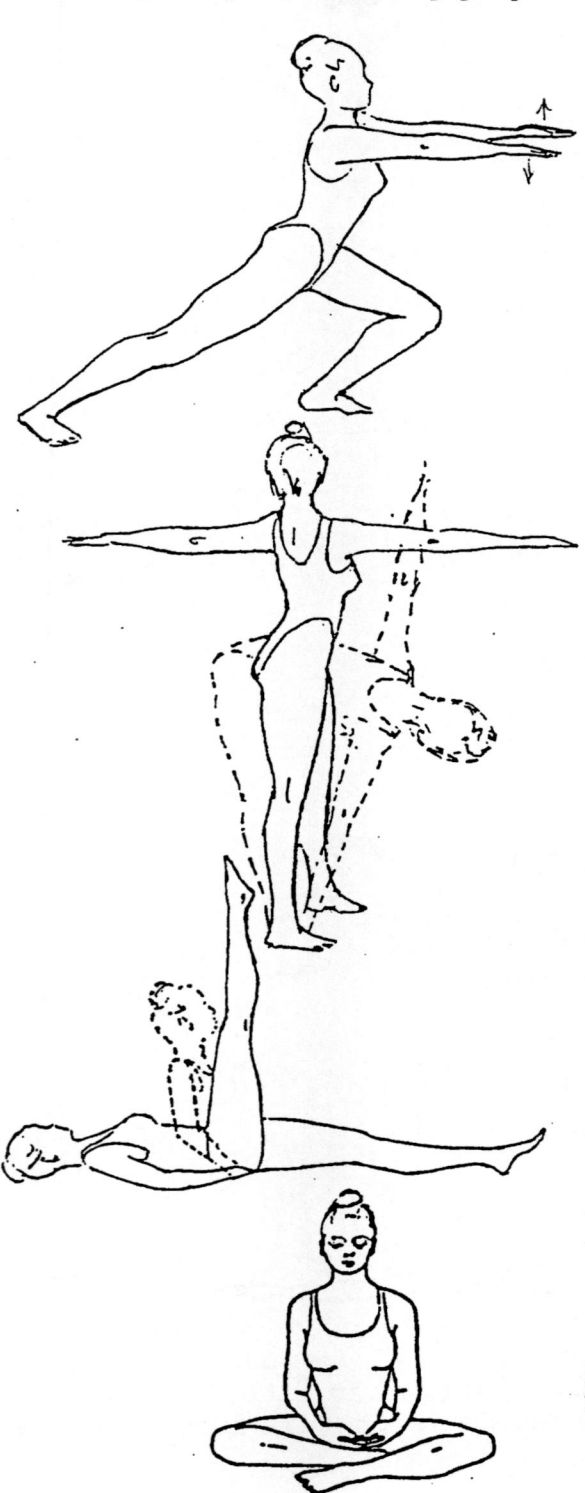

1. Stand with feet hip width apart and move one leg back as far as it will go, placing the other slightly in front of the body. Stretch so that both feet are flat on the floor, and weight of the body is on front foot. (Either foot forward is alright.) Stretch both arms out in front at shoulder level and shoulder width. Face one palm down and the other up (either is OK). With long, deep breathing, hold this position for 3 minutes, menditating on a mantra if you wish. Relax in Easy Pose for 3 minutes.

2. To flush toxins out of the liver, stand with feet shoulder width apart and arms straight out to the sides, eeping them exactly opposite each other and twist slowly to the left, stopping when right arm points straight ahead & left, straight back. Then bend over to nearly touch the floor between the feet with the right hand. You'll feel tremendous pressure on the liver area. Hold, without moving, with long, deep breathing for 3 minutes and relax in Easy Pose for 3 minutes.

3. (This isn't obligatory, but if you can do it, fine. It is very difficult, but give it a try. It is called INTERLOCKED POSTURE, and is intended to make the liver work more effectively.) Lie on the back, placing hands, palms down, under the buttocks and raise the right leg to 90°, toe pointed, leg straight. In that position, sit up, keeping left leg flat on the floor, and touch the nose to the right knee and hold for 3 minutes. Relax in Easy Pose.

4. In meditation pose, with a straight spine, chant:

Sat Narayan, Wahe Guru
Hari Narayan, Sat Nam.

(Time unspecified).

LIVER SET FOR HEPATITIS

1. In Rock Pose, lie down, resting the hands in Venus Lock on the stomach with Breath of Fire for 2 minutes. Inhale, hold the breath in & relax.

2. Sit on the left heel, and place right foot on left thigh. Balance with fingers of the left hand on the floor, and right hand is straight up in Guyan Mudra. Do Breath of Fire for 2 minutes. Deeply inhale, exhale and relax.

3. Stand with heels together, and place hands in Venus Lock at the groin, bending at the hips to form a 60° angle with torso. Through puckered lips (Beak Breath, panting) do Breath of Fire for 2 minutes. Inhale, hold for 10-15 seconds, exhale and relax.

4. In Easy Pose, stretch arms straight out to the sides, and rock from side to side palms down, rock side to side on the buttocks, keeping the arms parallel to the ground for 2 minutes with Breath of Fire. Relax.

5. Life Nerve Stretch with left foot on right thigh, grabbing right toe, with Breath of Fire for 2 minutes.

6. Camel Pose with both hands behind hips, and right leg stretched out in front, with Breath of fire for 2 minutes.

7. Life Nerve Stretch, both legs out in front. Grab toes, inhale deeply, exhale completely pulling Root Lock and pump the stomach in and out as long as possible. Inhale, exhale and repeat.

8. Relax for 2-5 minutes.
(Times added by G.K.)

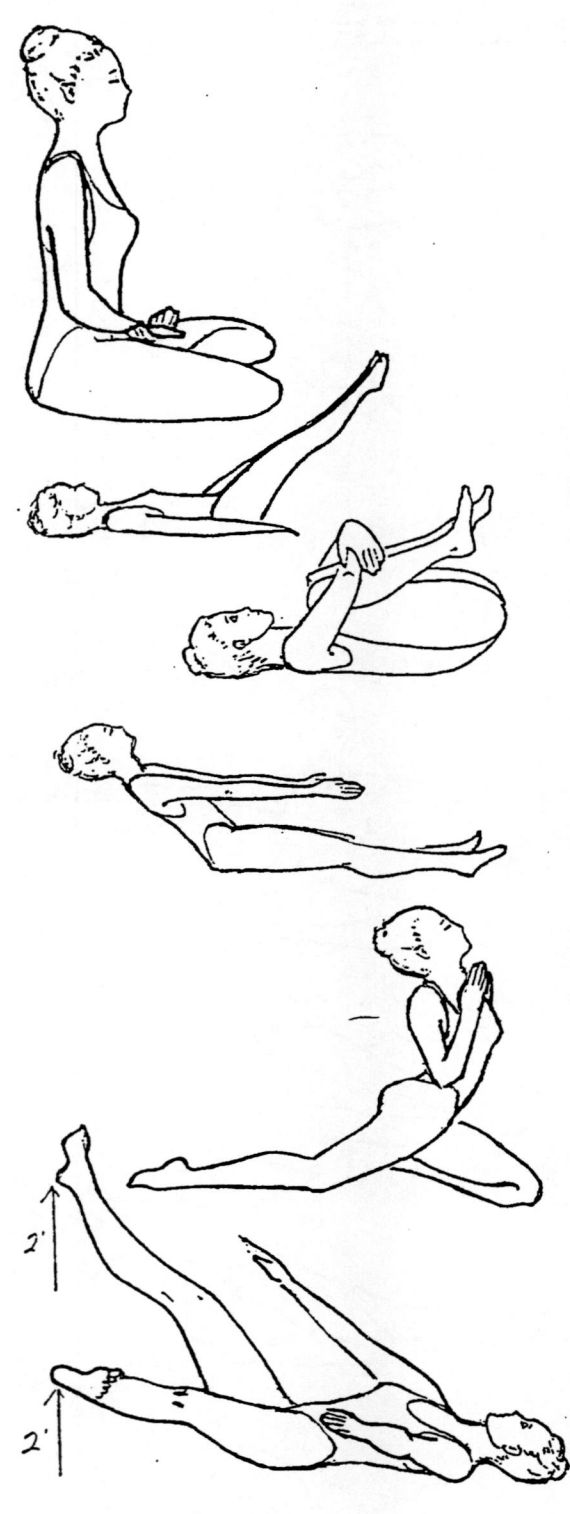

LIVER SET

1. Easy Pose, hands in lap, inhale for 5 seconds, exhale for 5 seconds, hold breath out for 15 seconds and pump stomach. for 5 minutes. Relax for 5 minutes.

2. PAVAN SODHAN KRIYA: Lying on back, inhale, raise legs to 60°, hold for 15 seconds. Exhale, brings knees to chest, hold 15 seconds, and repeat from beginning, then exhale and lower legs to the floor for 15 seconds, 1 cycle complete. Do 8 cycles, and relax for 5 minutes.

Pt. 2: Inhale and raise body from waist up to 60°, hold for 15 seconds, and exhale down, holding breath out for 15 seconds. As you rise, roll eyes to 3rd eye point, and as you come down, lower eyes. Keep spine straight and feet on the floor.

Completely relax.

(NOTE: PAVAN SODHAN KRIYA was given at UCLA on October 8, 1971. Part one is to be done for 31 minutes, with a 10 minute relaxation period. "Do every morning for 31 minutes after moving bowels, and you will conquer old age." It works on the liver, sex organs, navel point and diaphram.)

3. Rock Pose, but extend one foot back, and arch the neck, looking up. Hands in Prayer Mudra at neck. Hold for 5½ minutes on each side.

4. On back, spread legs three feet apart, and raise them two feet from floor. Arms are 3 feet apart and raised too. Hold with Long deep breathing until you shake.

5. In Lotus, ½ Lotus or Rock Pose, lie back, and relax with Long, deep breathing for 3 minutes.

LIVER LOVER
August 15, 1969

1. Sit on heels, and lie back down, head on floor, hands clasped in Venus Lock on the stomach (Supta Vajrasana), with Breath of Fire.

2. Squat on one foot, with the other foot on the thigh. Balance with the opposite hand, the other hand in Guyan Mudra, arm rounded out to the side with Breath of Fire for 2-3 minutes. Repeat on the opposite side.

3. Squat in Crow Pose, hands extended straight out between knees, and clasped in Venus Lock. Make a small "O" of the mouth, and do Breath of Fire through it for 2-3 minutes. Relax. Cooling and healing.

4. In Easy Pose, extend arms straight out to sides, parallel to the floor, palms down. Move upper body left and right, side to side with Breath of Fire for 2-3 minutes. Inhale, hold, exhale and relax. Keeps you young, and revitalized.

5. Life Nerve Stretch: Legs outstretched, bend and bring left on in to thigh. Right finger hooks right big toe, and left hand is placed under the right heel. Breath of Fire in that position. Then Inhale, hold and draw the nose to the knee, exhale, relax. 2-3 minutes.

6. Sit on left heel, right leg stretched forward and raise it as high as pssible, supporting the body with the hands behind hips on the floor, and drop head back. Breath of Fire for 2-3 minutes. Inhale, hold, exhale hard, drop right leg, and bend forward to grab toes. Inhale, exhale, apply Mulbhand, inhale and relax.

EXERCISE SET FOR THE LIVER, COLON AND STOMACH

1. With feet 2 feet apart, hands on hips, bend from the waist to the right chanting "Sa", to the left chanting "Ta", to the front chanting "Na", and to the back chanting "Ma". Hold each position 1 second and continue for 5 minutes. Opens up the hip area and prepares you for next exercise.

2. Legs 2 feet apart, hands on hips, roll the upper torso in big circles to the maximum in each direction for 2-3 minutes, one roll per second. Then chant "Har Hari" with each roll and continue for 2 more minutes. Stimulates gonads.

3. Legs apart A) Bring arms up and cross them parallel to the ground and grasp opposite upper arms. B) Lean back and raise arms up and back pulling breast muscle. C) Return crossed arms to parallel to ground D) Relax arms down to sides. Coordinate the movements with "Sa Ta Na Ma" for 3-4 minutes, 2-3 seconds for each cycle. Relieves lower back pain and pressurizes the lymph area.

4. Arms crossed and raised parallel to the ground as above, squat into Crow Pose, knees drawn into chest, soles of feet flat on the floor, and arise, chanting "Sa Ta Na Ma" powerfully with each 2 squats, for 3 minutes. Balances body energy and relieves pain in the lower back.

5. Place thumbs on Mercury mounds below the little fingers and make hands into fists, arms out to sides and swing the arms back in large circles, moving the shoulders, chanting "Har Har Har Har Har Hari" with each 2-3 circles for 2-3 minutes. Balances the psyche and enhances communication skills.

6. Stand on the balls of the feet with hands on hips and alternately kick feet forward in a fast jogging, shuffling motion, chanting aloud, "Hum Dum Har Har, Har Har Hum Dum" once every 3-4 seconds, coordinating movement with mantra for 3 minutes. Balances the metals in the body.

7. Immediately lie down on back and perform Cat Stretch to each side. Keeping shoulders on the ground, bend one knee and touch it to the ground over the straight leg, and repeat on alternate sides, powerfully, for 1-2 minutes. Pressures the liver and removes toxins. It also consolidates the effects of the previous exercises.

8. In ½ Cobra Pose on forearms with chin out, palms and forearms flat, elbows under shoulders, heels together, inhale and kick buttocks with alternate heels at a moderate pace for 3-4 minutes and at a rapid pace for another minute. For regulating calcium/magnesium balance in the blood and body (which is controlled in thighbone which also controls sexuality). Also applies maximum pressure to thyroid and parathyroid when neck us up & chin is out.

9. Squat in Frog Pose with heels raised and touching each other, arms straight between legs, fingertips on ground, head up, and raise buttocks, dropping head as you inhale, and return to squat allowing buttocks to strike heels as you strongly exhale and chant "Sa Ta Na Ma" every 2-3 seconds for 2 minutes. Works on the knees.

10. Stand, cross legs and sit down in Easy Pose, raise to a stand again and repeat movement 4 times balancing prana & apana.

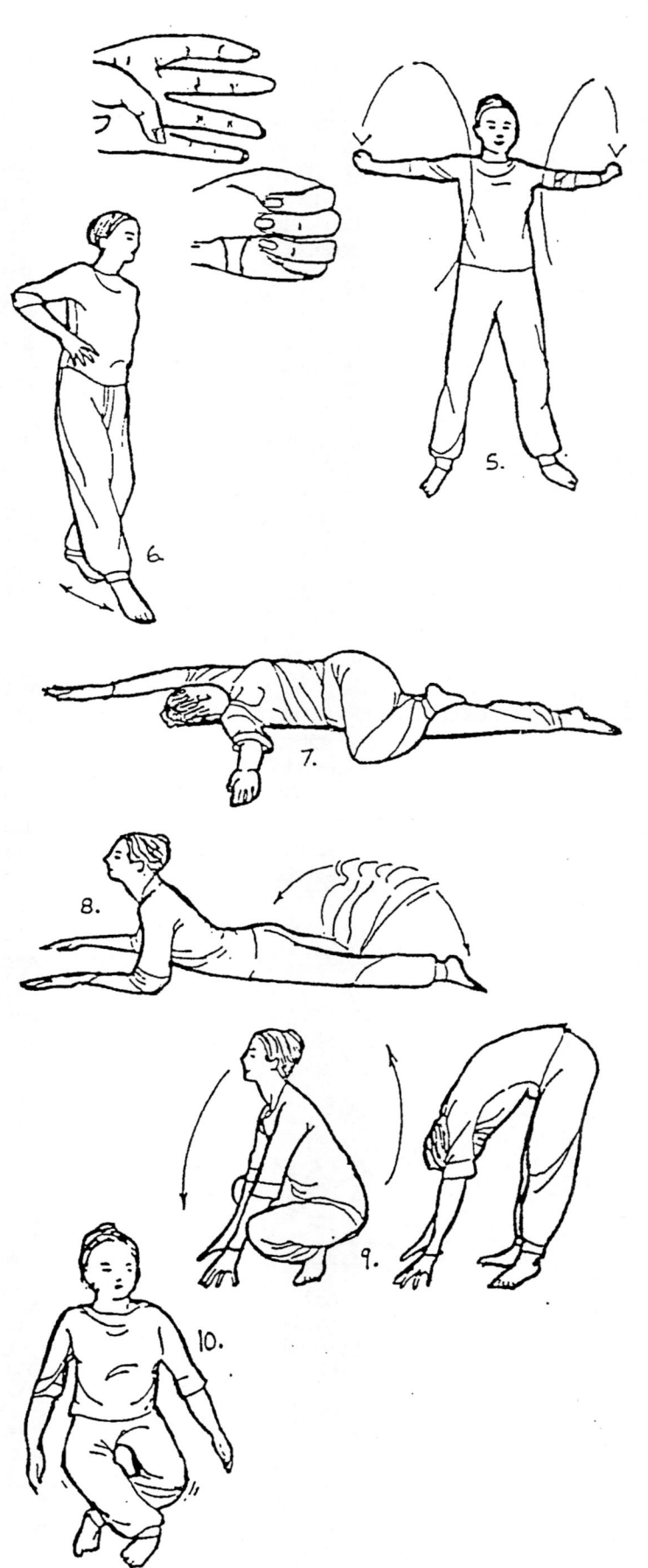

11. Repeat Frogs for 30 seconds.

12. On back, raise straight legs, grab toes and for 1-2 minutes inhale through a rolled tongue, exhale through the nose to cool the body.

13. In Easy Pose, arms at shoulder level, meet fingertips at center of chest palms facing out and straighten alternate arms out to the sides with a jerk to the elbow and return to center for 3 minutes. Works on the forearm which regulates the colon.

14. Spinal Flex in Easy Pose with hands on knees, inhaling as spine is arched forward, exhaling as it contracts back, shoulders relaxed, head straight for 4 minutes. For lymph area and it is reported to prevent breast cancer. If done correctly it will create sweat on the face & unusual pressure on the neck behind the ears insuring that the entire nervous system and Shushmana is being stimulated.

15. Make loose fists of hands with thumbs inside and place them at shoulder level. Inhale and rapidly extend arms up, exhale and return fists to shoulder level for 2-3 minutes, for spine and sciatic nerve.

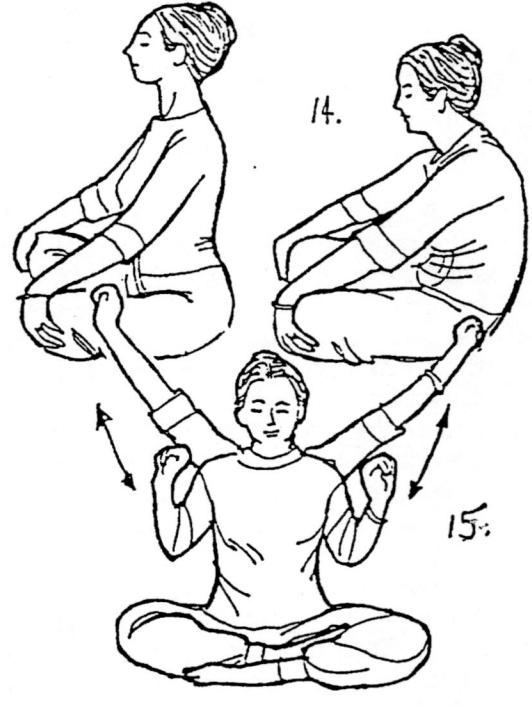

16. In Easy Pose, raise crossed arms to heart level, and as you chant "Sa Ta Na Ma" bend the head right, center, left, center, completing one cycle every 2-3 seconds for 1-2 minutes to adjust the neck.

17. In Easy Pose, sing "Nobility" for 4 minutes or meditatively breathe long and gently. NOTE: The beautiful, original drawings have been retained.

FOR ELIMINATION
March 7, 1972

1. Sit and bring soles of feet together, heels close to the groin. Holding toes, allow head to fall back and touch the spine, with long, deep breathing for 7 minutes. THEN SHAKE VIGOROUSLY, ALL OVER.

2. Sit on left heel, with right leg straight out in front. Hold right foot with both hands, and arch neck up and back to look at the sky, with long, deep breathing for 7 mins. THEN SHAKE VIGOROUSLY ALL OVER.

3. Sit in Lotus Pose, if possible, and Guyan Mudra, and meditate at the 3rd eye for 7 minutes. Then, place hands next to hips and lift entire body off the floor, and hold. Inhale and exhale 3 times, and SHAKE ALL OVER. Then lie down and relax.

4. Sit on heels, and make a fist of the right hand, grab it with the left hand and press it into the navel point, tightly. Inhale as you press up, exhale as you press down and dig in, 5 times.

5. In Easy Pose and Guyan Mudra, inhale, chanting

　　　　Hoooo

exhale chanting

　　　　Laaaa

5 times. Then stretch legs.

6. Legs out straight, place hands at sides, and raise left leg to 60° chanting
　　　　Raaaa
Raise right leg, chanting
　　　　Maaaa

Repeat and continue for 11 minutes. "In 11 minutes you are Rama".

7. Seated in Easy Pose and Guyan Mudra, meditate.

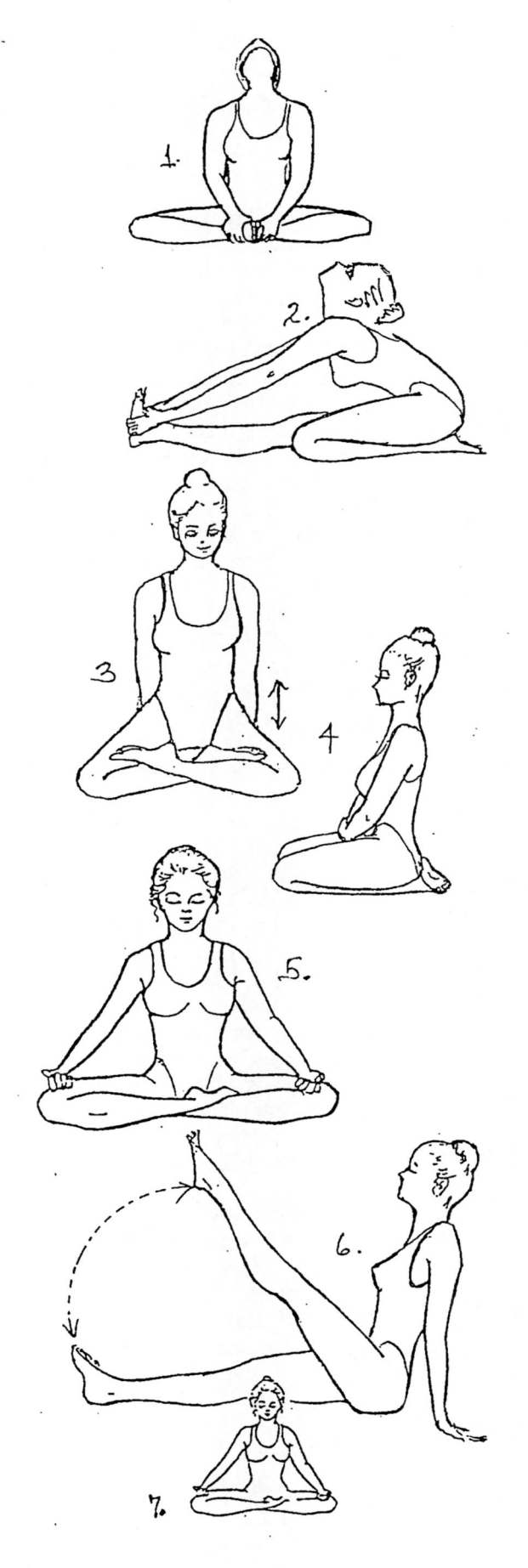

ELIMINATION (APANA) EXERCISES

1. Vatskar Kriya: Sit in Easy Pose with hands on the knees. Make a beak of the mouth and "drink" as much air as you can into the stomach, using short, continuous sips, as if you were swallowing. Pull in and hold, applying neck lock. Roll the stomach to the left until the breath has been held for half its maximum time, then reverse directions and continue for as long as possible. When the breath cannot be held any longer, straighten the spine and exhale slowly (not powerfully) through the nose. Repeat the exercise 2 more times. Always do this on an EMPTY STOMACH, and NOT MORE THAN TWICE a day. Adjusts acid-base balance in the stomach but it must be done regularly without missing a single day.

2. Sit on the heels, and keeping hands at the side, touch forehead to the ground. Imagine that there is a big tail coming off the end of the spine and wag it. Imagine the tail weighs 100 lbs. and try to break the wall. Continue for 3 minutes followed by 5 minutes of rest. Strengthens the heart.

3. Lie down on the back, and pressing the toes forward, lift both legs up 3 feet, and hold with long, deep breathing for 2-3 minutes. Inhale, hold briefly and relax. Slims waistline and cleans gall bladder.

4. Lying on the back, bring the legs overhead and catch the toes. Holding on to toes, roll back and forth on the spine from its base to the neck for 3 minutes. Flushes circulation and balances the nerves.

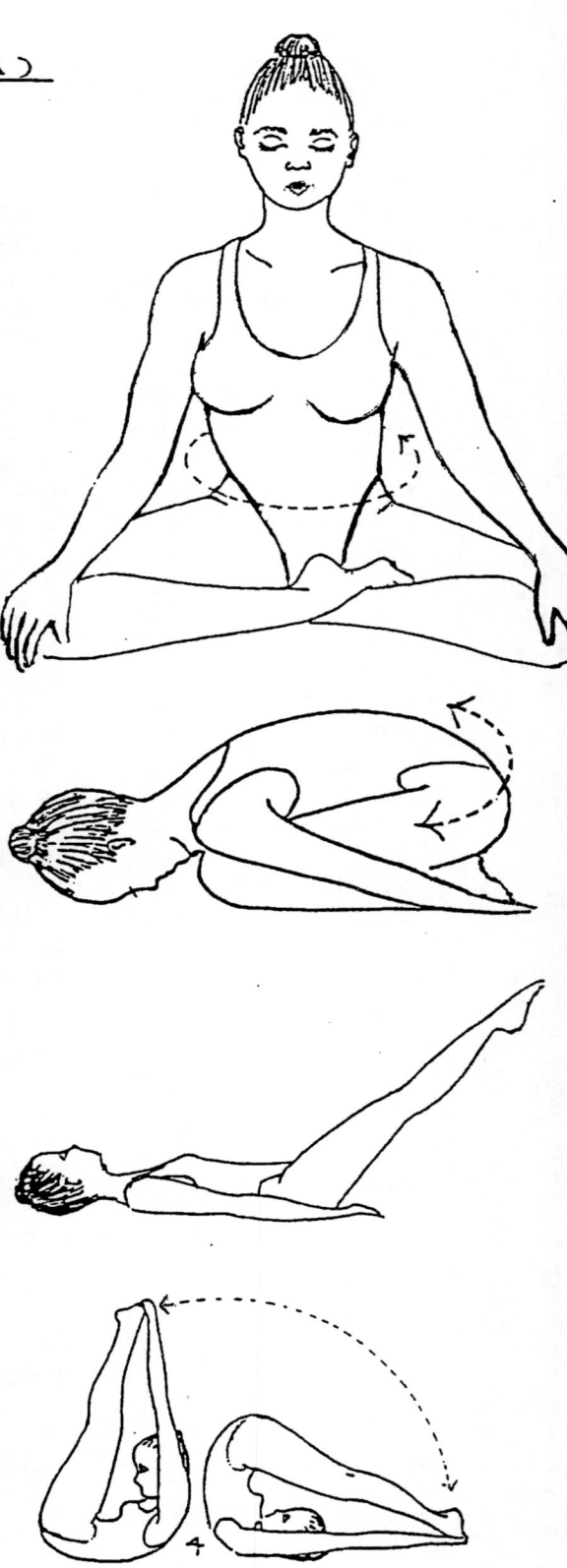

5. Sit up immediately in Easy Pose. As calmly as possible, make a "U" of the right hand and close the right nostril with the thumb, and the left nostril with the little finger. Inhale through the left nostril and exhale through the right for 3 minutes. Then inhale through both nostrils, hold and feel the energy radiate throughout the body, giving health and life.

6. In Easy Pose, place the Venus lock (hands interlaced, right thumb on top) in front of the chest at heart level with palms facing the chest. Inhale and turn the head left, chin over the shoulder, and exhale as you turn the head right, for 3 minutes. #5 & 6 distribute pranic force and stimulate the thyroid and parathyroid.

7. Then spread arms out to the side, parallel to the ground. Swing them back (as though swimming the backstroke) in large circles for 1 minute. Then inhale, hold the breath and bend the elbows bringing the fingertips to the shoulders, thumbs in back. While the breath is heald the electric current (aura) is remagnetized. Exhale and let the energy flow to all parts of the body and feel refreshed.

COMMENTS: This is a good example of a simple but powerful series that was kept secret by those few yogis who learned it. This enables one to completely master the digestive system and give a youthful appearance to your skin. Aging does not start with years; it begins with nutritional deficiency, intestinal problems and an inflexible spine that disrupts the flow of spinal fluid.

THE NAVEL CENTER & ELIMINATION

1. On back, bicycle alternate legs 1-1½ feet from the ground with long, deep breathing, 1-2 minutes.

2. Inhale, rasing legs to 90° and exhale, lowering them, rapidly for 1 minute. Rest for 30 seconds. Repeat twice.

3. On Stomach, raise up into Cobra Pose and try to kick buttocks with alternate legs, exhaling as you kick one leg, inhaling as you kick the other.

4. In Bow Pose on stomach, rock back and forth with the breath for 2 minutes.

5. On the back, clasp knees to chest and roll back and forth on the spine for 2 minutes.

6. In Rock Pose, sitting on heels, grasp heels and bend forward in Gurpranam with navel breathing for 1-2 minutes.

7. In Stretch Pose, raise heels and head 6" off the ground, keeping arms and legs straight, hands pointing to feet, eyes fixed on toes, and hold with Breath of Fire for 1-2 minutes.

8. On stomach, hands in Venus Lock and stretched overhead, arms hugging ears, raise arms, head, chest and (straight) legs and hold with Breath of Fire for 1-2 minutes.

9. Stand, arms at sides and sway like a pendulum, inhaling as you bend left, exhaling as you bend right for 2 minutes.

10. Still standing, inhale and twist the body to the left, extending the left arm, right hand to heart, then exhale as you twist right, right hand extended, left hand to the heart. Continue briskly for 2 minutes.

11. Standing, exhale and touch palms flat on the ground before feet, thumbs crossed. Then inhaling straighten up and arch backwards, holding the breath in for 10-20 seconds. Repeat 10-20 times.

12. Repeat bicycle exercise for 1-2 minutes.

13. On back, hands in Venus Lock behind the neck, raise alternate legs to 90° at a fast pace for 2 minutes.

14. In Rock Pose, hands in Venus Lock on the lap, inhale **Sat** and exhale **Nam** with a soft, rhythmic breath for 1-2 minutes.

15. Then perform Sat Kriya (see page   ) for 2 minutes. (Hands in Venus Lock, index fingers extended, or palms together overhead, exhale "Sat" pulling in navel, and inhale "Nam" relaxing it.)

16. Stretch arms and legs straight out in front with Breath of Fire for 2 minutes.

17. In Easy Pose, hands raised overhead, arms hugging ears, palms together, look to 3rd Eye and chant

**Ek Ong Kar
Sat Nam
Siri Wa (he) Guru**

for 3-5 minutes. Then relax.

RAISE KUNDALINI IN QUICK ORDER
(December 9, 1969)

1. **TABLE POSE:** Squatting, with feet 1½-2 feet apart, pass upper arms between thighs and calves, inside thighs & outside calves), and place hands under heels, thighs resting on the elbows, spine parallel to the floor. Hold with long, deep, breathing for 2-5 minutes. Then inhale, exhale and apply Mulbhand. (balances the sex glands.)

2. In EASY POSE, holding onto the shins, stretch and contract the spine up and down from the base for 2-3 minutes. (Without back & forward movements. There may be pain near the kidneys.) Inhale, exhale and apply Mulbhand.,

3. Spinal twist, using shoulders, with hands on shoulders, fingers forward, thumbs back. Feel it at the navel point. Continue for 2-3 minutes.

4. Spinal twist, with palms together overhead, arms traight up for 2-3 minutes. (For 9th vertebra.) Then inhale, exhale and pull Mulbhand.

5. BODY DROPS in Lotus Pose, if possible, or with legs stretched out in front. Weight is on fists beside the hips which lift the buttocks and drop them down again for 2 minutes.

6. Legs stretched straight out in front, stretch body forward and relax down, head on knees for 2-3 minutes. Then inhale, exhale and pull Mulbhand.

7. In EASY POSE, cross arms and place hands on opposite knees. Inhale deeply, pulling the arms and stretching the shoulders, hold the breath in, and exhale and relax.

8. FINGER LOCK at Heart CEnter, with long, deep breathing. Pull hard for 2-3 minutes. Then inhale, stretch arms above head and hold, exhale and apply Mulbhand.

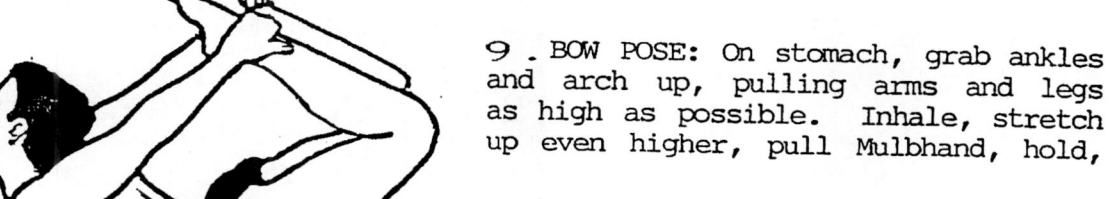

9. BOW POSE: On stomach, grab ankles and arch up, pulling arms and legs as high as possible. Inhale, stretch up even higher, pull Mulbhand, hold,

10. MEDITATION: Fix eyes on top of the skull, and press the tongue on the roof of the mouth. (There may be pain in the nose.) Dedicate self to the Divine.

COMMENTS: This is an excellent preparation for deep meditation. G.K. (Some times were added by G.K.)

OPPORTUNITY & GREEN ENERGY SET

As taught by Gurucharan Singh Khalsa

1. **SPINAL FLEXES:** Sit on heels, mentally inhaling **Sat**, (concentrating at the 1st vertebra or chakra), and exhaling **Nam** (concentrating on the 4th vertebra or 3rd chakra), for 2-3 minutes.
To end: Inhale, pull Mulbhand, exhale, pull Mulbhand and hold 10 seconds. Repeat 3 times.

2. **BODY DROPS:** Stretch legs out in front, hands on floor besided hips lifting body (and heels) off thefloor, and letting it drop, rapidly for 2-3 minutes.

3. **CROW POSE:** With arms straight out in front, fingers interlaced, forefingers extended, pointing out to infinity before the heart, with Breath of Fire for 2-3 minutes.
To end: Inhale, hold, project out from the Heart Center, end exhale.

4. **RUNNING IN PLACE:** Run vigorously pulling knees up high, with a good punching motion for 3-5 minutes.

5. **KUNDALINI LOTUS:** Balance on buttocks holding on to big toes, back, legs & arms straight, with Breath of Fire for 2-3 minutes.
To end: Inhale, hold, draw energy up the spine, exhale.

6. **TREA KRIYA:** Sitting on left heel with right foot on left thigh, hands cupped below the navel, lift up the diaphragm and chant **Ong So Hung** strongly from the heart, and hear the sound at the heart.

7. **ARMS OUT PARALLEL:** In Easy Pose, arms out to the sides, parallel to the ground, palms up, concentrate on the energy coming in the left palm and going out the right, forming a powerful arch between the hands, with Breath of Fire for 2-3 minutes.
To end: Inhale, hold feel the energy continue to enter the left palm, course through the shoulders, leave the right palm, and arch overhead. Exhale and relax.

8. **BOWING TO THE INFINITE:** In Easy Pose, hands in Venus Lock behind the neck, exhale and bring the forehead to the floor, inhale bring the forehead to the floor silently chanting Sat, and arise, inhaling, silently chanting Nam, for 2-3 minutes.

9. **ARM LIFTS:** Extend the arms straight out in front, palms down. Raise alternate arms from parallel to 60°, inhaling as right arm goes up and exhaling as it comes down, (almost a Breath of Fire), 2-3 minutes. To end: Arms together at level of 3rd eye, inhale, hold and project from the 3rd eye out to infinity. Exhale and relax.

10. **COSMIC CONNECTIONS:**

(A) Hands in Venus Lock 4 inches above the Crown Chakra, palms down (Shakti Pose), focus the eyes up and out of the Crown Chakra with Breath of Fire for 2-3 minutes.

(B) Hands remaining in place, point the forefingers straight up, continuing to focus out the Crown Chakra, breath long and deep for 2-3 minutes.

(C) Without lowering the hands, place the fingertips together with the palms apart (like a teepee), and continue to project in and up, with Breath of Fire for 2-3 minutes.
To end: Inhale, hold project out, exhale and relax.

11. **GREEN ENERGY PRODUCTION:** Arms at sides, bend forearms up, palms flat and faced forward, comfortably relaxed, visualizing green energy, chant from the heart, feeling a slight pull at the navel:

    Hari Hari Hari Har
    for 2-11 minutes.

To end: Inhale, exhale and relax in Guyan Mudra. Meditate and think of all the things you can be grateful for, sitting in a shower of energy coming to you. Love every breath that comes, and love all things, known and unknown.

COMMENTS: This set attracts opportunities and opens up the Heart Center. It allows one to approach prosperity from the Heart Center consciousness or plane of attraction. This consciousness can be summarized as follows: "The more I open myself, the more I can attract. I don't need to struggle; I have the ability to attract opportunities."

Start realizing that opportunites and prosperity can come in different forms than you have previously imagined. Believe that you <u>deserve</u> prosperity, and that God loves you.

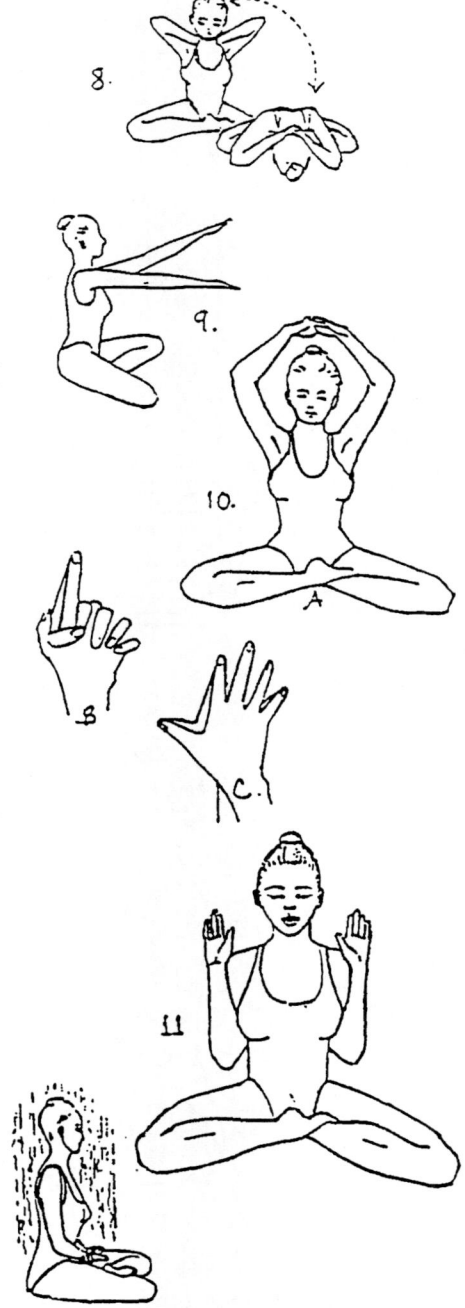

SIMPLE EXERCISE FOR SPIRITUAL HEALING
For Developing the Power of the Hands
September 7, 1974

1. Sit with a straight spine and raise arms up to 60°, rubbing the fingers on the palms for 2-5 minutes.

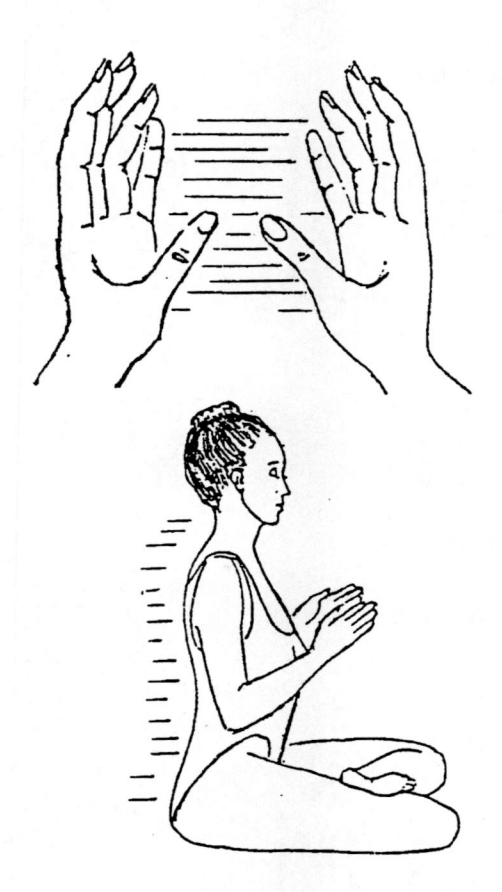

2. Face palms towards each other, 6" apart at chest level, and concentrate on the energy between them, and on the Silver Cord (the psychic channel from the rectum to the vocal cord), very straight and shining for 5 minutes.

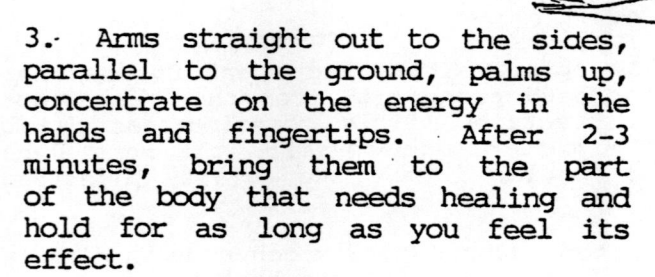

3. Arms straight out to the sides, parallel to the ground, palms up, concentrate on the energy in the hands and fingertips. After 2-3 minutes, bring them to the part of the body that needs healing and hold for as long as you feel its effect.

Relax and Renew

In Only Two to Eleven Minutes!

SEEK GOD WITHIN! Experience every act as a god for one day!

October 21, 1969

Start loving yourself. God gave you the gift of life; fall in love with it. Go crazy for it. Value it, feel it, have it, understand.

There is no God, no divinity and no religion, nothing, if you cannot fall in love with yourself.

Man to Man, XII

TRUST AND LOVE: We have so much to fear from childhood - we must disconnect from the past so we can have a future. Love- is a trust of selflessness within the self. Trust first, love later. Love is as Universal as God is. But our being is not sure what it is, causing doubt, anger, misery and death. One has to have mental training for release (death), and one who dies not knowing who he is, does not know where he is going.

June 19, 1972

THE ATTITUDE OF GRATITUDE is the highest yoga.

June 22, 1972

STRESS REDUCTION IN 2-11 MINUTES

All Kundalini Yoga Sets and Meditation alter mental and physical states, and ultimately restore balance, serenity and relaxation as well as yielding dynamic health and expanded consciousness. Some take long practice, and even years to produce such effects. Those that follow, however, yield dramatically effective results in from 2-11 minutes. The must be experienced to be believed!

In just 2-11 minutes one can regain serenity, emotional equilibrium and tranquility, re-energize, neutralize negativity, tension and anger, and regain control of the mind. These priceless gems, when practiced, will quickly add to efficiency, effectiveness, and the sense of dominion as well.

Pranayama, (breathing) often a specific component of the sets and meditations, is essential for stress reduction. If you can control the breath, you can, quite simply, control the mental and emotional climate, as the following exercises will clearly demonstrate! In fact, management of stress is as simple as management of the breath.

The body must be balanced and calm in order to deeply meditate. (That is why we do yoga before meditating.) When time is limited, however, there are some exercises that very quickly induce a state of deep meditation. These meditation facilitators, which appear at the beginning of the meditation section, are in themselves powerful stress removers, as they free one from dualistic thinking and align the mind with universal thought.

Finally, this section includes tips for self-protection, and for dealing with crisis situations, and an effective problem-solving visualization technique.

BREATH: Breath consciously! Breath is the tender charge of the Divine ...a limited life force. Control the source of energy (breath), and control the earth with a superior consciousness that no negativity can enter.

October 27, 1969

REDUCING STRESS THROUGH PROPER BREATHING

We can quickly alter emotional states and reduce stress by using the breath. Proper breathing is a prerequisite for stress management. We get more energy from the air with long, deep breathing from the navel, at a rate of 8 or fewer breaths per minute. Shallow, rapid breathing constantly calls upon the adrenals for added energy, burning them out.

The rhythm and depth of the breath correlates to different states of consciousness and emotion. To maintain the proper balance of oxygen and carbon dioxide, and avoid hyperventilation, it is important to breathe only through the nose, unless otherwise specified.

LONG DEEP BREATHING

Long, deep breathing, or the complete breath is the most natural and simplest of all breathing exercises, but we normally breathe irregularly, rapidly and shallowly, resulting in an emotional stance, chronic tension and weak nerves. The lungs are the largest organ in the human body. Besides supplying oxygen and removing carbon dioxide from the body, the respiratory system helps regulate PH balance (acidity and alkalinity), and excretes water vapor, hydrogen and small amounts of methane. An average pair of lungs can enlarge to a volume of almost 6,000 cubic centimeters, but we normally use only 600 to 700 cubic centimeters of that capacity. If the lungs are not expanded to their full capacity, small air sacs, the alveoli, cannot clean out their mucous linings so that we do not get enough oxygen to flush out toxic irritants that can lead to infections and disease.

Begin breathing exercises by a complete exhalation, contracting the chest until the lungs seem empty, then strongly contracting the abdomen to pressure out the last bit of stale air.

To take a complete breath, inhale by first expanding the lower abdomen, and follow by expanding the chest. As you exhale, let the chest deflate, then pull the belly in to finish. The diaphragm drops down to expand the lungs and admit air, then contracts upwards to expel it. To extend inhalation (implementing slower than 6 breaths per minute) place the tongue on the roof of the mouth, admitting only a small amount of air. This breath should be silent. Its practice automatically relaxes the mind and body.

To learn this breath, lie down on the back and move the hand with the inhalation, from the abdomen to the neck, and feel the inhalation from the bottom to the top.

BREATH OF FIRE

This is an energizing breath, in which the focus of energy is at the navel point in the abdomen. The breath is rapid (2-3 breaths per second), continuous without pause between inhale and exhale, and powerful. As you exhale, the air is pushed out by contracting the abdomen at the navel point, towards the spine, with the chest relaxed. As you inhale allow the abdomen to relax, briefly, creating a vacuum to suck air effortlessly into the lungs. This is a balanced breath with equal power in the inhale and exhale, but effort is exerted only on the exhale.

Breath of fire is a cleansing breath which purifies the blood and releases old toxins from the lungs, mucous lining, and cells. Regular practice expands the lungs. You can start with 1 to 3 minutes and build up to 11 minutes. Begin alternating 2 minutes of Breath of Fire with 1 minute of rest for 4 complete sets. If you feel dizzy, just relax the breath a moment and then continue.

RIGHT NOSTRIL BREATHING
(TO ENERGIZE)

If you are tired, falling asleep and need more energy, breathe through the right nostril. Right nostril breathing can be done two ways: (1) Block the left nostril with the left thumb, and inhale and exhale long and deeply through the right nostril only. (2) Inhale through the right nostril, and exhale through the left. With the left hand, block the left nostril with the left thumb to inhale, and then block the right nostril with the left ring finger to exhale. Repeat 3-4 minutes. To end, inhale through both nostrils, holding the breath 10 or more seconds, then exhale Sit calmly and enjoy the energy and the space.

Right nostril breathing energizes, and levels out an irritated, depressed or weird mental state.

LEFT NOSTRIL BREATHING
TO RELAX

Left nostril breathing can also be done 2 ways: (1) Block the right nostril and inhale and exhale through the left nostril only, using long, deep breaths. (2) Inhale through the left nostril, using the right thumb to block the right nostril, and exhale through the right nostril, blocking the left with the right ring and little fingers. Continue, pausing slightly between breaths. To end, inhale through both nostrils, hold a moment and exhale. Remain calmly seated and relax.

Do this breathing to calm the mind and cool the nerves. It is soothing to do it before going to bed.

ALTERNATE NOSTRIL BREATHING
TO BALANCE

Make a U-shape of thumb and index finger on right hand. Block the right nostril with the thumb. Inhale through the left nostril. Pause. Block the left nostril with the index finger as you release the thumb from the right nostril. Exhale through the right nostril, and (still blocking the left nostril), inhale through the right nostril. Pause. Block the right nostril again, and exhale through the left nostril. Continue in this way for 2-5 minutes.

This is a meditation in itself. It will make you feel calm, as well as energized and centered. It balances the brain and is excellent for clearing the sinuses. Inhale "SAT" and exhale "NAM". Focus attention on the breath. To end, inhale through both nostrils, hold 10 seconds and exhale. Meditate. You can also hold the breath out or in between breaths.

BREATHING TO CHANGE NOSTRILS AT WILL
& ALTER MENTAL STATES

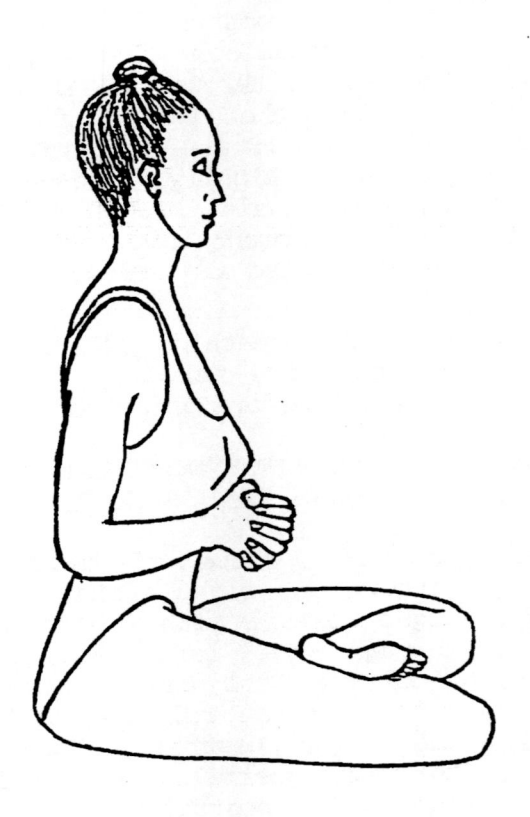

How to Do It: Sit in a comfortable meditative posture with your spine straight. Interlace your fingers with your right thumb on top. Place your hands at the center of your diaphragm line, touching your body.

Close your eyes. Concentrate on your breath at the tip of your nose. See from which nostril you are breathing. Within 3 minutes you should know. Then change it. If you are breathing primarily through your left nostril, consciously change to your right nostril. Be sure to keep your shoulders completely relaxed. You should have a pressure at your hands, but none at your shoulders.

Practice changing this breath back and forth for as long as you like. 1 minute is a good time. You can do up to 31 minutes.

What it will do for you: This exercise will alter your energy by changing the active nostril. If you are thinking something neurotic, and find that you're breathing through your right nostril, start breathing through the left nostril, instead. (This changes the energy from fire to cool). If you cannot relax or sleep, change to the left nostril. But if you are irritated, depressed, or in a wierd mental state, start breathing through the right nostril. If you are tired and need extra energy, change to the right nostril. In 3 minutes you will be a different person.

This ability to change nostrils should be taught to children within their first 3 years. Exercising this ability can prevent nervous breakdowns.

NOTE: With practice, you can switch nostrils simply by concentrating and shifting the gaze to the side you want to breathe through. Another technique is to lie down on the side of the operating nostril and put a small cushion under that armpit, pressing it with the weight of the body. The science of the nostrils is called Swara Yoga. It teaches that when one nostril is dominant, the opposite hemisphere of the brain dominates. The left nostril and right hemisphere of the brain are considered lunar, and the right nostril (and left hemisphere), solar. It is recommended to change nostrils at the first sign of disease.

BASIC BREATH SERIES

1) Sit in easy pose. Make an antenna of the right hand fingers and block the right nostril with the thumb. Begin long deep breathing through the left nostril for 3 minutes. Inhale--hold for 10 seconds.

2) Repeat the first exercise, but use the left hand and breathe through the right nostril. Continue for 3 minutes. Inhale--hold for 10 seconds.

3) Inhale through the left nostril, exhale through the right using long deep breaths. Use the thumb and the little finger to close alternate nostrils.

4) Repeat exercise 3, except inhale through the right nostril and exhale through the left.

5) Sit in easy pose with hands on knees, thumbs and forefingers touching, elbows straight. Begin breath of fire. Totally center yourself at the brow point. Continue with a regular powerful breath for 2 to 7-1/2 minutes. Then inhale, circulating the energy. Relax or meditate for 5 minutes, then chant long "Sat Nam's," at least 3, but up to 11, minutes if you want.

Sa -a -a -a -a -a -at Nam

Comments: This set opens the pranic channels and balances the breath in the two sides of your body. It is often practiced before a more strenuous, physical exercise. It is great to do by itself whenever you need a quick lift and a clear mind. It strengthens the nervous system, energizes, calms and balances.

ANTI-HYPERTENSION MEDITATION
July 2, 1986

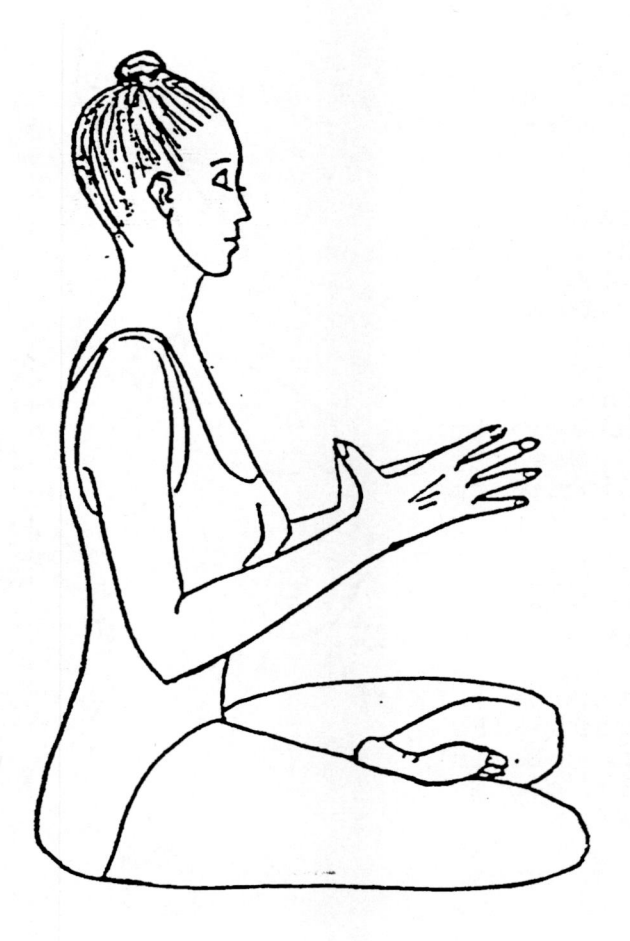

In Easy Pose, place fingertips together forming a tepee, at the heart level. Apply reasonable pressure to fingers and thumbs.

Inhale through the mouth to the maximum, and exhale through the nose. Breathe affectionately and beautifully as though you were drinking honey. Listen to the tape of "Rakhe Rakankaar", and feel the rhythm in your heart, and in every cell in the body. Keep the eyes 1/10 open, and focus at the tip of the nose or at the 3rd eye for 11-31 minutes. (If for 31 minutes, sleep afterwards.)

To end, sit quietly and listen to the sound chant back to you. Feel protection and victory.

PIKHANA BHAKTI MEDITATION
August 6, 1975

Through the closed eyes, look at the tip of the nose. Then, on a mental screen, project the picture of anyone you know well and love - holy man, Diety, friend, teacher. Relax and meditate on the figure you've created.

Gives one the power to see the creative consciousness of another. An enjoyable, devotional meditation.

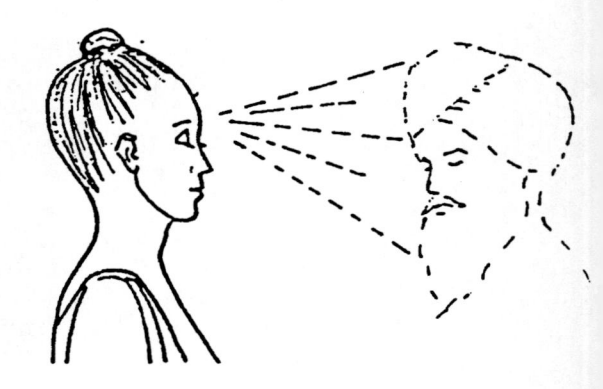

ANTI-STRESS BREATHING

In meditation posture, press tips of the thumbs and little fingers together. The other fingers touch each other on the same hand, but do not touch the opposite fingers, and are extended straight out between the navel and the heart center with the arms comfortably relaxed at the sides.

Eyes focus on the tip of the nose.

Inhale through the mouth with a long, deep and powerful breath, and exhale through the nose. Then inhale through the nose and exhale through the mouth. Continue the cycle for 11 minutes and do this meditation for 90 days.

EFFECTS: Balances the pituitary so that you don't receive every bit of information. Balances the 1st & 5th bodies. Calms inner tension. It takes awhile to begin working.

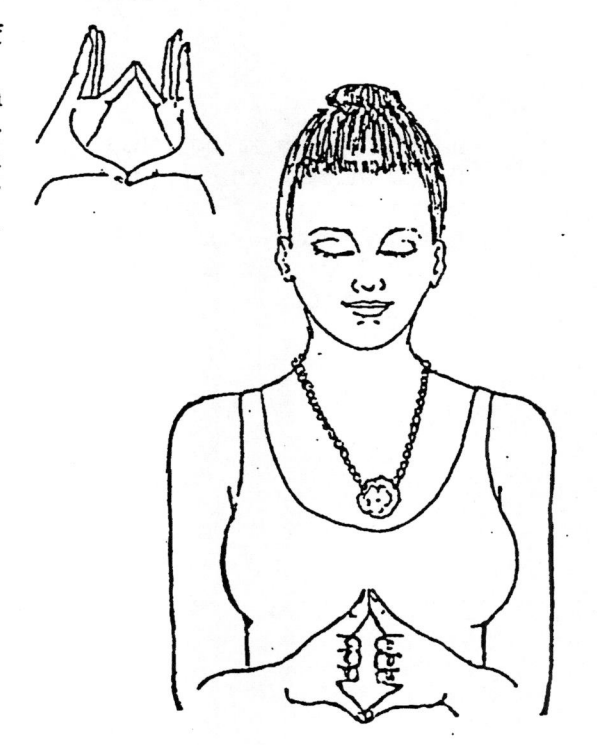

ENERGY & RELAXATION FOR NERVES
October 12, 1969

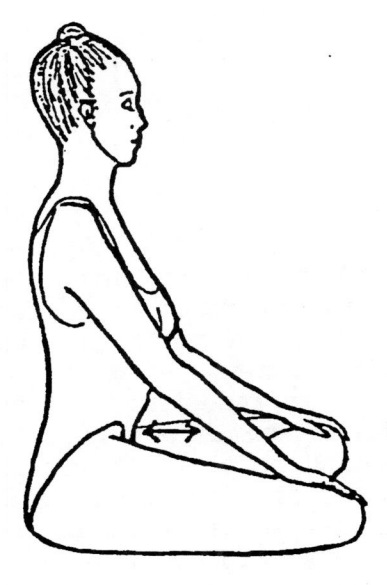

1. In Easy Pose, inhale, hold, pull and release Mulbhand 3 times, exhale, and repeat for 1 minute. Then stretch the legs.

2. Inhale, exhale, hold the breath out and pull and relax Mulbhand 3 times, inhale and repeat for 1 minute. Relax the legs, stretching them out.

3. Unite with the Universal Spirit (current). Let go, if only for an instant. Union cleanses negativity.

COMMENTS: Try 40 days without negativity. Offer all action, all thought to the Creator. Energy that is drawn from the navel is that given by the mother, and not paid back. Use nourishing channels of the navel as when in the womb.

EMOTIONAL BALANCE
Sunia(n) Antar
August 12, 1977

Before practicing this meditation, drink a glass of water. Sit in Easy Pose, place the arms across the chest and lock hands under the armpits, palms open and against the body. Raise the shoulders up tight against the earlobes, and apply Neck Lock, closing the eyes. The breath will automatically become slow. Continue for 3 minutes, gradually increasing to 11 minutes.

This meditation is very good for women and essential at times when one is worried or upset and doesn't know what to do, or when one feels like screaming, yelling and misbehaving. When out of focus or emotional, attention should be given to the body's water balance and breath rate. Humans are approximately 70% water, and behavior depends upon the relation of water and earth, air and ether. Breath, representing air and ether is the rhythm of life. Normally we breathe 15 times a minute, but when we are able to rhythmically slow down the breath to only 4 breaths per minute, we have indirect control over our minds, and it eliminates obnoxious behavior, promoting a calm mind regardless of the state of affairs. When there is a water imbalance in the system, and the kidneys are under pressure, it can cause worry and upset. Drinking water, pulling the shoulders up to the ears and tightly locking the entire upprea creates a solid break that can be applied to the four sides of the brain. After 2 or 3 minutes, thoughts will be there, but one does not feel them. This is a very effective method of balancing the functional brain.

MAN SUHAAVE MUDRA KRIYA
To Tranquilize the Mind in 3 Minutes (February 28, 1980)

Sit in Easy Pose with a straight spine. Bend elbows and bring the hands up and in until they meet before the Heart Center. The elbows should be held up almost to the level of the hands. Bend the index fingers into the palms. Join them with each other so that they press together from the first to the 2nd joint. The middle fingers extend and meet at the tips, and the other fingers curl into the hands, thumbs meeting at the tips. Hold the mudra about 4 inches from the body, with the extended fingers pointing away from the body. Gaze at the tip of the nose.

There is no mantra given for this meditation. Inhale completely repeating a mantra of your choice 11-21 times. Exhale, hold the breath out, and repeat the mantra an equal number of times on the held out breath. Continue for 3 minutes.

COMMENTS: This hand position is called, "the mudra which pleases the mind". Buddha gave it to his disciples for control of the mind. It works to tranquilize the mind within three minutes.

EVERYONE IS BORN A SAINT, innocent. Be innocent and be humble. Flow. Share with others. Share your information but do not push. Every individual has to grow. Live most relaxed and feel a FUN about everything.

March 21, 1974

KRIYA TO BALANCE & RECHARGE THE NERVOUS & IMMUNE SYSTEM
March 23, 1987

This is the most sacred kriya in yoga. It balances the 3 powers, the three systems of the body: parasympathetic, sympathetic, and nerve-active system. These are very important and must be in balance.

Do this kriya so you will never be in pain. It will slowly and steadily build very strong steel-like stamina in you. You'll think better, act better and be precisely accurate in life. You will become intuitive so you can subtly pick up messages, and you won't have to go to psychics for your sensitivity. This kriya is for the spine, which controls the nervous system. It is like taking a huge vitamin pill (so you won't need vitamins either), and it will balance every molecule in your body.

1. In Easy Pose, place arms out straight, parallel to the floor, at 30 degrees forward from the sides in a line with the thighs. Right Hand: with palm facing forward, keep index and middle finger stiff and straight, bending the ring and little fingers into the palm, held by the thumb. The arm and the extended fingers remain straight and rigid like steel and do not move throughout the meditation. (Imagine you are shooting a derringer.) Left Hand: Keep the elbow straight with palm facing the floor. Move the left arm rapidly up and down (about 9" total), the breath becoming like Breath of Fire, and the Belly Button automatically jumping. (This breath from the base of the navel will burn out the garbage.) The breath should sound like a steam engine.

After 11 minutes, inhale, solidify the body and keeping the attention at the 3rd Eye, tense every molecule to rebuild the body. Hold 30 seconds, and exhale. Immediately inhale and hold 20 seconds. Rapidly exhale, inhale and hold 10 seconds. The last time, rapidly exhale, inhale and hold 5 seconds. Then exhale and relax.

COMMENTS: If you get cramps during this exercise, your calcium is off; if you get tired, your magnesium is out of balance. If the arm hurts, take 2 bananas because the potassium is out of balance. If your lower back hurts (and you are a woman), menstruation is impaired, and if you are a man, you are on the verge of impotency. If the head hurts it means the flow of blood to the head is obstructed and nutrition is not right.

2. In easy pose, lock palm over palm, with right palm facing body, fingers overlapping the back of the opposite hand at Heart Center. Inhale and press hands together so hard that the hands, arms and rib cage begin to shake. Hold 15 seconds and exhale. Repeat twice more (3 times total), and then relax.

COMMENTS: This exercise brings the navel area into balance and recharges all the pranic areas and the immune system of the body. It will put you into a deep meditative state, even if done for only a few minutes.

THE 4/4 BREATH FOR ENERGY

Sit straight placing the palms together at the Heart Center with the fingers pointing up,. Focus at the Brow Point with eyelids lightly closed. Inhaling, break the breath into 4 equal parts or sniffs, filling the lungs completely on the 4th. As you exhale, released the breath equally in 4 parts, completely emptying the lungs on the 4th. On each part of the inhale and exhale, pull in the navel point. (The stronger you pump the navel, the more energy you will generate.) One full breath cycle (In and out) takes about 7-8 seconds. Codntinue for 2-3 minutes. If you press the hands together very hard, and do it vigorously, 1 minute will recharge you and alter your mental state. If you are anxious or confused, add the mantra "Sa Ta Na Ma" mentally on both the inhale and exhale.

TO END: Press the palms forcefully together for 10-15 seconds, creating a tension in the whole body by pressing as hard can. Hold as long as possible. Exhale powerfully and repeat (inhale, hold and press). Exhale, relax and feel all the tension in the body vanish. If you need rest, immediately lie on the back with the eyes closed and allow each area of the body to relax for 2 more minutes. Take a few deep breaths, stretch and you will be ready for action.

WHAT IT WILL DO FOR YOU: Do this at a break in the action or the game. It will relax and energize you, and help combat encroaching fatigue or emotion. In games or sports it can rejuvenate corrdination and spirit, and possibly avoid injury. This is a great quick pickup when you have only a minute. If you do it 2 or 3 times a day at strategic times (before meals, meetings, driving home, etc.) and when you begin to feel tired, you will notice a big difference in the way you feel. Do it at 3:00 p.m. to avoid the "3:00-pass-out-syndrome".

HASSELS: Hassels aren't of the people. They are of the age - the duality. One must stand to the truth for we are not liberated by hassel.

March 3, 1970

MEDITATION FOR THE LOWER TRIANGLE
To Repair Stress Damage

Sit in Easy Pose. Make sure the spine is pulled up and stretched straight. Extend the right arm straight up hugging the ear. Extend the left arm up to 60 degrees from horizontal, with the palm facing down. On both hands, put the thumb onto the mound just below the little finger. Keep the eyes slightly open, and look down toward the upper lip. Press the elbows straight. Stretch the arms up from the shoulders. Continue for 11 minutes.

COMMENTS: This meditation alleviates any problem in the lower spine. It is a direct healer for the kidneys and adrenal glands. Consequently, it helps repair the energy drained by long term stress. This kriya also helps the heart. Although there is no breath specified, the breath will automatically become longer and deeper as you continue. It is important to hold the arms perfectly still to receive full benefit.

DHRIB DHRISTI LOCHINA KARMA KRIYA
Silent Meditation to Center and Balance
October 10, 1973

Sit with a straight spine, hips and shoulders in a line. Lock the tips of the front teeth together. Focus the eyes on the tip of the nose with the tongue touching the upper palate (which should occur automatically within about 1 minute). From the 3rd Eye (between the eyebrows) silently project the mantra

Sa Ta Na Ma

Beam it out, creating an internal harmony. Coordinate the mantra with the breath. Usually one or two repetitions of "Sa Ta Na Ma" are used with each inhale and each exhale. Continue for 31 minutes.

COMMENTS: "Dhrib Dhristi Lochina Karma Kriya" means "the action of acquiring insight into the future". This powerful, simple meditation was first taught on the eve of a full moon, when the effects are gretest as the subconscious mind is then fully open to its vibratory action.

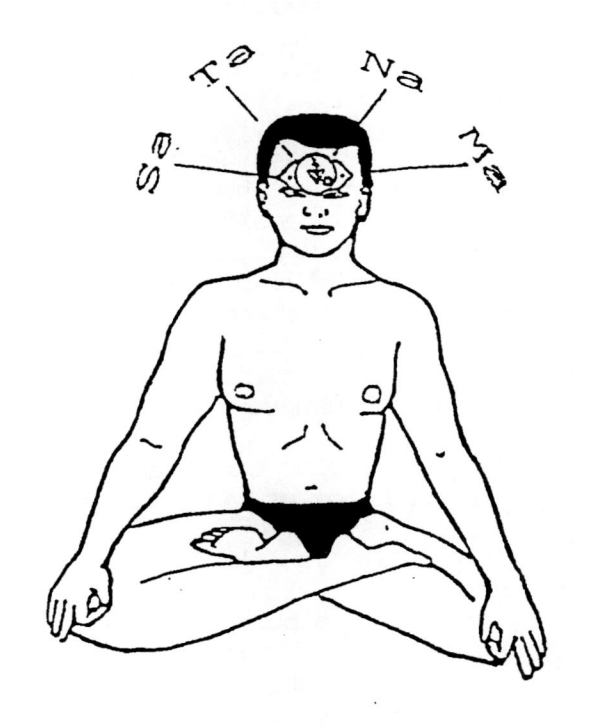

Although most meditations require long periods of practice for mastery, it is possible to master this one in a single or several sittings, because of the wide range of individual differences in practitioners and the uniqueness of the meditation.

Though the meditation should be practiced for at least 31 minutes at a sitting, the minimum (compromise) time is 15 minutes, and to master it, you should practice for 1½ hours. Three hours practice will open up the psychic capacities. But, in only 3-11 minutes practice, you can go inside, tune out external distractions and center yourself. You can do it on the bus or standing in line, or at work when you can't be alone.

Honestly practice it for the longer times, and the following things will happen: Your eyes will have the power to heal anyone. Your words will have the power to penetrate deeply. You will learn to talk inspiringly, and your words will always represent the truth of a given situation ("vac siddhi"). You will be able to project your personality or your bodily sensations anywhere. Lastly, you will know the consequences of any sequence that you may start.

VATSAR KRIYA
For Acid Stomach

1. Kneel in Rock Pose, keeping spine straight, and rest the forehead on the ground before the knees. Extend the arms straight overhead, resting them on the ground. Hold the position for 1 minute or more with normal breathing.

2. Sit in Easy Pose with a straight spine resting the hands on the knees. Pucker the mouth into a beak and inhale through it until the lungs are completely filled. Hold the air in and churn the stomach around in a circle until you can no longer hold the breath. Exhale through the mouth and repeat twice more.

Drink 2½ kilos of water in the morning and 2½ kilos of water in the evening.

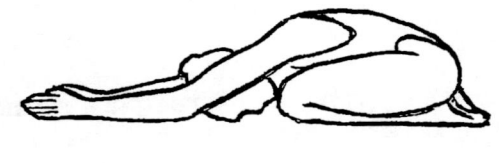

COMMENTS: This kriya causes the life force at the 4th vertebra to cure the body. It must be done on an empty stomach. Exercise 1 brings increased blood flow to the pineal and pituitary glands, stimulating secretions of the glands which brings wisdom. Exercise 2 eliminates acidity in the stomach. But if it is repeated more than 3 times, the system will become too alkaline. Avoid hot foods such as peppers and curry.

SICKNESS: Most sickness comes because you listen to negativity. Protect the self – don't indulge in negative conversation.

March 11, 1970

SITALI PRANAYAM

Sit in a comfortable meditative posture with a straight spine. Curl the tongue up on the sides and protrude it slightly past the lips. Inhale deeply and smoothly through the rolled tongue and exhale through the nose. Continue for 5 minutes. Inhale, hold, pull the tongue in and relax. Then repeat for 5 more minutes. (Variations include: 2-3 minutes periods, and the practice of 52 breaths daily, 26 in the morning and 26 in the evening.)

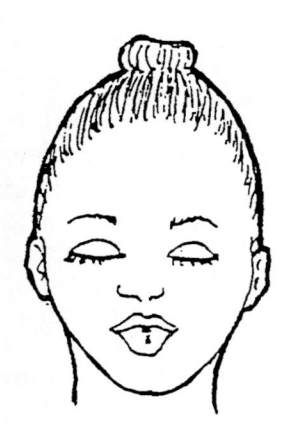

Sitali Pranayam is a well-known practice. It soothes and cools the spine near the 4th, 5th and 6th vertebrae, which, in turn, regulates the sexual and digestive energy. This breath is often used for lowering fever (and it can cool you in warm weather). Daily practice of 26 breaths in the morning and 26 breaths in the evening can extend the lifespan. The tongue may taste bitter at first, a sign of toxification, but as you continue the tongue will taste sweet and you will have overcome all sickness inside.

It is an excellent kriya to do before chanting the Siri Gaitri Mantra ("RA MA DA SA SA SAY SO HUNG").

It is said that people who practice this kriya have all things that they need come to them by planetary ether. In mystical terms, you are served by the heavens.

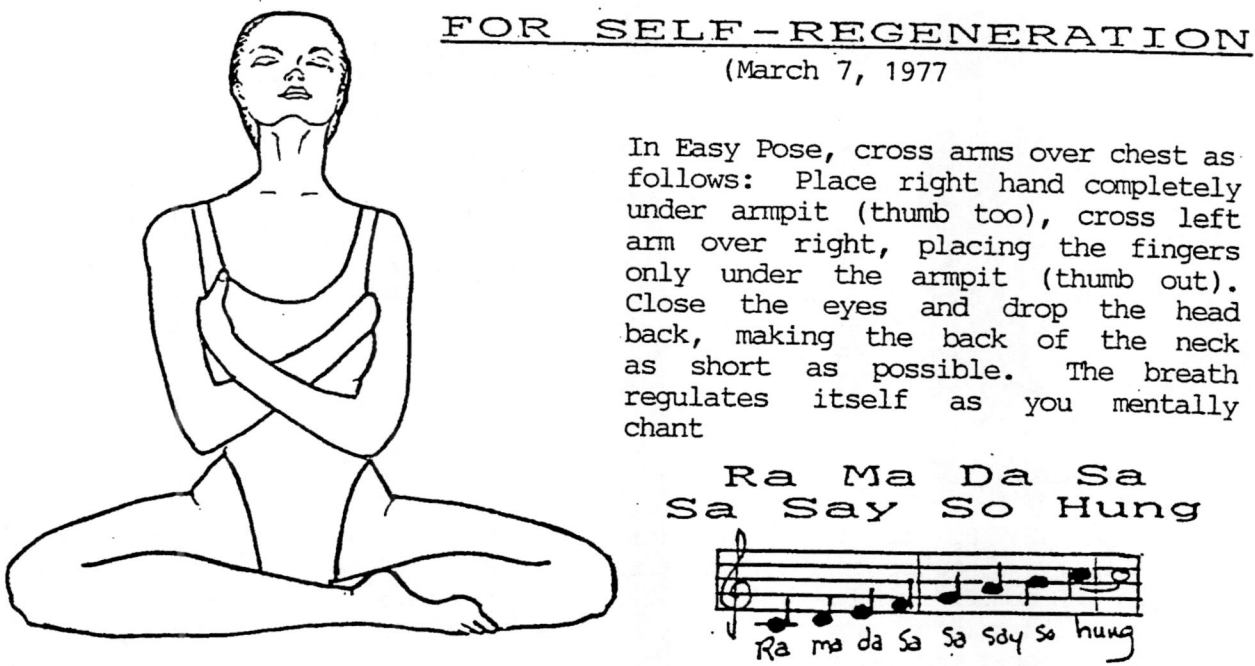

FOR SELF-REGENERATION
(March 7, 1977

In Easy Pose, cross arms over chest as follows: Place right hand completely under armpit (thumb too), cross left arm over right, placing the fingers only under the armpit (thumb out). Close the eyes and drop the head back, making the back of the neck as short as possible. The breath regulates itself as you mentally chant

**Ra Ma Da Sa
Sa Say So Hung**

for 3 minutes. Self-regenerating.

LONG SAT NAMS
To Neutralize Tension

Sit straight and relaxed and bring the forearms up and in until the hands meet at the heart level. Face both palms up and cross the right hand over the left palm with the fingers extended and joined to each other. Place the left thumb in the right hand.

The eyes are 9/10 closed and as the meditation progresses, they may close completely. Inhale deeply and exhale completely as you chant

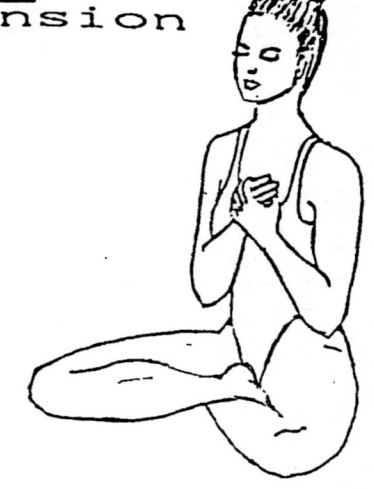

   Saaaaaaaaaaaaaaaaaaaaaaaaaaaaaaaat
   Naam

Ratio of "Sat" to "Nam" is 35:1. Begin with 11 minutes and build to 31.

COMMENTS: This is an extremely relaxing meditation. It completely neutralizes tension and puts you in the most relaxing situation you can possibly imagine. By doing it for 40 days you can revitalize your glandular system and re-establish glandular equilibrium.

FOR CONCENTRATION IN ACTION
& To Learn to Meditate

Sit comfortably with a straight spine. With the four fingers of the right hand, feel the pulse on the left wrist. Place the fingers in a straight line, lightly, so that you can feel the pulse in each fingertip. Focus the lightly closed eyes at the Brow Point (between the eyebrows). On each beat of the heart, mentally hear the sound

   Sat Nam

for 11 minutes, building to 31.

COMMENTS: If you don't know how to meditate or you want to develop the ability of concentration in action, this is a beautiful technique. This is THE meditation for someone who can't meditate. It allows you to control your reaction to any situation and can bring sweetness and one-pointedness to the most outrageous and scattered mind.

7 WAVE "SAT NAM" MEDITATION

Sit in Easy Pose, palms together in Prayer Mudra, with the eyes closed and focussed at the Brow Point. Inhale deeply, and with the exhale, chant the mantra in the "Law of Seven" or "Law of the Tides":

Vibrate **Saaaat** in six waves

and let **Naam** be the seventh.

On each wave, thread the sound thru the chakras, beginning at the base of the spine in the rectum. On "Nam", let the energy and sound radiate from the 7th chakra at the top of the head through the aura. As the sound penetrates each chakra, gently pull the physical area it corresponds to. The 1st is at the rectum, the 2nd at the sex organ, the 3rd, at the navel, the 4th at the heart, the 5th at the throat and the 6th is between the eyebrows. Continue for 15 minutes.

COMMENTS: If you can build this meditation 6 seconds a day to at least 31 minutes, the mind will be cleansed as the ocean waves wash the sandy beach. This is a bij (seed) mantra meditation. Bij mantras such as "Sat Nam" are the only mantras which can totally rearrange the habit patterns of the subconscious mind. We all have habit patterns, and couldn't function without them. But some patterns we have created are unwanted. You have changed, so you want the habit patterns to change. By vibrating the sound current "Sat Nam" in this manner, you activate the energy of the mind to erase and establish habits. Consequently, this meditation is a good introduction to Kundalini yoga. It will open the mind to the new experience. A long-time student will do it to clear off the effects of a hurried day before beginning another deep meditation. After chanting this mantra, you will feel calm, relaxed and mellow.

PURPOSE: No one is on earth without purpose. Chances are given to raise consciousness.

March 3, 1970

MEDITATION FOR POWERFUL ENERGY
May 17, 1976

Sit with a straight spine in a comfortable meditative posture. Place the sun (ring) fingers together and interlace all the other fingers with the right thumb on top. Hold the hands several inches out from the diaphragm with the sun fingers pointing up at 60°.

Close the eyes. Inhale deeply and powerfully. Exhale as you chant

$$Ong$$
$$(Oooooonnnnnng)$$

with the mouth open but the air flowing out through the nose. The sound is far back and up in the soft palate. (In group chanting, each person should use his own breath rhythm.)

COMMENTS: The power of this chant, when correctly done, must be experienced to be believed. Only 5 repetitions are necessary to completely elevate consciousness. When you have a hard day to face, this meditation will give you absolutely powerful energy and it will balance your most effective computer - the brain. It can also be done when you can sleep afterwards. It *is* the best thing to do for "brain drain". (The only thing better is to do this exact mantra and mudra in shoulder stand, with a wall for support.)

ONG SOHUNG: In higher consciousness, there is no duality, no difference between you and God.

The difference between you and Him is simply ignorance and attachment.

A constant, permanent connection with the Creator is all you need. Then time will serve you and you will not serve time.

December 15, 1969

GYAN BHAND
For Self-Healing, Tuning up Nervous System, Disease Resistance
October 23, 1975

Sit with a straight spine and extend the left arm straight out in front and up at a 60° angle from horizontal. The palm faces down and the fingers are straight. Hold the right hand with the palm forward at the height of the ear, 8-10 inches from the head with the fingers pointing up, and the thumb and index finger in Guyan Mudra. Focus at the brow point with normal breathing. Mentally vibrate

Wahe Guru

silently and rhythmically at the 3rd eye for 3-5 minutes. Then switch arms and repeat. Feel the distinct difference in the sides of the body. Feel in complete control of the nervous system.

COMMENTS: This is an excellent self-healing meditation. You may feel a pressure in the eyes, shoulders or spine as the nerves adjust. It is a very advanced state of meditation. It can tune up the entire nervous system and build resistance to disease. It will give the power to ward off negative thoughts. This simple meditation gives the mind the power to penetrate into a deeper meditation. It is good for the digestive system and helps prevent heart attacks. Helps fight any disease from the diaphragm up.

ONG IN VIRASAN
For Negativity

Sit in Virasan, with left heel in perineum, right foot even with the left knee. Raise arms overhead and clasp hands in inverted Venus Lock (palms facing up), arch the spine up and back, and perform chin lock. Continuously chant

Ong Ong Ong

for 3-31 minutes. (Guru Gobind Singh sat in this pose chanting for 2½ hrs.)

TO REMOVE NEGATIVITY
January 19, 1973

1. Clasp fingers in Venus Lock, but curl Mercury (little) and Sun (ring) fingers into the palms instead of crossing them. Then hook left Saturn (middle) finger over right Sun (ring) finger and pull, hard. Focus at the 3rd eye, continuously pulling hard on the finger lock for 1-3 minutes. Removes anger and enthrones the neutral mind.

2. Fit base of palms under the cheek bones and push as hard as you can for 1-3 minutes. It doesn't have to hurt, but if it does, you have the right spot. Makes you feel happy!

3. Grasp left wrist with the right hand and pull the left arm as far to the right as possible, and then some more!, for 1-3 minutes. Removes tension across the shoulder blades.

4. Make wrist lock behind the back with the hands touching the spine and try to bring elbows together. Pull! Arch the spine forward and apply chin lock for 1-3 minutes. Raises energy up the spine and elevates you!

COMMENTS: This short set leaves you feeling great! Perfect for depresion, anger, fatigue or stress. G.K.

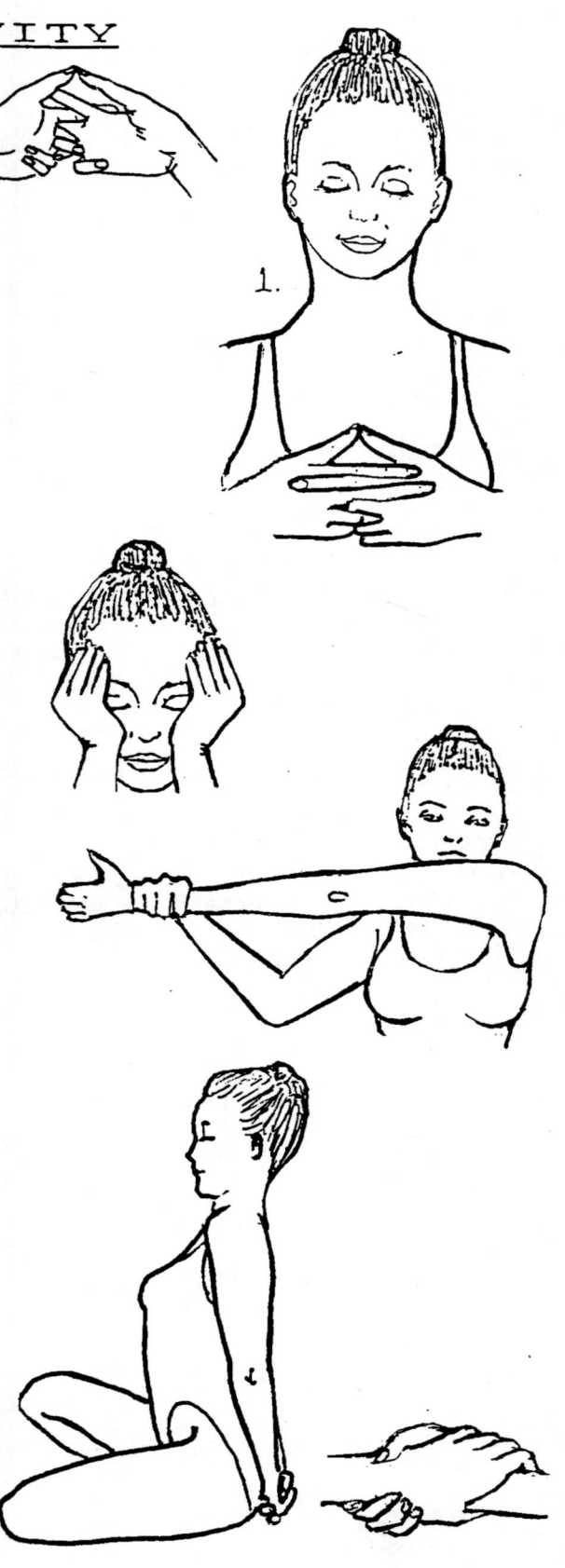

STRENGTHENING THE NERVOUS SYSTEM
(Not a Set)

TRIANGLE POSE: Stand with feet about hip-width apart, and bend over placing the palms flat, 3-4 feet from the toes about shoulderwidth apart, forming a triangle with buttocks at the apex. Stretch the body straight from heels to buttocks and from buttocks to wrists, (no bending at knees, shoulders or elbows) allowing thead and neck to relax in a line with the hips. Relax in this position with long, deep breathing for 2-5 minutes. (Deep breathing eliminates discomfort.) To end, inhale deeply, hold for 10 seconds, exhale and relax in a comfortable position with the spine straighing still aware of the breathing, eyes closed to heighten inner attentin.

This exercise strengthens and revitalizes the nervous system, aids digestion and gives extra energy. You will be surprised at the difference if you do it every day for several weeks. It is also good for when one is short tempered or impatient and it relaxes most of the major muscles, is an outlet for frustration and builds patience. This is great for the office - just close the door and be revitalized in just 5 minutes.

NOTE: The exercise can also be done on the fingertips, which is very powerful for strengthending the nervous system. Stay on fingertips as long as possible and then return palms to the floor to continue.

Follow with **GURPRANAM:** Sit on heels in Rock Pose, bending down to rest forehead on the floor before the knees. Stretch the arms straight out ahead, palms together and rest there with long, deep breathing for 1-2 minutes.

HUMILITY: Project maximum light but be humble. You may achieve something and go a little crazy, mistaking the mid-spiritual shelter for the destination. You should remain a student always! It is difficult to be aware and not show off.

February 10, 1970

QUICK ENERGIZERS
(Not a set)

CROSSCRAWLS: Standing, raise the left leg to the chest while raising the right arm straight up. Then alternate arms and legs, coordinating with a powerful breath for 1-3 minutes

On the back, raise left leg to 90°, with right arm overhead on the floor, and alternate with powerful breathing.

Crosscrawls establishes balance in the right and left hemispheres of the brain, and strengthens the magnetic field. (Walking with arms swinging naturally at the sides keeps energy balanced and strength intact, but carrying things weakens us. It has been shown that people laden with packages are more vulnerable to assault, partly due to the weakened electromagnetic field.)

COLD SHOWER: For cleansing the aura and lively energy, there is nothing like a cold shower. Yogi Bhajan cautions women to wear thigh covering pants so as not to upset the Ca.Mg. balance, and men to wear pants that cover the genetals.

SHOULDERSTAND: A quick way to revitalize as well as relax is to perform shoulderstand for at least 3 minutes, for it alters the flow of blood to give a burst of energy, stimulates the thyroid, and stretches the cervical and thoracic vertebrae removing tension in the shoulders and neck, and stimulating circulation to the brain. Follow with Plow Pose and deep relaxation on the back.

Quick Insomnia Relief
(Not a set)

Do 10 minutes of "Shakti-Bhakti" meditation to relax the solar plexus and wake up refreshed.

108 Frogs, just before retiring can knock you out cold!

Long, deep breathing through the left nostril for 3-5 minutes will relax you and put you to sleep.

Sleep on the right side to activate the left nostril. (Sleeping on the left sifde activates the right nostril energizing you, and it stimulates the digestive system.)

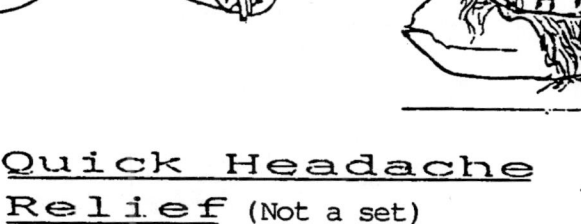

Quick Headache Relief (Not a set)

Pressing the heels of the hands into the temples relieves some headaches.

Headaches caused by neck displacements can be relieved by exercises that adjust the neck. As you do such an exercises, be aware of where it hurts, and try to align the vertebrae. (See appendix.)

Headaches from eye strain can be alleviated by eye exercises, especially "Looking Out the Back of the Head" (see eye exercises in sets, meditations and appendix).

Nature's asperin is grapefruit. Try eating one to ease or eliminate even severe headache!

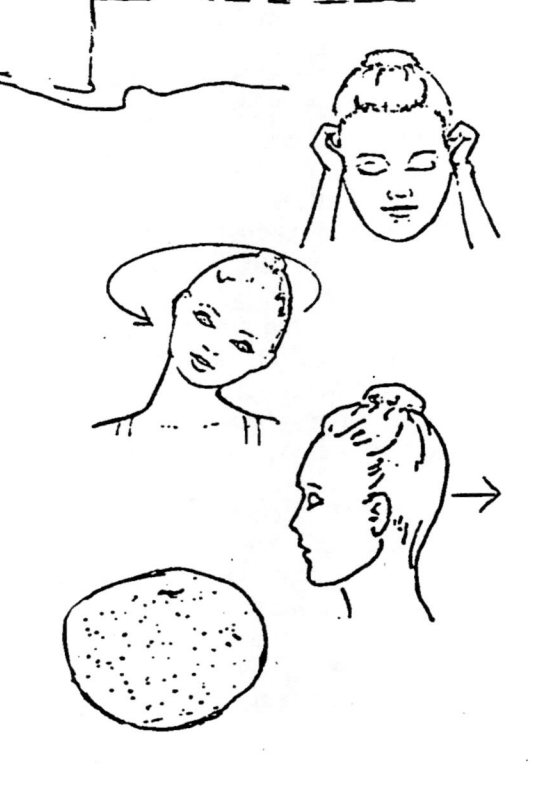

Dealing with Crisis Situations

In a crisis we sometimes find it necessary to deal with a situation on the spot, without even 5 minutes to withdraw and collect ourselves. The following techniques can get us through such times.

1. DRINK AN 8 OZ. GLASS OF WATER in one breath (bottoms up - no sipping!) to automatically calm you. It slows the breath, lowers the temperature, centers you and lowers the blood pressure A pause in the middle of crisis gives one a clearer, more neutral perspective, making him a part of the solution rather than part of the problem.

2. MONITER THE BREATH AND SLOW IT DOWN to 4-8 breaths per minute for steadiness and patience and on the spot stress reduction. Observe the breath and feel its rhythm. (Loss of rhythm is one manifestation of stress and an early indicator of disease.) Breathing fewer than 8 breaths per minute always calms you, and silent repetition of a mantra like "Sat Nam" (I am the truth) with the prolonged inhale and exhale is effective, for both centering and detaching you from negative thoughts. Long, deep breathing also relaxes the muscles, including the heart, slowing down its beat. Listen inside for you rhythm, your inner silence, and your heartbeat

3. SWITCH NOSTRILS to alter your mental state. Just close off the most open nostril and breathe powerfully through the other one, or see "Breathing to Change Nostrils at Will" in this section.

4. SWITCH FROM THE NEGATIVE TO THE POSITIVE MIND by repeating the following mantra 5 or more times:

Ek Ong Kar
Sat Gur Prasad
Sat Gur Prasad
Ek Ong Kar

5. BREAKTHROUGH BREATHING is an effective technique for emotional crisis, little known even among students of the science of breathing. It affects both the sympathetic and parasympathetic nerve centers and is used for emotional emergencies, when a situation seems impossible. It can also be used to break nicotine addiction.

Use it anytime, anywhere but don't overuse it, for this powerful, effective should be treated with care! First, clear the nasal passages, with a tissue if necessary. Then, inhale long and deep through the nose, lifting the rib cage several inches. Then force all the air out through the nose, in one explosive exhale. Do it just a few times to experience its benefits. The minimun number of breaths is 3, and it shouldn't be done more than 10 times at any given time.

6. MATCH BREATHS WITH A VICTIM, patient or client to calm the other down. Matching breaths causes a sympathetic bond which enables you to transmit calm and healing energy. Once your breaths are synchronized, begin slowing down yours, making it possible for his breathing to follow yours. If you are in physical contact, look at the person and talk quietly to him.

Self-Protection Tips

1. Much energy interaction between bepole takes place from the navel area. It is therefore important to have a strong navel center for self-protection (as is well known in the martial arts. Please see Transitions to a Heart-Centered World for sets to strengthen the navel area.) One effective technique is to wear a soft cotton cummerbund around the middle, one long enough to go around 3 times. A wide, colorful wrap-around sash is easy to integrate into a woman's wardrobe. Men can wear it under the clothing.

2. Because of this powerful navel energy, do not confront a negative or dangerous person fact to face or navel to navel. If you cannot get away, stand to the side to avoid his havel energy.

3. Imagine an impenetrable, protective shield of light around you.

4. The electro-magnetic field surrounding you is protection against every kind of danger. It can quickly be strengthened by all the breathing exercises, crosscrawls and triangle pose. (Again, see Transitions for exercises and meditations specifically to develop and strengthen this energy field.)

5. When you are in a position to heal or help others, you can protect yourself from possible negative consequences by prayerfully asking:

A) To be an agent of the higher good. (Release worry by asserting that you are there to serve and are not responsible for negative or positive outcomes.

B) To be a channel of love and light.

C) That the outcome be for the good of all concerned.

D) And adapt an attitude of gratitude for the opportunity of serving and helping others.

LEARN MARTIAL ARTS: It is our duty to help the weak. We must equip ourselves with the art of self-defense. Be steady, strong and beautiful.

June 19, 1972

VISUALIZATION FOR ACTUALIZATION

Although most movie stars, lottery winners and self-made millionaires had childhool fantasies of fame and fortune, only a very small percent of all those who dream of such things ever actualize their desires. What is it that makes one person's dreams materialize in the physical world, while most of us only fantasize without hope of fulfillment? The answer lies in INTENT & RESOLVE.

Visualization without intent, decision and resolve is mere fantasy. To validate a fantasy for actualization, empower it with "gut level" intention: the firm decision to acquire or attain a desired condition! In Kundalini Yoga this means involving the Navel Chakra, the empowering center of the subtle body. Prove it to yourself: Fantasize a cherished desire and flesh in the details (how it will look, smell, sound and even imagine touching things in the image). Then validate it! Hold the image and pull firmly on the navel point (allowing navel energy to join the picture) as you firmly decide to actualize it. Do you feel a difference?

The following technique is most effective with an open Heart Chakra, and a powerful Navel Center (See Transitions to a Heart Centered World for Heart & Navel exercises), and especially in the moments following meditation when the positive mind can effectively project desires and solutions.

1. First, clearly see and experience where you are now, aware of each cell in the body, connections to the environment and to the past and future. (Living in the past or future without connections between them or an anchor in the present can cause anxiety. Serenity, conversely, arises from awareness of the here and now, relationship to surrounds, connections to goals, and absorbtion in what we are doing. Contact with reality can be made by simply looking at one's hand or by feeling oneself sitting. Verify this by remembering a situation in which you were calm and notice how well-connected you were then.)

2. Next, clearly see and experience where you want to be - a destination, a resolved problem, a realized achievement or cherished desire. Feel as you will feel, see what you will see, hear what you will hear, and touch something. Experience satisfaction and serenity from being where you set out to be.

3. Hold the vision and add resolution by firmly pulling in on the navel point and beaming a bright golden light from your 3rd Eye between where you are now and where you want to be. Feel the connection between present and future and try to feel them as one, in the same time dimension - the present.

4. Finally, visualize the steps you will take to get where you want to be. Make a visual plan. If the process is a simple one, one set of steps is enough. A complex project may require several possible plans. As soon as you see the appropriate steps, you will begin to feel calmer.

  a. Be sure not to add negative qualifications or doubts that may block manifestation, like "but I don't have enough money to do that".

  b. Establish a positive image of yourself, with the sense that you deserve the desired condition, and that others (especially spouse or parents) will support this decision, for we can block manifestation by negative programming such as feeling unworthy or that others think you are undeserving, or unlucky.

  c. The visualization may be as general or specific as feels appropriate. If specific steps must be taken, include them but if you can feel that "it is being taken care of by the Universe", you needn't specify each step.

  d. Allow each step or problem to be resolved along the way, merge into the light and feel it transform problems into solutions

5. Now, relax and let the Universe go to work. Let go of any concern and feel confident and optimistic and then forget it for now, adapting an attitude of gratitude for a happy result. Relax and allow you positive feelings to attract the result - feel your whole body merge into a golden light and project this energy from the 3rd Eye and the Heart Chakra. Vibrate with the Universe, acknowledging its benevolence and love.

MEDITATION FACILITATORS
(Not a set)

When you want to meditate but don't have time to do a complete yoga set first, try one or more of the following exercises before sitting. End each by inhaling, pulling Mulbhand, holding and exhaling (or inhale, exhale and then pull Mulbhand and hold

FROGS to stimulate the 1st & 2nd chakras and help you sit: Squat on the toes, heels raised and touching each other, arms between legs fingertips on floor, and head up. Raise buttocks, allowing head to drop and look at knees and repeat 26-52 times. Follow with forward bend.

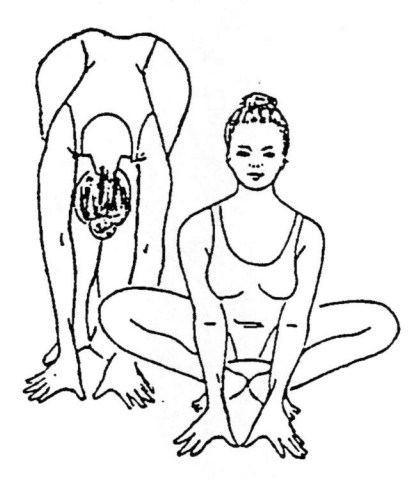

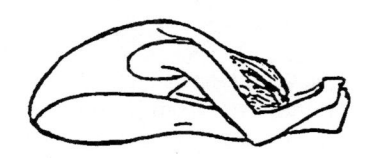

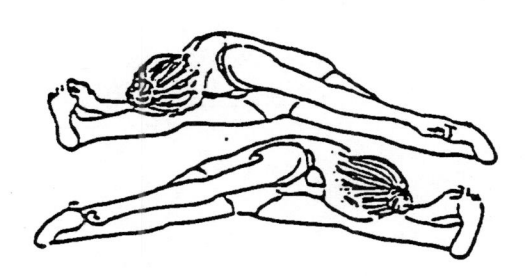

FORWARD BENDS to stretch legs, stimulate the life nerve and navel energy: Sit with legs stretched out in front, bend over grasping toes and exhale as you pull the head to the knees, inhale as you come up, and continue. Or, sit with legs spread wide apart, touching head to alternate knees for 1-2 minutes.

CROW SQUATS to stimulate and circulate energy from the 1st & 2nd chakras, and to make sitting easier: Squat, extending the arms straight ahead (or place hands in Venus Lock on top of head), and stand, repeating for 26 or 52 times. You'll be glad to sit down.

INVERTED CAMEL LIFTS to raise kundalini energy up the spine: On back bend knees drawing heels to buttocks feet flat on the floor. Grasp ankles and arch the pelvis up, lifting the navel towards the sky on the inhale, returning to first position on exhale and continue 26 or 52 times.

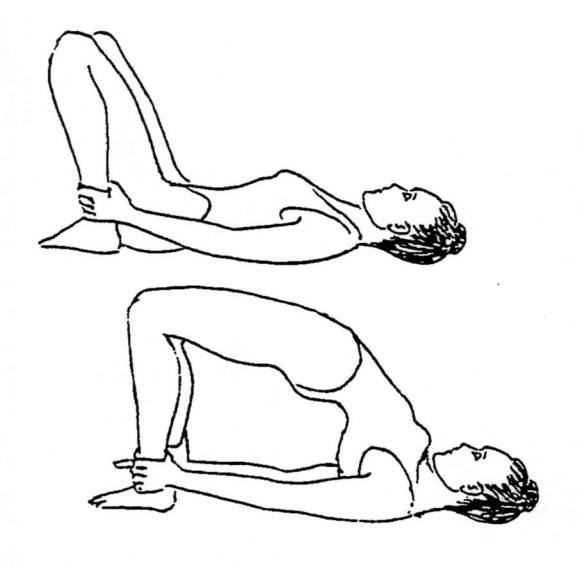

GURPRANAM to stimulate pituitary and pineal glands and 6th and 7th chakras: Sit in Rock Pose and rest the forehead on the floor, stretching the arms out in front, palms together, and hold with long, deep breathing for 2-2 minutes.

TRIANGLE POSE to stimulate the pituitary and relax the spine and the mind: With feet hip width aprt, bend over and place hands shoulder-width apart about 3 feet in front of the feet. Raise buttocks in a triangle, arms and legs perfectly straight, and hold with long deep breathing from 3-5 minutes End by pulling Mulbhand on the held inhale. Follow with Gurpranam.

CHAKRASANA (or Wheel Pose) to stimulate all the chakras and energize the spine: On the back, place fingertips just under the shoulders, pointing them towards the feet, and bend knees bringing heels to buttocks. Inhale and lift torso into an arch, keeping the arms straight and try to straighten the knees. Arch the neck and look at the hands, and hold with Breath of Fire for 30 seconds-1 minute, or as long as possible. The spine tingles with excitement after this.

YOGA MUDRA for moving energy up and opening the spine: Sit in Lotus Pose or Siddhasana, and lower the head to the ground clasping the hands in Venus Lock on the back, breathing long and deep for 1-3 minutes

ADHA SHAKTI CHALNEE KRIYA to stimulate the 6th & 7th chakras: Kneel and bring head to the ground, lifting feet and shins up off the ground and balance with the hands in Venus Lock on the back. Meditate at the Brow Point for 3 minutes.

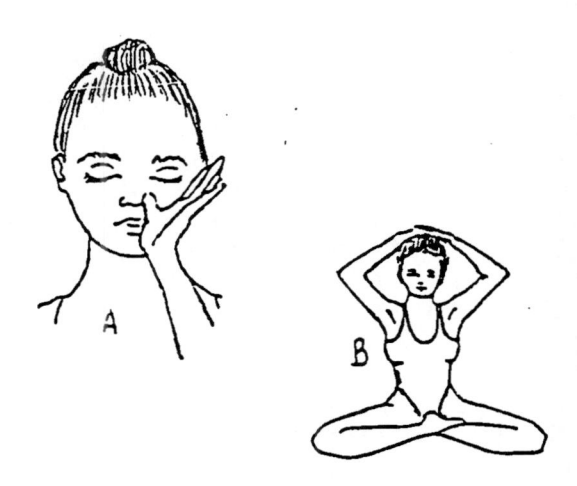

AFTER ANY OF THE FACILITATORS assume or continue in meditation posture with a perfectly straight spine and slightly tucked chin. Place tongue on the roof of the mouth and begin long, deep breathing (4 or fewer breaths a minute) and presto! Instant higher consciousness

JANUIRASANA for concentration: Sit with the left heel in the perineum and the right leg stretched forward. Inhale, stretching arms overhead, and exhale as you slowly bend forward and touch the head to the right knee, clasping the toes of the right foot with both hands. Breath long and deep for 2 minutes and then reverse legs and repeat. This is a classic meditation facilitator.

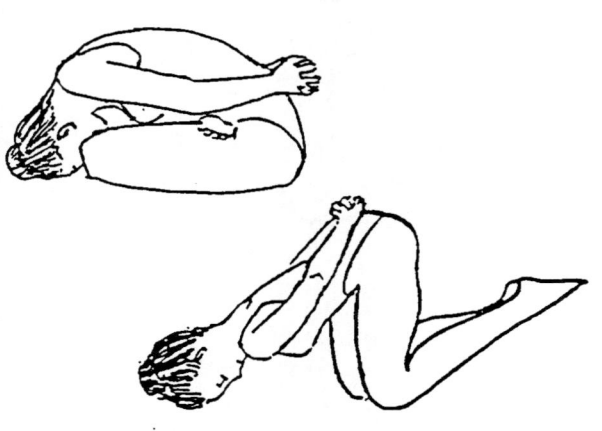

TO OPEN THE CROWN CHAKRA: A) Right hand in Guyan Mudra on left knee, block left nostril with thumb of left hand, fingers pointing straight up, with Breath of Fire through the right nostril for 3-5 minutes. Inhale deeply, hold and savour the space, exhale, relax and meditate. For a clear, focussed mind.
B) Hands in Venus Lock on top of the head, with Breath of Fire for 3-5 minutes, focussing eyes on the crown chakra, tongue pressing roof of the mouth.

THE COSMIC TEDDY BEAR

AFTER MEDITATION

After any exercise set or meditation, before and/or after the deep relaxation, go deep within to feel and experience that space of peace and silence. Listen for the silence or the vibration of the mantra, or for the cosmic sound.

Be at home - you are home. You are at one with God. God and you are one. Feel secure, cozy, love yourself and love your soul. Feel that you are begin hugged by the Cosmic Teddy Bear. Love it, nourish it, feel it in every cell of your body.

Yogi Bhajan said at Ladies Camp, "if you have difficulty experiencing God, feel that He is a teddy bear."

ON SELF BLESSING: One secret: When you get up in the morning, BLESS YOURSELF! I do it all the time. I do it like this: When I take my first 'curl', I say 'blessed are my hands and blessed is my head that brings them over me, and blessed are my eyes that see them. And blessed is my body that has awakened from the spell of infinite death unto activity. I shall tell the whole world how beautiful is Guru Ram Das, and how God is working in personality through this 'pipe' to give his people the miracle beyond what is written in their destiny.' And then I curl around and I sleep a little more, and then get up again. And I always do it secretely, thrice. And once I got caught by my own teacher.

December 29, 1985
(This is on tape)

Meditations

MEDITATION is the concentration on one point of mind to your own universality.

Meditation is the greatest purification.

Meditation is to draw mental energy thru all the nerve centers in one being and project them into the Superior Being in such a way as to feel projected. All diseases will go away. Focus all mental energy on your own purity - you will be divine.

March 11, 1970

BEGINNING & ENDING A DAY: My friend, learn never to wake up without meditation, or without thanking your own unknown - your God. And never sleep without meditation and relating to your own unknown God, who knows if tomorrow shall come. Keep the account clear. Start the day with God, see the day with God, and then God will take care of it. Isn't that simple? And at the end of the day, give yourself to God and sleep. If the morning dawns on you again, get up and live moment to moment, day to day, and walk away with the precious gift of life. Life is a precious gift!

July 14, 1975

DIVINE LIGHT: God's Light only comes when you learn to meditate on the self and feel the flow of Divine Light within. Consider yourself as a pure channel of Divine Spirit. Do it for 3 days constantly, and see what beauty it brings.

March 11, 1970

MEDITATION IN KUNDALINI YOGA

Meditation in conjunction with the practice of Kundalini yoga is the most powerful, safe and effective means of achieving altered states of consciousness. The practice of Kundalini yoga strengthens the nervous system and the entire physical, mental and emotional being to receive and utilize the higher frequencies induced by meditation. Therefore, practitioners of Yogi Bhajan's technology do no experience destructive, traumatic, spontaneous Kundalini arousals, common among those who practice other types of meditation and yogic traditions. Instead, they experience the gradual, repeated, safe and almost imperceptable ascent of Kundalini energy, with its attendant pleasures and talents and without the traditional fireworks and pain.

The Kundalini Yoga/Meditation combination brings the meditative mind into everyday life and elevates day to day living to a higher plateau. Yoga without meditation is like cake without frosting, and meditation without yoga practice is like the dessert without the dinner.

These meditations are actually pre-meditations. Each focuses consciousness to implement specific effects through the mantras and mudras. The real meditation begins AFTER the chanting is done. (So be sure to savour those precious post-chanting moments to enjoy a conversation with God or your higher self, or to use the heightened awareness to survey the body and take stock of its needs.) Most of all, this is the time to listen and know.

MANTRAS

Mantras are the repeated words, sounds or phrases in one of the sacred languages (Sanscrit or Gurmuki - so designated because in these languages the sound of the word vibrationally approximates the concept it represents). Yogi Bhajan has given us several mantras in English, too.

Though affirmations have a powerful effect on the mind, taking one from a negative to a positive mind-set, mantras take you from the polarities of the positive-negative mind to the Universal, neutral mind, and link the finite self with the Infinite Self.

Prayer is another powerful tool, but it is usually a one-way affair, (asking for blessings, or thanking or praising God for those already bestowed). Chanting mantras opens up a two-way communication, tuning us into cosmic frequencies, enabling us to listen and receive, as well as press our cause.

The sounds of mantras affect the cosmic spheres as well as individual consciousness. The meaning, (though unintelligible to the Western conscious mind), has a powerful impact on the subconscious mind. The touch of the tongue on the palate, additionally, reflexes to impact the brain in a scientific and precise manner, when the mantras are correctly chanted. Repeated repetition makes the effect "kick in" despite blocks and scepticism, too. Lastly, the music that often accompanies the chanting, touches the heart and opens one's sensitivities. This is called "Nad Yoga" or "the yoga of the mind".

It is of paramount importance to chant a mantra correctly. To enjoy its full effect, ask your teacher for the correct pronounciation, rhythm and the prescribed breathing, melody and meaning.

Two ways to empower mantras are (1) to visualize the mantra written on a screen before the closed eyes as it is intoned, and (2) to listen to the mantra while inhaling between repetitions. You may also feel the mantra - pulsated at the heart, vibraing in the head, circling up the spine, or penetrating the body down to the cellular level.

During the course of chanting, take your time. Attend to one thing at a time - if visualizations are specified, first set the breathing and chanting on "automatic pilot". Then add pictures, movements of energy or pulsations. After a little practice you will find it is possible to hold several things in the mind at once, and this will be useful in all phases of life.

MEDITATING AT HOME

1. First, "tune in" (with the Adi Shakti Mantra: ONG NAMO, GURU DEV NAMO) Then do warmups, especially spinal flexes. Follow with a Yoga set of your choice. Then relax a few minutes on the back before meditating.

2. Sit in a clean, quiet place. Meditating at the same time and in the same place everyday, gradually sanctifies the area. But if you are meditating in a subway, or standing in line, imagine a sanctified place and program yourself to tune out distractions. Nature offers good settings like under a tree, beside a stream or the ocean, and churches are ideal retreats.

3. The very best time to meditate is in the early morning before sunrise as yogis do. (Sadhana!) 2½ hours before sunrise is the usual time to begin - the "primal hours". Other powerful times are at 4:00 P.M. and at sunset. Bedtime is a must! Meditation and yoga actually replace sleep, so you will find you need less sleep when you do a morning and evening routine (which processes the subconscious fears and concerns of unsettling sunrise dreams).

4. A timer of some sort is useful to avoid "clock watching", and or wondering.

5. The hair should be worn up, in a knot on top of the head (to prevent energy 'leakage'), and you should be seated on a natural surface - ie. wool, cotton, wood. The feet should be bare.

6. You may wish to begin with short meditations (some are as short as 3-5 minutes in this book) and proceed to longer ones with practice. It is recommended to practice one meditation daily for 40 days to achieve its effects. 90 days can break a habit pattern. If you like variety, sample a different one every evening, perhaps, but stick to the same one every morning for at least 40 days.

7. Most of Yogi Bhajan's meditations are designed to attract or deliver specific results. You can program yourself with prayer or visualization of the desired results, before and after the meditation, consolidating the entire effect. But, during the meditation, concentrate on the specified techniques and absorb yourself in the sound and the energy.

8. What you may encounter: Because of a misconception that one can simply sit down and quiet the mind for meditation, many people are discouraged from meditating. The mind generates one thousand thoughts per wink of the eye, and when we sit to meditate, we become acutely aware of these thoughts. That is why we use mantras - to focus the mind. Distractions

are the rule. Just keep going back to the mantra, the breath and other points of focus. You may feel uncomfortable during meditation, but you will feel much better afterwards. Since meditation is also a cleansing process, a lot of "garbage" may come up. This is normal, and in fact, desireable. It means that the process is working. Don't expect to sit in bliss every time! When thoughts come up, don't reflect or act on them. Just let them pass like the flow of a river. You may even become negative or emotional. Fine. Experience whatever happens and let it go to the universe. The process is working. Over a period of time, you will be pleased at how much lighter you feel and how certain things no longer bother you.

9. Be sure to keep the spine perfectly straight and apply Chin Lock (see Appendix), for the alignment of the chakras and to facilitate energy flow, during all meditations unless otherwise specified.

10. Have patience with yourself. Perhaps you will achieve only a minute or two of fully focussed consciousness during the first attempts. It comes with practice.

11. To repeat, meditation really begins in the spacious moments after pranayama or chanting. It is rewarding at that time to sit for a few minutes and experience the effects of the previous effort. You may listen to the mantra chanting back to you, allow physical effects to develop (like watching the energy you have engendered pursue its own course) or simply commune with yourself at a cellular or super-conscious level. Enjoy that time and space!

12. Daily practice for only 10-30 minutes can change the course of your life, transform your personality and help you to become your own best possible self! Even meditating only once a week produces a more illumined and evolving consciousness.

YOU ARE THE UNIVERSE: If you are not beautiful and graceful, there is nothing beautiful or graceful. This is a truth, for you are the universe and the universe is you.

October 14, 1971
("Sermon on 2 Cushions")

Be BRIGHT. Be BRAVE. Be BEAUTIFUL!

November, 1988

SHABD KRIYA
April 1, 1974

Sit in Easy Pose with a straight spine, hands in lap in Buddha Mudra, right on top of left, thumbs meeting and facing forward. With eyes focussed at the tip of the nose and half opened, inhale in 4 equal parts, mentally vibrating

Sa Ta Na Ma

Then, holding the breath, vibrate the entire mantra 4 more times (16 counts). Exhale in 2 equal strokes, mentally projecting

Wahe Guru

Continue for 15-62 minutes.

The best time to practice this kriya is before bed. If practiced regularly, once a week or as often as every night, sleep will be deep and relaxed, and the nerves will regenerate. After a few months, the rhythm of your breath will be subconsciously regulated and eventually will hear the mantra in daily activities, and you will think better, work bett, share better, love better and even fight better.

There cannot be enough praise of the meditation's effect on the personality. It gives the mind the power to stretch tinfinity, promotes radiance and patience and practical universality.

LAUGHING is one exercise to raise your consciousness and it is a comfort to the heart.

Beads of Truth
(Undated)

MEDITATION FOR THE CENTRAL NERVOUS SYSTEM

October 16, 1979

Sit in Easy Pose with a straight spine. Relax the arms down with the elbows bent and raise the forearms until the hands are near the shoulders, facing the palms forward and in Guyan Mudra. Eyes are 9/10 closed. Inhale, exhale, and with the breath held out, mentally vibrate

Waahe Guroo

as you first pull root Root Lock, then Diaphram Lock and then Neck Lock in a continuous wave-like motion, with each repetition of the mantra. The whole spine will undulate. Repeat a total of 9 times (9 mantra repetitions and 9 undulations) on the held out breath. Inhale, exhale and repeat.

Begin practicing for 11 minutes and slowly build time to a maximum of 31 minutes.

COMMENTS: Nothing is better than this for the Sushmana Nadi and the Central Nervous System. It will bring elaborate changes in an individual who practices it.

DIVINITY: There is nothing quick in this world. Pay off your karma gracefully - the Divine shall help you. Have no doubt, no duality: <u>YOU ARE THE INCARNATION OF GOD.</u> Every mind has the possibility of expanding to Infinity.

June 22, 1972

REBIRTHING MEDITATION
March 9, 1982

Sit in Easy Pose with a straight spine. Bring the hands up until they meet at the diaphragm level and interlace the fingers, pressing the palms into the body over the heart. Forearms are parallel to the ground, sticking out like wings.

Purse the lips and breathe through the mouth. Inhale powerfully and fast with such a force that the cheeks are sucked into the teeth. Put all the power into the inhale, but keep the exhale short too, allowing for about 20 breaths a minute. Continue for 2 minutes, then inhale and hold the breath briefly.

2nd Part: Concentrate on the 3rd Eye and imagine yourself as a candle flame, burning away your ego, all dirt, the past, the present, and all negativity. Just be positive and imagine the positive thought of yourself burning away all the negativity through the candlelight. Continue for 3 minutes. On the final inhale, hold the breath and bring in a very pure, positive thought.

THE SUBCONSCIOUS: Being a conscious person, one must free the subconscious mind. Subconscious mind is like a camera, recording everything that comes to you in dreams and hangs on to you. One cannot enter the neutral, conscious mind (the path to Supreme Consciousness) until he frees the subconscious. Without labor there is no liberation. Surrender the lower self to the higher self which liberates the subconscious mind.

June 19, 1972

NATAL REBIRTHING MEDITATION

March 22, 1982

Sit in Easy Pose with a straight spine, arms at sides, hands up to solar plexis level, palms up. Lock index and middle fingers under the thumbs with the other fingers straight and relaxed, pointing towards each other about an inch apart.

Inhale and exhale through the open mouth, creating the sound

Akkkkkkhhhhh

in the throat. Rhythm is fast, about 40 inhales and exhales per minute for 3 minutes.

Then inhale, lock the teeth, concentrate and hold the breath for 20 seconds and exhale. Repeat twice more and on the last breath retention, feel and circulate the breath throughout the body.

To end, simply smile, silently, for 2 minutes. Then laugh, gently for 3 minutes.

COMMENTS: Do not jump up after this meditation for at least 10 minutes. This meditation involves reducing yourself to the size of spermatazoa. It will allow you to lose a lot of garbage. As you are smiling, don't think of anything except that which will make you smile. Feel good, feel elevated, feel blissful. It will totally recuperate your personality. Within this energy we have to heal our very selves - the sad self, the destructive self and the negative self. When laughing, it is as if you are seeing something wonderful happening and you are enjoying it.

MEDITATION TO BRING UP THE PAST

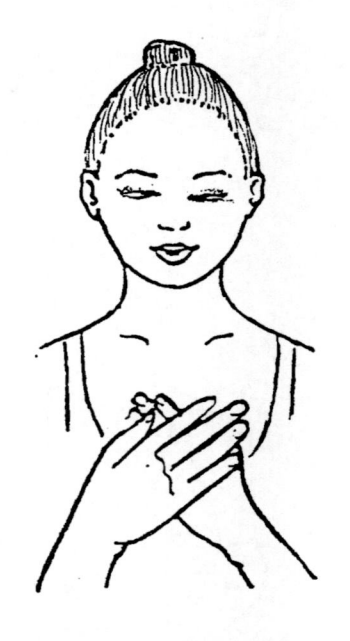

In meditation pose with a straight spine, cross hands, palms facing chest (bases of palms a little above the nipples) and out a few inches from the body. Either hand can be on top.

Eyes focus on the tip of the nose.

As in the Kirtan Kriya (see page 131) chanting aloud, bring each syllable in through the top of the head and out the 3rd Eye in an "L" shape:

Sa Ta Na Ma

for 15-31 minutes. To end, inhale, hold the breath and press the eyes up, hearing the mantra echo inside the head. Relax or meditate for 10-15 minutes so that the past will come up. FEEL the emotions as they arise and release them through the 3rd Eye, mentally chanting "Sat Nam".

COMMENTS: You may see colors! Feel and experience any event, seeing and hearing them. Then relax and release those feelings, pictures and sounds to infinity. See them travel away on the light and on the vibration of the mantra, knowing they are returning to their origin. All things come from God and all things go to God. Send them back with blessings, and free yourself from an unwanted and non-existent past.

This meditation not only rids you of past garbage, it establishes your relationship to the past and balances it with the present. It also enhances intuition and you become aware of your age.

> SUBCONSCIOUS MIND is a part of the mind which is silent, which observes and which records. Mind is like an onion - there are many layers. Anyone who does not know the secret of the subconscious remains a fool.
>
> June 20, 1972

MEDITATION FOR SURRENDER
Establishing the appropriate relationship between the ego and the Infinite Self

Sit in meditation pose with straight spine, hands in Buddha Mudra (left palm in right so that forefingers meet at about the first knuckle at a 90° angle, thumbs touching) in the lap. Eyes are 1/10 open, looking straight ahead, and focussed at the 3rd Eye.

Inhale in 8 equal parts so that the lungs are filled on the 8th sniff, and chant as you exhale (but not necessarily using all the air),

Wa He Guru

Ennunciate clearly and project out of the 3rd Eye for 15-31 minutes.
(On the inhale, I like to silently chant "Guru Ram Das, I surrender"-G.K.)

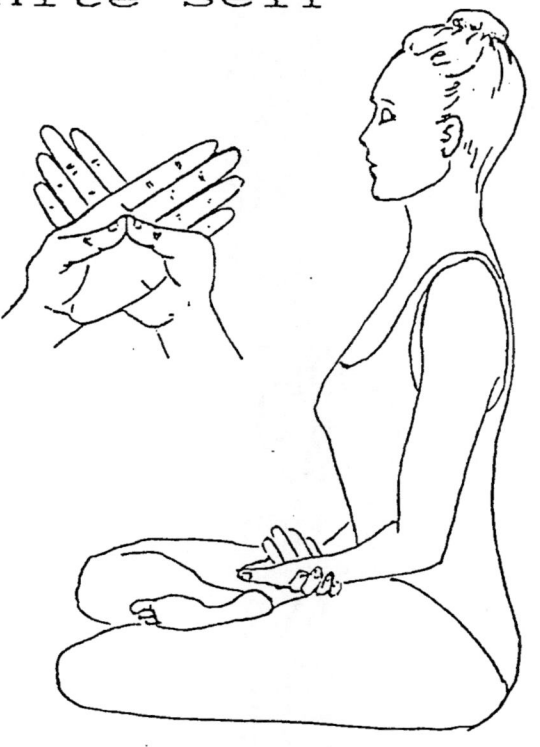

This meditation is very energizing if the breath is taken seriously and is pumped from the navel point. To get maximum benefit (especially when doing it for shorter times) pull Mul Bhand and feel the energy go up the spine to the 3rd Eye as you chant "Wa He Guru".

> SELF SURRENDER: We must have faith, whatever is written in our fate. The moment you forget you are a self, problems come. So long as man lives in self, God lives in him. The truth of self-surrender is to give yourself to God - there is nothing else. Out of that nothing comes everything.
>
> June 19, 1972
>
> LIVE LIFE not as you think it should be, but as it should be. Merge your will with the Will of the Creator.
>
> Undated

For Setting the Physical Plane in Order
SERABA SUD MEDITATION
February 6, 1975

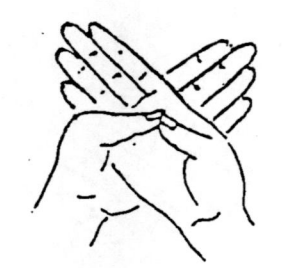

To begin, stretch the body well and feel good all over. Then, sit with a straight spine and place the right hand on top of the left hand, pressing the thumbs together. Hold this mudra at diaphragm level, take a deep breath and chant:

```
Ha ri, ha ri,
Ha ri, ha ri,
Ha ri, ha ri,
Haaaaaaaarrr.
```

The chanting is long and slow. The final "Har" is chanted until the breath is out. "Ha" and "ri" are two separate sounds.

Focus the closed eyes on the Brow Point, looking out through the 3rd eye. As the mind settles you may see various colors flash onto your mental screen. At first some black, then a little red. Finally you will start seeing green. When you do, meditate on that color, letting it fill the entire consciousness with a vibration of health & productivity.

COMMENTS: This is one of a number of meditations that is particularly effective for those who want to practice self-healing and for those who deal with other people's mental problems. It is good for wives who do not want a divorce in their lives, because its main effect is to set the physical plane in order. Stress is the product of practical concerns and this meditation will work on the problem, and impart the peace of mind that comes with doing something positive about a situation as well. Meditating on the color green is good for those who want divine green energy in their home. Practice and understand the power of the meditation and it will lift your spirit in a real practical way.

UNGALI PRANAYAM

May 1, 1975

Sit like a yogi, straight and simple, with the spine erect. The hands are in Guyan Mudra. Inhale, breaking the breath into 15 equal segments. On the exhale, break the breath into 15 more waves. Now add the Panj Shabad form of "Sat Nam" with the breath,

inhaling
SaSaSaSaSaSaSaSaSaSaSaSaSaSaSa
and exhhaling
TaTaTaTaTaTaTaTaTaTaTaTaTaTaTa
and inhaling
NaNaNaNaNaNaNaNaNaNaNaNaNaNaNa
and exhaling
MaMaMaMaMaMaMaMaMaMaMaMaMaMaMa

This is done mentally with the breath. One cycle of "Sa-Ta-Na-Ma" takes about 30 seconds. Continue this cycle for 3 minutes. Inhale, exhale and relax. Enjoy the conscious state. Practice this meditation up to 31 minutes but build gradually from 3 minutes by adding one minute per day.

COMMENTS: This is a powerful meditation in the ancient technology of pranayam. It has not been openly taught before and should be practiced very properly. When you begin, deeply exhale and then start inhaling. (If the nerves aren't slowly prepared, 31 minutes of this meditation can make you faint. So someone should stand by in case you overdo it, to give you water immediately if necessary.)

As you mentally hear the basic sounds of the mantra, do not think of them as familiar. Instead, create a sound to be listened to by your innermost potential and guiding Self. Ask the inner self how it likes and reacts to it. These sounds and the rhythm communicate in the language of the inner self and will produce a definite result.

The body is made to do yoga. The postures and angles create certain pressures to stimulate reactions in the brain accessing the unlimited self by the extension and alteratiion of thought patterns. Yogi Bhajan says, "The whole body has been made to adjust to all the complications of postures that activate the brain's thought, extension and performance so that man can experience what he wants to know, and that is the unknown of himself. This kriya is the 'SIMRAM PRANAYAM' in which you have the authority to expand your consciousness and your ability and your brain cells. You can start making a hole in the five sections of the brain, right and left sides, so that the central channel can look over all this seen by you." So, this meditation activates the central nerve channel, the brain, pituitary, pineal and fontenal areas to coordinate and transcend the individual functioning of the 10 regions of the left and right brains. (It is also excellent to reduce body weight when accompanied by an appropriate greens diet!)

To Connect with the True Self
SEHAJ SUKH DIHAN
With Mul Mantra

SEHAJ SUKH DIHAN means 'happy way, slowly, with little exertion.' "Sukh" means comfort, and "Dihan", meditation. The MUL MANTRA is tthe highest of all mantras and the root of all mantras. It is a '90 pad' mantra.

Sit in meditation posture. No mudra was given. Inhale, feeling the breath pass through the eyebrows and the root of the nose, while mentally taking in 2 repetitions of the mantra. Hold the breath, mentally chanting 1 repetition of the mantra. Exhale with 2 mental repetitions.

EK ONG KAR	God is One
SAT NAM	Truth is His Name
KARTA PURAKH	Creator
NIRBHAO	Fearless
NIRVAIR	Without Enmity
AKAAL MOORAT	Immortal
AJUNI	Unborn
SAI BHANG	Self-Illuminated
GUR PRASAD	By Guru's Grace
JAP.	Meditate.
AAD SUCH	True in the Beginning
JUGAAD SUCH	True through the Ages
HAI BHEE SUCH	True at Present
NAANAK HOSI BHEE SUCH.	Nanak shall ever be True.

Repeat 108 times and you can redeem yourself from 8.4 million incarnations. In human life, you can consciously do this mantra and be free. VARIATION: Inhale with 1 mantra, hold for 3 and exhale with 1.

COMMENTS: To repeat this mantra and go into its depths, is to be entranced by the depth of your own soul. It is a compass at points to God, describing the Human-in-God-Consciousness. It orients you, sets you on the right path.

This mantra has everything in it. It is both a mantra and a sutra. It creates a sound which is like a ladder of consciness. It is also a technology and a description. It forms the basis of the consciousness we wish to acquire - that consciousness that exists in our very souls.

To Raise Kundalini & Bliss Out
LAYA YOGA #7
August 21, 1970

In MAHA SUK MUDRA (sitting with the left foot under the right thigh, and the right foot on top of the left thigh), stretch the neck and the spine straight. Pull Root Lock and Chin Lock. Tune into the vibration of Yogi Bhajan and chant:

Akal

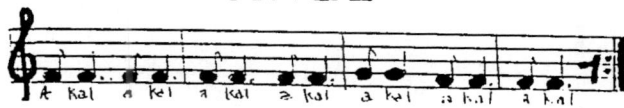

Akal means undying, and it frees you from death. Chant it seven times and on the 5th time, raise the pitch. Continue for 5 minutes.

SECOND PART: For 3 minutes, spin the 3½ cycle Adi Shakti Mantra up the spine:

Ek Ong Kar A
Sat a Nam A
Siri Wha A
He Guru

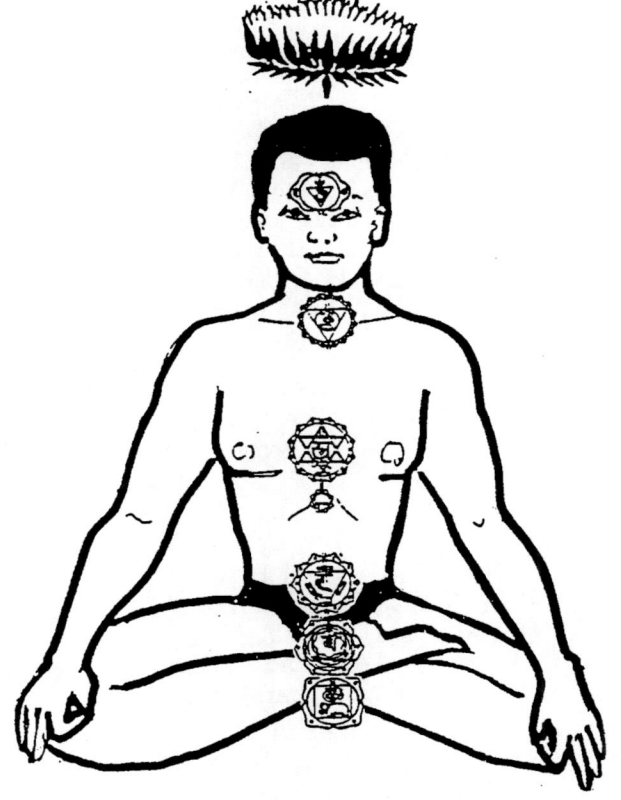

(There is one Creator whose name is Truth. Great is the Ecstacy of that Supreme Wisdom.)

On "Ek" pull the Navel Point. On the first "A" pull Mulbhand (so that energy descends from the navel to the rectum), on the 2nd "A", pull Diaphragm Lock (still holding Mulbhand) and visualize energy spiraling up the spine. On the 3rd "A" pull Neck Lock as the energy goes from the 3rd Eye to the Crown Chakra, and on "Hey Guru", relax all the Bhandas. Repeat and continue (usually for 11 minutes) strengthening the energy visualization inhale, hold the breath, and feel the energy continue to spiral up the spine without any conscious effort on your part, immersing you in bliss.

TO END: Chant long "Sat Nam's" 3 times, (see page 96)

Sat Nam

and then once, with meaning, chant

God & Me   Me & God   are one.

MEDITATION FOR INNER & OUTER VISION

A) Stretch legs straight out and lean back 60° with palms in back of hips. Press eyes up and back looking out through the tope of the head and meditate for 8-11 minutes with long, deep breathing. Inhale deeply, hold up to 1 minute and exhale.

B) In Easy Pose, interlock fingers like hooks (Bear Grip), left palm facing out. Press the eyes up slightly, and meditate through the Brow Point for 3 minutes. Then Mentally project a beam of light from the Brow Point out to infinity for 8 minutes. Then deeply inhale and exhale a few times, then inhale, and hold the breath up to 1 minute, and exhale.

C) In Rock Pose, focus on the point on the back of the skull opposite the Brow Point, and meditate for 3 minutes. Inhale deeply, exhale completely and apply root lock, holding as long as comfortable, and then relax the breath.

D) Sit as in B and roll the eyes up and circle them around to see all four corners of the inside of the skull for 2 minutes. Then deep inhale while still circling the eyes and hold up to 1 minute. Exhale and completely relax on the back.

The eyes are keys to inner world vision as well as outer world vision. This series of exercises uses the eyes and eye pressure to create different states of consciousness. Each eye position alters the basic frequencies and the way thoughts are transformed in the mind. This kriya brings deep relaxation and calmness. It causes tension in all the eye muscles to relax and decreases abnormal vision.

TRATAKAM FOR THE EYES

SET 1

1. After a pranayam, sit & gaze without blinking at the red, rising sun, up to two diameters from the horizon, only. With Long, deep breathing draw energy from the sun to the eyes and optic nerves.

Inhale, close eyes, cup palms over eyes and meditate on the energy vibrating and shining in the eyes. Many eye problems will clear up.

SET 2

1. In Panther Pose (with fingers wide apart and arched, like claws), open eyes wide and fix them on the horizon. Begin long, deep breathing, and focus on breath and pranic flow in the eyes for 3 minutes. Inhale, close eyes, and hold for 20-30 seconds.

2. In Rock Pose, leaning back to 60°, without blinking, fix eyes on the horizon, and breath long and deep for 3 to 31 minutes. Brings pranic energy to eyes, digestion, nerves and personality control.

3. Legs stretched out in front, lean back to 60°, supported by hands behind hips, and drop head back, and gaze straight up, without blinking. For clowdy vision and cataracts.

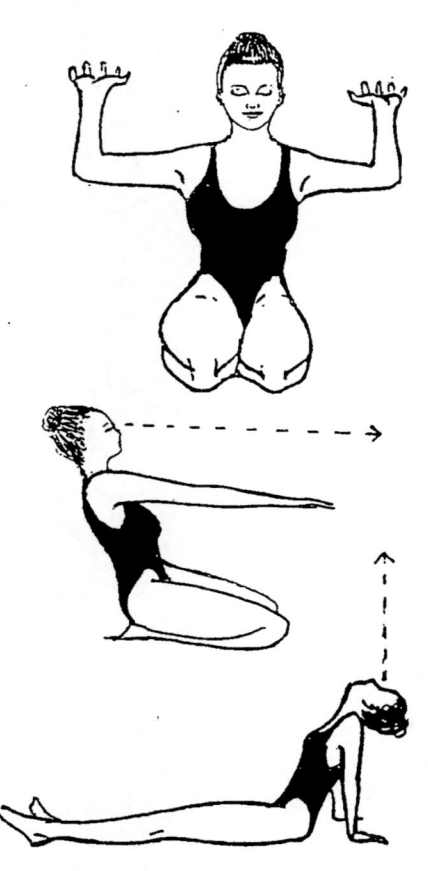

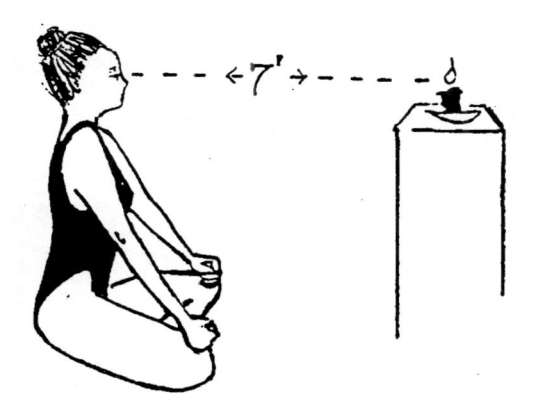

SET 3

Place a lighted candle on a table so that flame is level with the root of your nose, when seated, 7 feet from it. Look at the dark spot under tip of flame for at least 31 minutes. Inhale, close eyes, and place image at brow point.

MAHA AGNI PRANAYAM
To Reorganize Brain Secretions & Counteract Marijuana Effects
March 23, 1974

Sit in Easy or Lotus Pose, placing the palms together 9-12 inches before the Heart Chakra. Inhale and swing the head from the right shoulder, across the chest, to the left shoulder, and then pull the chin in returning head to center. Then focus at the 3rd Eye and silently project the mantra

Ra Ra Ra Ra
Ma Ma Ma Ma
Ra Ra Ra Ra
Ma Ma Ma Ma
Sa Ta Na Ma

Exhale and immediately swing the head again as you inhale. The head swing should be quick and give a little pull at the base of the skull. Continue for 11 minutes, building the time of practice to 31 minutes.

COMMENTS: This meditation reorganizes the brain secretions. The finger position (little fingers touching from base to tips) stimulates the heart meridian correlating your desires with what you can achieve through action, and you can become a more effective human being. The head motion recirculates spinal fluid, which is often blocked at the base of the neck, especially in those who have used a drug like marijuana. "Ra" is the sun, "Ma" is the moon. Try to set up a rhythm in reflection of Cosmic Rhythm. This kriya is most effective on the 4th & 11th days after the new moon, when there is a special pressure on the endocrine system. Take advantage of these days for its maximum benefits.

ANTI-DEPRESSION & BRAIN SYNCHRONY MEDITATION
For former Marijuana abusers

In Easy Pose with a straight spine, raise the upper arms parallel to the ground, hands in Guyan Mudra, but with index finger ON TOP of the thumb. Raise mudras in front of the eyes, and stare through them with wide open eyes, beyond the hands to the horizon. Inhale deeply as you separate the hands 36-45 inches out to the sides, while keeping the eyes fixed on the horizon. Exhale back to the original position. Keep the elbows relaxed. One cycle takes about 4 seconds. As the hands go out, mentally vibrate "Sa", as they return, "Ta", out "Na", return "Ma" and so on. Meditate on the life energy in the breath. The mental feeling of stretching the breath from a single point to the width of the arm spread is essential. After 2-3 minutes, increase speed to 3½-4 seconds for each cycle of "Sa-Ta-Na-Ma", and continue for 3 more minutes. Then inhale and relax, arms and shoulders totally dead. No mudra is needed, just RELAX. Or meditate at the crown chakra, and focus all your energy at the anterior fontenal on top of the skull. Put all of your energy into total relaxation or on that one square inch on the skull. Continue for about 15 minutes.

COMMENTS: You were born to be positive and creative. The creativity of your existence is unlimited. Since we have not extablished the habit of constancy in thought and action, we create negative patterns of thought, and depression. This meditation will let you evuate and measure how positive or negative you are and it will make you positive and happy. It focuses on the range of the breath. In the subconscious, breath and life are synonymous. Be meditating this way, depression can be alleviated. If you do it correctly, there will be tremendous pressure at the lymph glands. The two sides of the brain are separated and coordinated. Those unfortunate who used marijuana at any time in their life get the hemispheres confused. The effect is periodic scatteredness, lack of motivation, depression or alienation. This can recur anytime in life, even after years of abstinence. The body needs to be readjusted through an appropriate beet and banana fast. This exercise will also re-coordinate the brain functions. Increase the time of the meditation slowly. Ultimately you can do it for 11 minutes, followed by the relaxation of 31 minutes.

TO BREAK A COCAINE HABIT

A) Sit with the arms bent up and at the sides, hands in Guyan Mudra, and shoulder blades pressed together in back. Eyes are closed. Inhale and hold the breath in for 1 minute. Exhale. Repeat twice.

B) Relax the arms down and breathe normally for 2½-3 minutes.

C) Resume mudra and inhale, pressing the tongue with all your strength against the roof of the mouth and apply Root Lock for 30 seconds. Exhale and do Breath of Fire for 15-20 seconds. Repeat the exercise one.

D) Inhale and press the tongue against the roof of the mouth for 1 minute. Exhale and relax.

COMMENTS: This kriya balances the nervous system and acts as a check on the parasympathetic nervous system. It helps break the cocaine habit and alleviates withdrawal symptoms. It is an especially good practice for women.

DRUGS: LSD opens the chakras and centers in the brain which are not ready to be open, and then are not properly closed. Yoga must close them. A good practice is "closing the gates". Marijuana affects the "ojas" supplied to the brain. All drugs are a rape of the body. They stimulate certain centers not ready to be stimulated. You are not earning it and must eventually pay the debt.

August 23, 1972

FOR EMOTIONAL BALANCE & REPAIR OF DAMAGE DUE TO COCAINE USE

(From <u>Man to Man XII</u>)

A) In meditation pose, with a straight spine, do Breath of Fire for 31 minutes.

B) Kirtan Kriya for 31 minutes: Meditate at the Brow Point, chanting the 5 primal sounds of the Panj Shabad

SA TA NA MA

(Sa: Infinity, cosmos, beginning, Ta - life, existence, Na - death, & Ma - rebirth)

Hands on knees, elbows straight, on "Sa" touch the Jupiter (index) finger to the thumb. On "Ta", touch the Saturn (2nd) finger to the thumb. On "Na" touch the thumb and Sun (ring) finger, and on "Ma", the (small) Mercury finger and thumb. Repeat and continue.

For the first 5 minutes, chant in normal (language of humans) voice, for the next 5 minutes, whisper (in the language of lovers), and for the next 10 minutes chant silently (in the divine language). For the next 5 minutes come back to the whispered chanting, and for the last 5 minutes return to the normal voice. (These are the 3 languages of consciousness.) Meditate on the 4 primal sounds in an "L" shape: Let each "Sa Ta Na Ma" enter through the Crown chakra and project it out to infinity through the 3rd Eye.

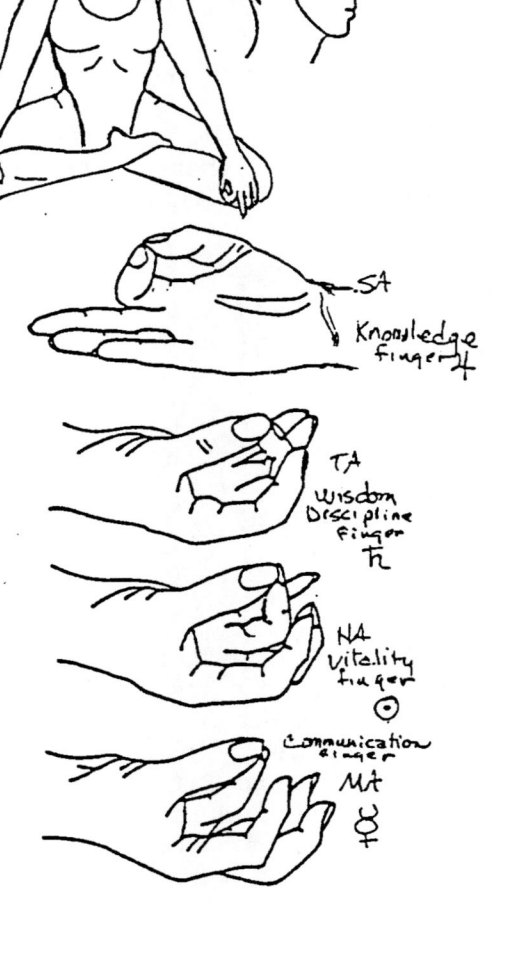

COMMENTS: All meditation stops at "Sa-Ta-Na-Ma". There is nothing beyond it. All pranayama stops at Breath of Fire. There is nothing beyond that. These are the most effective tools we can apply - the results are 100% effective. Kirtan Kriya is the most important meditation in Kundalini Yoga. Yogi Bhajan has said, "if you could do only one, this is it!" It does everything for you and in the proper order! It is powerful for emotional balance. If you can't 'get it together', do this meditation for 31 minutes and be totally balanced. Over a period of time, this meditation can be your best friend. GK

MEDICAL MEDITATION FOR HABITUATION

January 7, 1974

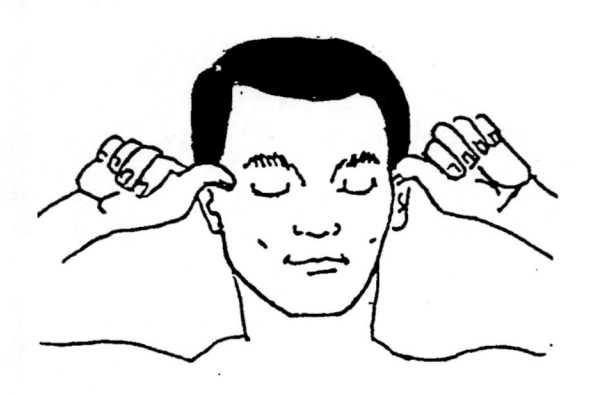

Sit with a straight spine, especially pushing the lower 6 vertebrae forward. Make fists, extending thumbs straight out and placer them on the temples. Lock molars and rhythmically press them feeling it on the thumbs and chanting

Sa Ta Na Ma

looking to the 3rd Eye and feeling the mantra there. Continue for 3-7 minutes gradually extending the time to 20-31 minutes.

Then place hands in Guyan Mudra and follow with 3 repetitions of

**Ad Gurey Nameh
Jugad Gurey Nameh
Sat Gurey Nameh,
Siri Guru Devey Nameh**

for comfort and protection.

COMMENTS: Thumb pressure triggers reflex current into the central brain, and activates the brain area under the stem of the Pineal Gland. It is an imbalance in this area that makes physical and mental addictions seem unbreakable. This imbalance alters radiance in the Pineal Gland, which regulates the Pituitary Gland. Particularly effective for drug dependence, mental illness and phobic conditions, it is also effective in tobacco, coffee, sugar and alcohol habits. NOTE: See "Breakthrough Breathing", page 104 for nicotine addiction.

YOGA MIXED WITH DOPE and a lot of sex is bad and people can freak out when the centers open (that way).

August 23, 1973

MOSES MEDITATION
For Memory
December 9, 1977

In meditative posture with a straight spine, raise arms in front of body so that right forearm crosses on top of left forearm a few inches above elbows, at chest level, and angled upward slightly. Fingers are held together with thumbs stretched away from hands, palms up and flattened.

Eyes are 9/10 closed. Breath as required to continuously chant

Aah Men

Both lips must meet on "Men". Rock forward to 45° as you chant "Aah", and rock backward to 45° as you chant "Men". Gradually work up to 31 minutes.

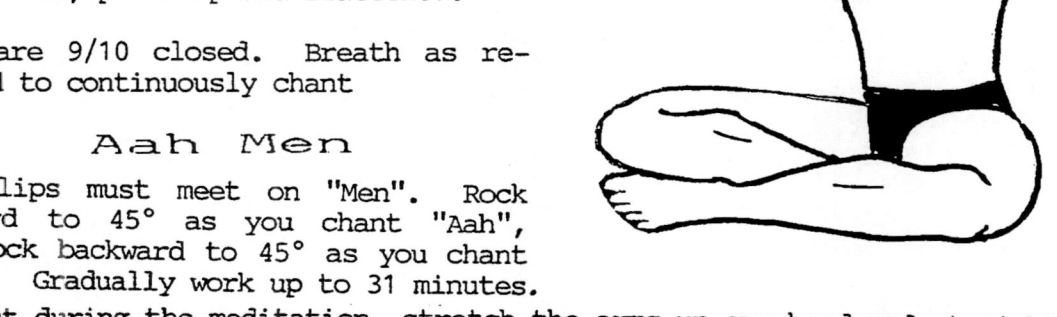

To rest during the meditation, stretch the arms up overhead and straighten them for a moment and then resume.

COMMENTS: This is how they used to memorize the Torah. One would speak and the others would listen to it and say "Aah Men", and the speaker would continue reading the scriptures. That is how they learned them by heart. People learn the Koran, too, like this, and remember the entire thing. Why? When the body leans, you feel out of balance and the middle ear, which has a kind of little sand in it sends a signal to the brain: "Alert!" All you need is an alert brain.

MEDITATION TO GET OUT OF DEPRESSION, & FOR THE CAPACITY TO DEAL WITH LIFE
October 3, 1979

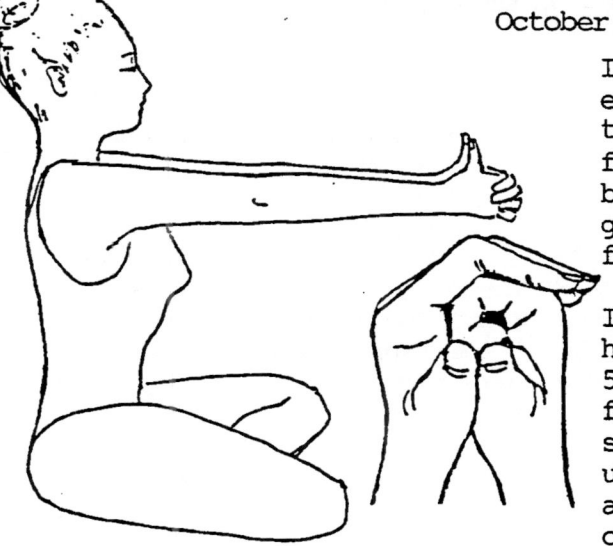

In Easy Pose with a straight spine, extend arms straight forward, parallel to the ground. Close right hand in fist, wrapping left fingers around, bases of palms touching, thumbs together and pulled up straight. Eyes focus on thumbs.

Inhale for 5 seconds, and without holding the breath in, exhale for 5 seconds. Then hold the breath OUT for 15 seconds. Continue the cycle, starting with 3-5 minutes and working up to 11. Progress slowly. You can also work up to holding the breath out for 1 full minute.

COMMENTS: This meditation totally recharges you and is an antidote to depression. It builds a new system, gives one capacity and caliber to deal with life, and establishes a direct relationship with the pranic body.

HEALING MEDITATION FOR ACUTE DEPRESSION
February 9, 1976

Sit in a comfortable meditation posture and place the hands back to back, with the fingers pointing away from the body between the heart center and the throat center, about 6 inches from the body. Be sure that the knuckles touch. Forearms are parallel to the ground and the thumbs point straight down, parallel to each other. This position creates a great deal of tension on the backs of the hands.

Eyes focus on the tip of the nose or on the upper lip. Inhale deeply and chant

Wahay Guroo

16 times on the exhale. One complete cycle takes 20-25 seconds. Begin with 11 minutes and gradually increase to 31 minutes.

COMMENTS: This meditation can cure the worst depression in just 11 minutes. If someone comes to you with a story of depression, don't just brush them off. Instead, help them out of their depressed state with this meditation. It is one of the best ways to cure the emptiness within within ourselves, too.

SELF ESTEEM AND GRACE: A terrible weakness is not to value yourself. You do not think you are graceful. If you think you are graceful, then you have to live gracefully and can't do all those weird things. We have to gracefully accept our grace, but we don't want to do it.

March 21, 1974

BREATH MEDITATION TO STRENGTHEN THE MIND & THE IMMUNE SYSTEM
April 15, 1986

Sit in Easy Pose, with left arm bent at elbow, hand up to side in Surya Mudra (thumb tip touching ring fingertip) at shoulder level. Right arm bent up, with index finger pointing up, blocking right nostril, thumb clasping other fingers in a fist. Do Breath of Fire through the left nostril to the rhythm of <u>Sat Nam, Wha He Guru</u> (by Singh Kaur) or about 3 breaths per second, strongly pumping the navel.

To end, clasp hands in Venus Lock before the face. Inhale, hold the breath and try to pull the hands apart, resisting as hard as possible, creating great tension. Exhale and repeat three more times.

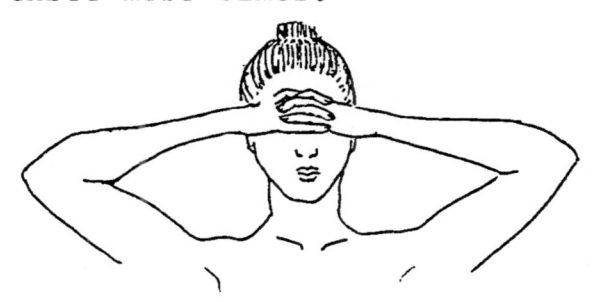

COMMENTS: To be healthy we must have moral and mental strength. If we don't have moral strength, we won't have mental strength. We are born with inherited strength which is equal to the power of God. Our projected strength is created or blocked, by ourselves, usually with anger, self-defeat and blame. To have strong projected strength, we must consciously work out what we are using to block it. Our psyche and energy centers have to be adjusted by us.

MEDITATION TO PERFECT THE POWER OF PRAYER, CONQUER SICKNESS, & BECOME A HEALER

January 19, 1976

Sit nicely with a straight spine and place the hands in Venus Lock at the diaphragm pointing away from the body. Position the right thumb over the left and tuck it into the hole between the palms, (the left thumb continuing to rest in the nook between the thumb and 1st finger of the right hand). Eyes focus on the ground.

Inhale the 4 stroke breath - each stroke filling up ¼ of the lungs. (Each stroke is thought to be 1 finger length long, traveling from the tip of the nose to the brow point.) With the inhale, vibrate

Sa Ta Na Ma
(Infinity, Life, Death, Rebirth)

The inhale should last 4-5 seconds. Then hold the breath for 16 mental repetitions of

Wahe Guru

in a gently pulsating rhythm (soft, then louder, then soft, etc.), for 16-20 seconds. Then exhale with the 4 part breath and again mentally vibrate

Sa Ta Na Ma

for a maximum of 11 minutes to begin with, and gradually build to 31 minutes, adding 1 or 2 minutes per meditation after sufficient practice.

COMMENTS: This is a very powerful meditation and should always be practiced with someone observing. You may loose all sense of time, space, body, everything. Be sure to remember to breathe!!, and have husband, wife or good friend consciously in attendance. (Switch roles afterwards, and in either position you are exactly part of the meditation, so meditate with your eyes open as you watch your fellow being.

When Yogi-ji taught this meditation, he had the class try to breathe thru the LEFT NOSTRIL (see page 84) without blocking the right, on both the inhale and the exhale. When you want to heal YOURSELF, breathe through the left nostril, and when you want to heal OTHERS, focus on the RIGHT.

If you perfect this meditation, you can perfect the power of prayer. It says in yogic scriptures that the practitioner shall become a spiritual healer.

REJUVENATION MEDITATION
December 1979

Sit in Easy Pose with a straight spine. Relax the arms down beside the body. Keeping the elbows snug against the body, raise the forearms up and in until the hands meet at the heart level, facing the palms up. Spread the fingers and thumbs and join the hands by pressing the sides of the little fingers together. Eyes are focussed at the tip of the nose and beyond, deeply into the ground.

Inhale deeply, through a semi-puckered mouth, and hold the breath in for 4 or 5 seconds, then completely exhale in 4 equal strokes through the nose, mentally vibrating

   Sa Ta Na Ma

Hold the breath out for 2-3 seconds and resume the cycle for 11 minutes. When you are competent, build time slowly to 31 minutes. DO NOT GO BEYOND 31 MINUTES.

This is a powerful meditation, best done before going to bed. Do not over-tax yourself and exceed limits.

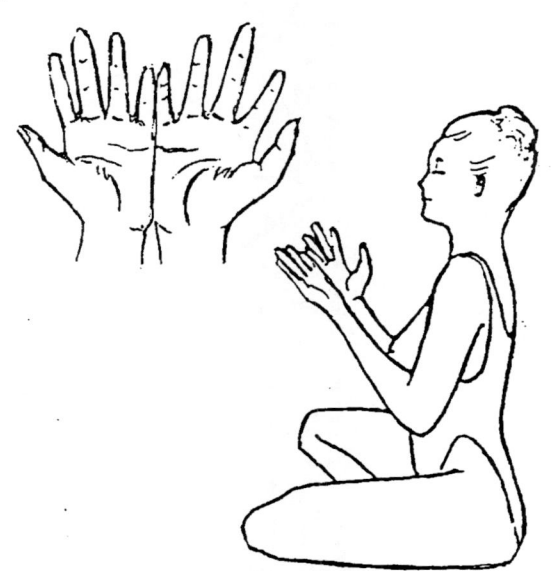

This is a very spacey meditation. Be sure to give yourself plenty of time afterwards to recover. If you push yourself too hard or too fast, the nervous system may go out of control. Working mainly on the glandular system, this simple but powerful meditation produces strong health and excellent regenerative capabilities. Do it simply be yourself, and experience for yourself the virtue of the breath of life.

MAHA KARMA SHAMBHAVI KRIYA

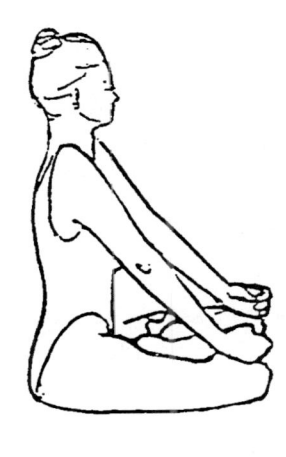

In Lotus Pose, if possible, look to 3rd Eye, roll tongue back and suck on it, with firm chin lock, and long, deep breathing. Silently chant Sat up the spine with Mulbhand, and Nam out the top of the head.

This purifies and opens the energy centers. For control of the breath, pain in the eyse, it coordinates the energy of the optic nerve. Irritations of the body leave. To harness the three powers of God!

SOLAM PAD PRANA KRIYA
Part I
March 6, 1978

Seated in Easy Pose or Rock Pose with a straight spine, pulling the navel in and pressing the chest forward, join the fingers of the left hand, palm down, hand and forearm pointing right at solar plexus level. The right hand is in Surya Mudra with the thumb and ring finger joined, other fingers relaxed, and rest the elbow on on the back of the left hand, right palm up, fingers stretching back towards the right shoulder. Both upper arms extend straight out from the shoulders, parallel to the floor, higher than in Kunchen Mudra

With the eyes focussed on the tip of the nose, deeply inhale and chant

Hari Hari Hari Hari
Hari Hari Hari Hari
Hari Hari Hari Hari
Hari Hari Hari Hari

16 times in monotone, as the breath is completely exhaled, in a steady rhythm THROUGH THE NOSE, only. (Do not speak through the mouth.) Continue for 11 minutes. Loosen up the shoulders before racticing the meditation, and practice only on an EMPTY STOMACH. (Even an excess of liquids can cause colic.) Group participants should sit in straight rows.

Use this meditation to transcend emotions and channel the vagus nerve. By focussing the eyes on the tip of the nose, the ida and pingala are stimulated, in turn stimulating the Shushmana at the Tirkuti (3rd Eye Point), where the 3 pathways meet. And then you've made it! It's a small thing. Do it right.

SOLAM PAD PRANA KRIYA
Part II

Everything is exactly the same as in the first part, but Jalandhara Bhanda is now applied. The chin and throat are contracted together, chin resting in the notch between the collar bones, without tilting the head. The exactness of the angles of the arms is very important (in both parts) and the meditation MUST BE DONE WHEN THE TEMPERATURE IS OVER 65° - never less. It should be practiced for several days for 11 minutes to understand the fluidness.

C.   . Yogi Bhajan's teacher sent him to a ogi who lived in a cave, heated by fire in the mountains in winter to learn this meditation. During this meditation the vagus nerve is stretched and balanced and the breath doesn't switch into neutral - the power of this pranayam. Pressure will be experienced from the wrist to the shoulder.

ADI SHAKTI MEDITATION
March 4, 1976

In Easy Pose, with chest out and chin pulled in, press fingers together from base to tips without touching palms. Press thumbs together pointing them straight up, fingers pointing straight out away from the body at diaphragm level, eyes looking straight ahead.

Inhale deeply and chant two repetitions of the mantra

```
     Adi   Shakti
     Adi   Shakti
     Adi   Shakti
     Namo, Namo.
    Sarab  Shakti
    Sarab  Shakti
    Sarab  Shakti
     Namo, Namo.
  Prithum Bhagawati
  Prithum Bhagawati
  Prithum Bhagawati
     Namo, Namo.
     Kundalini,
     Mata Shakti
     Mata Shakti
     Namo, Namo.
```

continuously exhaling, 2 repetitions per breath. If you run out of breath, stop there and begin again. Continue for 11 minutes, building to 31.

COMMENTS: Adi Shakti means primal (female) power. Sarab Shakti is all power, and Prithum Bhagawati means 'which creates through God'. Meditation on the primal, creative power of God magnifies ones pranic potency. The Motherpower mantra can also be chanted when stars are poorly aspected.

BHAGAUTI: The form of woman is Bhagauti, the Goddess with 8 hands walking on the back of a tiger (which represents ego). She has 4 hands bearing arms, swords and spears. The sword is defense, the spear distance.) In her other four hands she holds grace - flowers, beads and lotus blossoms for purity. So half of her represents gifts and half, defense. She is the symbol of compassion and power, self-defense and grace, knowledge and arms, this Goddess who rides on a tiger.

October 1971

MAHAN KAL KRIYA
(Given April 23, 30, & Oct. 5, 1973)

In Easy Pose, cross wrists over chest, as if dead, and pull the lower 3 locks (MAHA BANDHA). With chin pulled in focus at the top of the head, trying to look at the back of the head. Pain will come to the side of the jaws. It's O.K. Vibrate the mantra in the center of the head:

Akal Maha Kal
(Undying, great death)

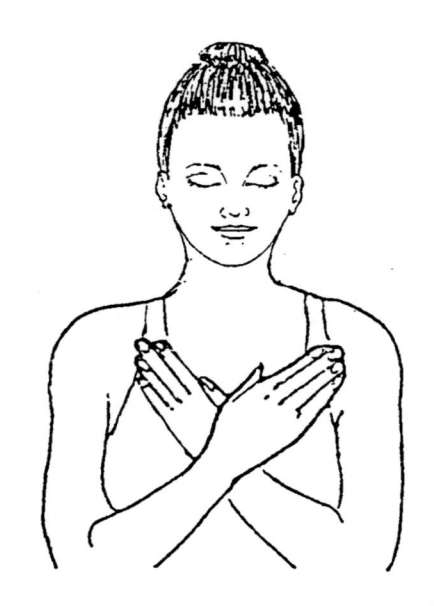

COMMENTS: This is a powerful meditation. It will bring innocence and dispel fear from the personality. It is said that with constant practice, all in the family will live to a ripe old age.

SHAKTI-BHAKTI MEDITATION
(Given May 3, 1973)

A. In SHAKTI POSTURE, (Easy Pose, hands in Venus Lock, palms down, over the solar center on top of the head) and chant:

Akal Maha Kal

B. In BHAKTI POSTURE, (Easy Pose, with both elbows at sides, and both hands in Guyan Mudra: Women place left forearm straight up, palm facing face, and right forearm straight out, parallel to the ground, palm up. Men reverse with right arm up, and left parallel to the ground.)

With eyes half-closed, again chant:

Akal Maha Kal

COMMENTS: No times were specified. This meditation produces physical euphoria, and the "great body" experience. Practiced for only 5 minutes (each part) at bedtime induces a most blissful and regenerating sleep. G.K.

1st SODHUNG MANTRA

For harnessing Ether
July 11 and August 4, 1975

1st Sodhung Mantra - mantra of God Purification. To be practiced at sunset for 40 days to obtain Siddhis.

In Easy Pose and Guyan Mudra chant

Dharti Hai

and visualize grey from the navel down. Then chant

Akash Hai

and imagine Blue Ether from the eyebrows up. Then chant

Guru Ram Das Hai

visualizing a brilliant white light at the heart.

COMMENTS: Best done in the evening in the red light of the setting sun. To know past, present and future. To know what a person thinks before he thinks it. To penetrate into the cosmos. Don't try to get at the meaning...just burn (this) candle to dispel the darkness.

TATTVA SIDDHI KRIYA

For control of the elements
given August 4, 1975

With right palm over Crown Chakra, and left hand in the lap, chant

Pritvi Hai
Akash Hai
Guru Ram Das Hai

On "Pritvi Hai", concentrate on the hand in the lap (and on the earth). On "Akash Hai", look up at the other hand (and the Crown Chakra). On "Guru" focus at the 6th Chakra (the "Third Eye"), on "Ram", on the Throat Chakra, and on "Das", at the Heart Chakra. The Mantra is chanted on one breath.

COMMENTS: Dharti and Pritvi mean earth. Akash is ether. These meditations were given together on August 4, 1975, and have been given separately on other occasions.

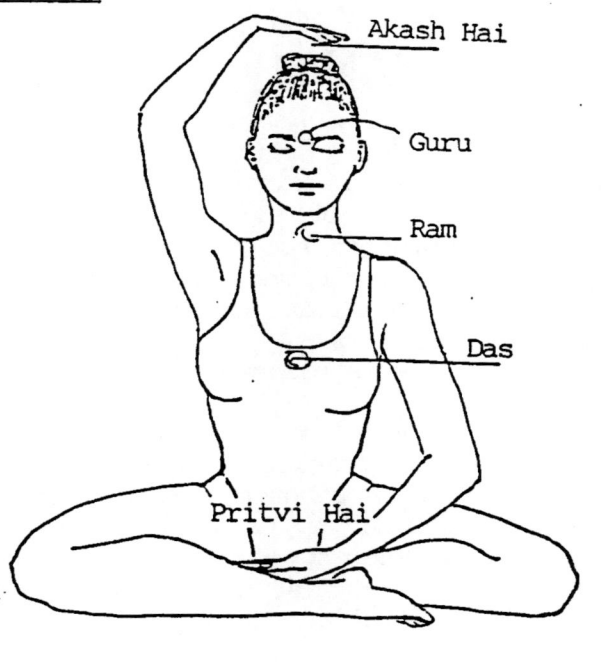

ASTRAL PROJECTION
(1976?)

A In meditation pose, with elbows at sides and forearms parallel to the floor, face palms in and bend fingers so that the tips touch pads. Point thumbs up and circle them for 3-5 minutes - 31 minutes if it is to be great!

B Left hand on heart, right hand raised more to the side than forward chant

    Sa Ta Na Ma

thumb pressing each finger, in turn (as in Kirtan Kriya - see "Kriya for Emotional Balance and Damage due to Cocaine Use") for 5-11 minutes.

C Astral Projection: Hold opposite arms, close eyes and look out the top of the head. With long deep breathing, inhale

Whaaaaaaaaaaaaa

and exhale

Guuuruuuuuuuuuuu

feeling the top 1/5 of the head. On 2nd repetition, focus 3" above the head. On the 3rd repetition, focus 6" above the head. Continue, raising the focus on each repetition to 1 foot, 3 feet, the ceiling level, above the roof, above the neighborhood, seeing the housetops below, seeing the whole city, the continent, the whole earth and then the rich blue ether. Then be surrounded by brilliant white light and merge with it!

After a pleasant interval, return the same way you left.

NOTE: A similar meditation was given on January 16, 1973: "Bring energy and consciousness to the 3rd eye and silently vibrate "Sa Ta Na Ma" for 21 minutes, 16 silently, and the last 5 minutes aloud. Then inhale, stretch up, and for a few minutes, chanting in the "3 voices" - aloud, whispering, and silently - see "Kirtan Kriya" as above), project out of the body going into the universe. Keep trying. Come out of the meditation the way you came in. Do this kriya when depressed."

ARJUNI KRIYA

April 13, 1978

In Easy Pose with a straight spine cross right thumb over the left thumb and close the hands over the thumbs with the fingers straight pushing the thumbs as deeply as possibler into the closed hands. The outsides of the hands remain firmly pressed together from the tips of the little fingers to the heels of the hands, and the index fingers are pressing each other at the tips. Fingers point straight up with their tips level with the lips. Elbows extend out to the sides and forearms are parallel to the ground.

Inhale deeply and completely exhale as the mantra is chanted. Be sure there is no breath left in the lungs after the mantra has been chanted. In a monotone, as the breath is exhaled, chant

EK ONG KAR SAT HARI

Be sure that all of the breath is exhaled with each repetition of the mantra There are seven beats to it - "KAR" gets three beats, and the other words each get one. Each repetition takes 6-8 seconds. Emphacize "HAR". Focus on the breath and on the mantra. The scripture this meditation should be practiced in a very lonely place, but Yogi Bhajan practiced it in a public place. Begin with 11 minutes and slowly build to as long as desirable.

COMMENTS: This meditation works very powerfully on the glandular system. It can take you to the 'third blue ether'. It can put a person to sleep, so precautions to stay awake should be made. The person who practices this meditation will develop the ability to fly through the air! Do not use this power for negative purposes. Once you start, you can't stop and it will eat you alive.

FULL MOON "SUCH SUCH" Meditation
April 28, 1972

Sit comfortably, with a straight spine and chant

Such Such Such

hearing "SSSSS....CHHHH" like a snake. (Time unspecified.)

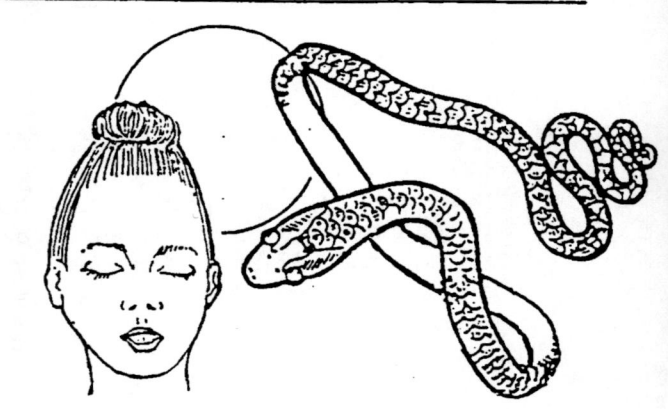

CHANDRA KRIYA MUDRA
July 19, 1975
TO BE DONE ON A FULL MOON IN A WATER SIGN

In meditation posture, interlace the fingers in reverse Venus Lock, palms up, thumbtips touching and chant:

Ek Ong — pulling navel point

Kar — releasing it

Sat Gur Prasad — at heart

Reverse. (Time unspecified.)

COMMENTS: Each pore of the body becomes an eye, an INDRA EYE, known as INDRANITRI. This opens the 3rd Eye, an the 3rd Eye of the opener of the 3rd Eye. It is opened all the way.

NOTE: The full moons in water signs occur when the sun is in earth signs, between August 23 & September 22, December 21 & January 19, and April 20 & May 20, when the sun is in the signs of Virgo, Capricorn and Taurus, respectively and the moon is in Pisces, Cancer and Scorpio. Notice that Yogi Bhajan, however, gave it one a full moon in an earth sign (Capricorn) since the sun was in the opposite water sign of Cancer.

PUSHMA KRIYA: FLOWER MEDITATION
April 19, 1976

Sitting in Easy Pose or any comfortable meditation posture, open the hands like flowers. This position is similar to the tiger's claw of Kung Fu and is formed by curving all the fingers and thumbs, spacing them evenly about an inch apart at the tips. Place this configuration about 10 inches out from the heart center, palms up. Press the Moon Centers (the base oof the palms) together. Now, tense the fingers as much as possible, keeping them as hard as rocks. Close the eyes and see two flowers at the forehead. When you tense the fingers properly, you will see lines of color at the forehead.

You will go through lots of changes and they start almost immediately. Keep the fingers stiff like steel and you will begin to sweat. Continue for 7 minutes. After 7 minutes, relax the hands onto the knees. Maintain a meditative mind as you relax.

Go higher and higher in your consciousness, beyond the sun, moon and stars and into the world beyond. Keep on expanding yourself. Keep the eyes closed and go to Infinity. Within this tiny world of your head, create an infinite world. Within the tiny world of your head, experience the Infinite World. Float and flow into yonder lands. See the unseen. Imagine the unimaginable. Know the unknown.

Inhale deeply and hold the entire world in this breath......Let it go......
Inhale deeply and experience the pranic energy in this breath.............
Let it go.......... Inhale, and utter the word,

Wha

> HARMONY: You are a product of harmony, because the creative power of God is harmonious. There is nothing in disharmony on this planet. There is no conflict!
>
> <u>Man to Man XII</u>

HAVE FAITH in the Creative Force, Truth. Every happening is a lesson, a message. Smile in the face of adversity. Only wish that God's Will be done. You belong to Him. He will provide for those who unite with Him.

October 10, 1969

LET GO! FLOW with the all-pervading current of the Universal Spirt (Cosmic Ocean). Unite with the One and the All.

October 10, 1969

IMPROVE with each breath. Every negative vibration returns 10-fold.

September 11, 1969

ANY ACT IN THE NAME OF GOD returns 10-fold! Action towards the spiritual enlightenment of others!

October 28, 1969

I AM - life is not an experiment!   October 19, 1973

A CLEAN BODY is a guarantee that you will have self-realization sooner. First take care of the gross self and then realize the self in God.

February 10, 1970

Appendix

HAPPINESS: Work, earn and share. Animals have a territory of space; humans have a territory of grace. We must not "get" if we can't first give - it is the Law of Grace. Every spiritual man must follow it - it is the first requirement of an enlightened mind. Deal with others as you want to be dealt with.

March 23, 1974

MEDITATE on God in the primal hours, earn by the sweat of your brow, share among your brothers, and live healthy, happy and holy lives as God has made us.

June 20, 1972

AM - PM: Give the morning to God and the evening to Happiness on this earth. Evenings are important; when the sun goes down, energy is low, and we need a good mood and good company to guard the evenings so that the mornings will be bright and beautiful.

PM: 90% of wrongs are done between 4:00 P.M. and 4:00 A.M. The rising sun holds you.

March 23, 1974

FAITH: Have faith in the Guru or learn at the hands of time. Be flexible in mind and adjust to truth.

June 15, 1970

SUPPELMENTARY EXERCISES

In addition to sets in this book, we have added exercises from other sets and notes for specific problems, for thorough coverage of yoga treatment for stress-related conditions.

Additional Exercises for Nerves

(Sets & exercises for nerves are on pages 44, 45 & 48, and for the memory, on 37, 46-48. All breathing exercises 84-95 and meditations on 96-99, 101, 116, 117, 123, 124, 130, 137-143 (actually ALL Kundalini Yoga and meditation is good for the nervous system.))

FOR AURIC BALANCE & NERVE STRENGTH: Stand, balancing on the left leg with the right leg in Lotus Pose on the left thigh (Tree Pose), arms outstretched to the sides, with left palm down and right palm up. Pull Mulbhand and focus at the 3rd Eye with long deep breathing. (Time unspecified NOTES)

FOR DRUG DAMAGE TO NERVES: On hands and knees, flex the spine up like a cat, exhaling and tucking the head, and down like a cow, inhaling and raising the head (Cat-Cow), with increasing speed for 3 minutes once a day for 40 days to repair drug's damage to nerves. During this time drink "Golden Milk" (see page 173)(SELFNUT & HEAL)

FOR NERVE STRENGTH: Sitting, spread legs wide apart, hands inside and under the thighs, and do body drops. (Time Unspecified.) (NOTES)

WHA GURU KRIYA FOR NERVOUS BALANCE: Sit in Lotus or Easy Pose with hands on knees in Guyan Mudra with the eyes nearly closed. Break the inhale into 10 equal parts or "sniffs". With each sniff, move the hands mechanically (in short jerks) 1/10 of the way toward the forhead, fingers straight, palms facing up. On the 10th inhale, the palms are on the forehead with the fingers pointing up. As you exhale, join the fingertips from base to tips of the 2 hands and lower they slowly, separating them at navel level and returning them to Guyan Mudra on knees. On each sniff of the inhale mentally vibrate

          Wha

and on the exhale,

          Guru

Continue for 3-11 minutes. This builds the nervous system so nothing bothers you. With weak nerves and aura it is difficult to act on your ideals. This helps. (SADA)

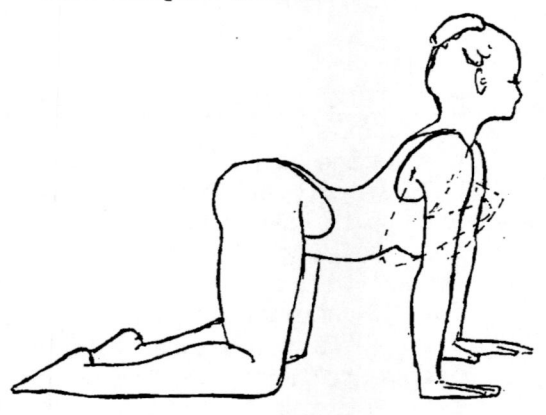

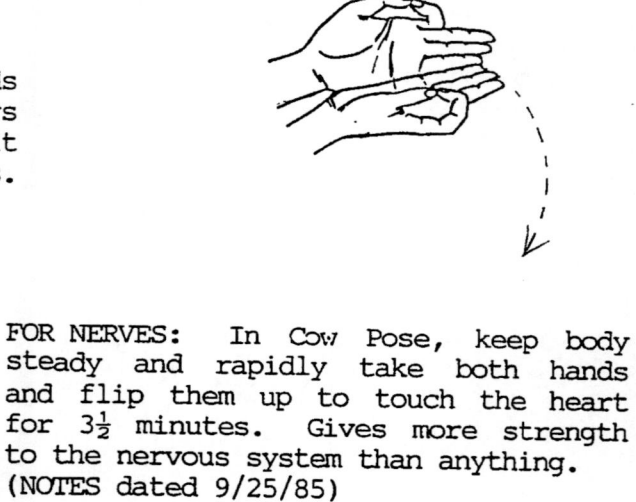

FOR NERVES: In Cow Pose, keep body steady and rapidly take both hands and flip them up to touch the heart for 3½ minutes. Gives more strength to the nervous system than anything. (NOTES dated 9/25/85)

FOR MEMORY: Reverse Cross-crawls - touch alternate heels with opposite hands behind the body for 2-3 minutes. (NOTES)

Additional Exercises for Spinal Adjustment

(Sets for spinal adjustment are on pgs. 26-32, 34.)

LOOSENS NECK MUSCLES, FACILITATING NECK ADJUSTMENT: In Easy Pose with hands on knees, rapidly shake the head from left to right ("no, no, no!") allowing the muscles of the jaw and face to relax for 3 minutes. As you loosen up and shake the pituitary gland and everything in the head will move, stimulating circulation to the capillaries and strenthening the cheek and jaw muscles. (JOY, "For the Lymph Glands".)

TO ADJUST THE NECK: In Easy Pose, pace the palm of the left hand on the left rear of the neck, and the palm of the right hand above the right ear, fingers extending to the back of the head. Look at the tip of the nose and push with maximum pressure with both hands for 2-3 minutes. Reverse. The breathing will become heavy. Adjusts neck. (MAIN-5/2/77)

TO ADJUST NECK & FACE MUSCLES: In Easy Pose, jut the lower jaw forward in an exaggerated underbite, smile and wrinkle the nose and cross the eyes. Raise shoulders to the ears and pull the head down to meet them. Then lower shoulders and stretch the neck up, maintaining the facial expression. Continue for 2 minutes. (MAIN-5/4/77)

NECK ADJUSTMENT: In Easy Pose, place right hand on right rear of head with palm pressing the head towards the left front and resist with the neck muscles for 90 seconds. Reverse sides. (MAIN, 5/4/77)

ALIGN & STRETCH NECK VERTEBRAE: Plow Pose or Shoulder Stand lengthens the spine at the neck, automatically making minor adjustments. Should be followed by Fish Pose or variation which arches the same area, stretching in the opposite direction. (TRADITIONAL)

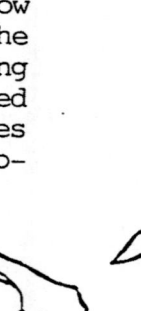

OPENS CIRCULATION TO HEAD & ADJUSTS NECK: Stand up straight and lock thumbs into tightly squeezed fists, arms hanging at sides. Gently and carefully allow head to fall back and stare at a point on the ceiling or in the sky, with Breath of Fire for 2-3 mins. Inhale deeply and slowly bring head forward and tuck the chin in. Then straighten the head and hold the breath briefly, exhale and relax. Sets the magnetic field, alerts the body and opens circulation to the head (and neck). (KEEP - "Ajna Stimulation Kriya"

ADJUSTS SPINE: In Easy Pose, fold arms across chest with upper arms out and parallel to the ground. Neck is straight. Meditate at the root of the nose and pull arms forward from the shoulders. This brings serum up the spine and adjusts it, giving a calm, quiet and peaceful attitude. Enables one to face tension and feel good about it. (MAIN 5/4/77)

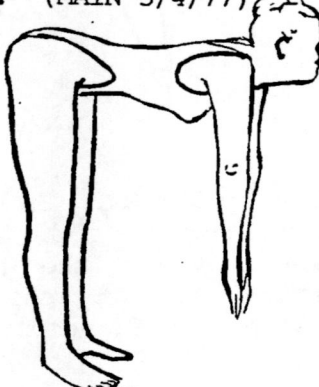

ADJUSTS VERTEBRAL DISCS: Stand with feet 2 feet apart. Keeping the spine straight, bend forward from the waist until the upper bvody is parallel to the ground, and relax the arms down. Roll the eyes up and raise the head only as high as is necessary to see straight ahead. Hold position for 3 minutes. (MAIN - 5/1/77)

FOR 3RD VERTEBRA & HIP BONE: In Easy Pose, place hands together in Prayer Mudra. Raise the left arm to the side at a 60° angle, palm up, as you also bring both knees up as high as possible. Return left palm, clapping palms together as you lower the knees. Repeat with right arm and continue alternating arms, and inhaling as one goes up, exhaling as it come down, for 4-5 minutes. Lift knees forcefully with powerful breathing, establishing a rhythm. (Y480 "For the Back)

ADJUSTS SPINE: Squat in Crow Pose with hands behind you, palms flat behind buttocks. Inhale and push hips up in modified Bridge Pose. Swing the head up and down as fast as possible with Breath of Fire for 15 seconds Then, continue Breath of Fire and powerfully and rapidly raise and lower the buttocks for 2 miutes. Works on thyroid and parathyroid and adjusts the spine. (Y480, "For Glands, Circulation and the Meditative Mind")

ADJUSTS SPINE: On hands and knees, drop the spine as in Cow Pose and extend left leg straight back, raising it as high as possible, and then lowering it to level, up and down for 3 minutes. Reverse and repeat. Come back into Cow Pose, open the mouth, stick out the tongue and do Breath of Fire for 1 minute. Adjusts spine in areas not accessible to chiropractic adjustment. (MAIN - 5/4/77)

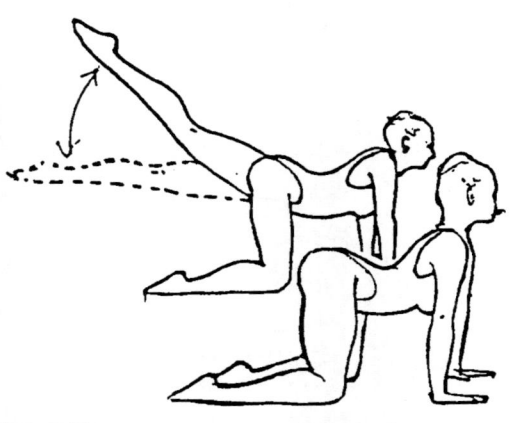

ALL THE BONES OF THE SPINE WILL ADJUST THEMSELVES: In Easy Pose, place palms together overhead, arms a little bent, and raise and lower them counting to "108" ("1" up, "2" down). Then, arms extended straight up, stretch the spine straight up from the base with long, deep breathing for 1-2 minutes. Inhale, hold and stretch for 15 seconds, exhale and relax. (K480 - "Kriya for the Colon, Spine and Organs")

Additional Exercises for the Eyes

(Sets & meditations for the eyes are on pages 37, 48-53, 124-5, & 135.)

ADHA SHAKTI CHALNEE KRIYA for CLEAR SPARKLING EYES: Kneel and bring head to the ground, hands in Venus Lock on the back, and raise feet and shins off the ground, near buttocks. Balance and meditate at the Brow Point for 3 minutes. Then place hands under the shoulders, extend left leg up and back to 60° and kick the buttocks with Breath of Fire for 2 minutes. Switch legs and repeat. Gives clarity of thought and clear, sparkling eyes. (MED - Transforming the Lower Triangle to the Higher Triangle)

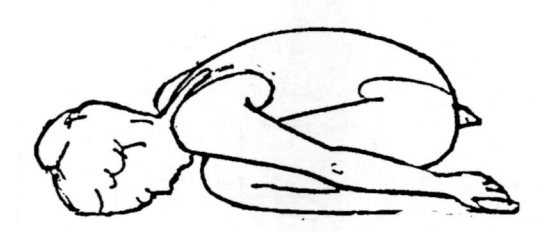

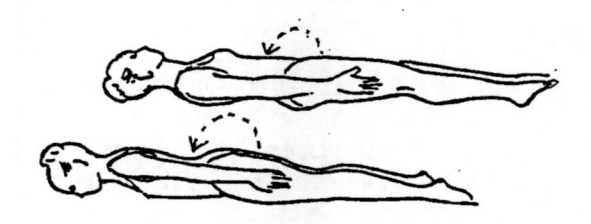

CLEANS EYES: In Rock Pose, spread knees wide and bring forehead to the ground, resting palms of hands on soles of feet. Focus at the 3rd Eye, consciously relax and breathe normally for 5-20 minutes. Then take several deep breaths and slowly come out of the position. This exercise subtly stimulates the Ajna Chakra and cleans the eyes. It MUST BE FOLLOWED BY BUNDLE ROLL: Lie on your back with arms pressed tightly against the sides and legs straight like a bundle of logs. Keep the body straight and roll over and over across the floor and then back again, for 3-5 minutes. Balances the Magnetic Field. Relax. (Do not do the first one unless you follow it with the 2nd. (KEEP "Ajna Stimulation Kriya")

GOOD FOR EYESIGHT: Frog Pose, done quickly for 3-4 minutes (180-210 repetitions) is good for circulation, hearing and eyesight. (See 'Skull & Pelvic Bone Adjustment for directions - Y480 - For the Lymph Glands)

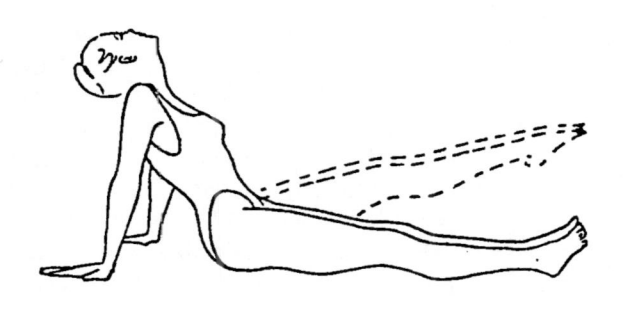

FOR HEADACHE & EYE DISEASE: Sit up and lean back 60°, palms behind you for support. Bend the neck and drop the head back to look at the ceiling, fixing eyes on one point without winking or blinking and do Breath of Fire for 2 minutes. Inhale and raise both feet up 12", keeping the vision steady and hold for 15-20 seconds. Exhale, lower feet and repeat the first part for 1 minute. Then inhale, raise feet to 12" again, hold 15 seconds exhale and completely relax on the back. Moves energy to the eyes and has helped cases of headache and eye disease such as cataracts. (SADA - Beginners Cleansing Set)

FOR PRANIC FORCE IN THE EYES: Lying on the stomach, hands in Venus Lock behind back, inhale and arch the torso up, lifting head, shoulders and chest with the eyes closed and hold for 30 seconds. Exhaling, lower body and open the eyes. Repeat 10 times. (NOTES)

INCREASES CIRCULATION TO EYES: In Easy Pose, inhale, hold the breath and puff out the cheeks as fully as possible. Keeping the cheeks puffed, breathe through the nose and release a little air as needed to maintain pressure for 1-2 minutes. Then, with cheeks still puffed, head stationary, move the eyes left, right, up and down for another minute. Good for complexion, it brings circulation to eyes & cheeks. (JOY - For Sciatic)

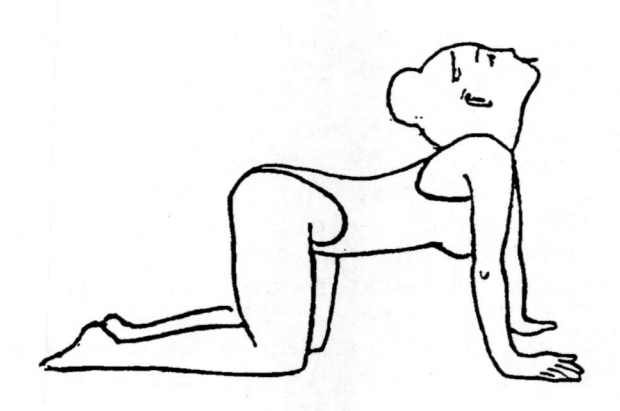

EYESIGHT: In Cow Pose on hands and knees, (hands and knees each shoulder width apart, arms straight and parallel to thighs) flex the spine down as if someone were sitting on it and arch the neck raising the head up. Roll the eyes skyward and stick the tongue all the way out, breathing powerfully through the mouth for 2 minutes. Eye position works on eyesight and tongue position helps adjust central vagus nerve. (JOY - Exercise Set for Circulation)

WORKS ON EYES: In Easy Pose, bend elbows out to sides at shoulder level, and spreading the fingers wide like a fan, cross hands in front of the open eyes, moving arms from the elbows, upper arm remaining parallel to floor, forcefully and rapidly for 3 minutes. (JOY - For Balancing Aura)

Additional Exercises for the Adrenals & Kidneys

(Sets for adrenals & kidneys are on 42, 43, 52, 56-62 & 94)

UDDIYANA BHANDA FOR STIMULATING ADRENALS: This is the diaphragm lock, applied by lifting the diaphragm high up into the throax and pulling the upper abdominal muscles back towards the spine on the exhaled breath. This creats a cavity that gives a gentle massage to the heart muscles and stimulates the hypothalmic-pituitary adrenal axis in the brain and the sense of compassion. It can give new youthfulness to the body. This powerful lock allows pranic force through the central nerve channel of spine on the exhaled breath. This creates a cavity that gives a gentle massage to the heart muscles. This powerful lock allows pranic force through the central nerve channel of the spine and up into the neck region, stimulating the hypothalmic-pituitary-adrenal axis in the brain. It can give new youthfulness to the body. The spine should be straight, and the contraction applied on the exhale. (Forcefully applied on the inhale, it can create undesireable pressure in the eyes and heart. SADA - p. 41)

WORKS ON KIDNEYS & ADRENALS: Sit in Easy Pose, bringing left hand to chest level forearm parallel to ground, palm facing body. Grasp left wrist with right hand from the outside without encircling left wrist with the thum. Close eyes to a slit and turning left palm slightly out, stare into it as into a mirror. Create muscular tension by pulling toward the chest with the right hand and resisting with the left. Continue for 2-3 minutes and do not reverse. This works on the kidneys and adrenals and causes excessive glandular secretion. Don't cheat or worry about competency - just go through it. (If you inhale and hold the breath the lungs will go through some changes. (MAIN 5/1/77)

FOR THE KIDNEYS: Place right foot on left thigh, left foot flat on the floor, knee bent up near the chest. Raise left arm straight up, hand in Guyan Mudra and place the right arm behind the hips, palm on floor. Raise the body up and balance on the right palm and left foot with Breath of Fire for 1-3 minutes. (HEAL)

KIDNEYS, BLADDER & ADRENALS: Sit on the heels, knees wide apart in with toes together. Place fingertips on the floor, arms straight and slightly lift the body up, supporting its weight on fingertips and forelegs. Inhale deeply, exhale completely, and holding the breath out, pump the navel point in and out 5 times. Inhale deeply, and holding the breath in, pump the navel 125 times. Exhale completely, and holding the breath out, pump the navel 15 more times. Then relax for 1 minute. (HEAL)

PRESSURIZES KIDNEYS, GONADS & ADRENALS: In Easy Pose, holding on to knees, inhale completely, stretching ribcage to the maximum and don't leak or sip in more air. Put the tongue against the upper teeth and the roof of the mouth, relax the spine and flex it until you can no longer hold the breath in, and then exhale. Gradually increases duration of held breath until you can hold it for 1 minute. Continue for 11 minutes. (JOY - Lungs & Bloodstream)

BUILDS ADRENALS: In Easy Pose, arms parallel to the ground, palms up, breath long and deep for 2 minutes, holding the position precisely. Then inhale, and holding the breath in for 15 seconds, stretch the arms out as far as possible. Exhale, relax. Builds heart, lungs, pancrease and adrenals. (K480 - Colon, Spine & Organs)

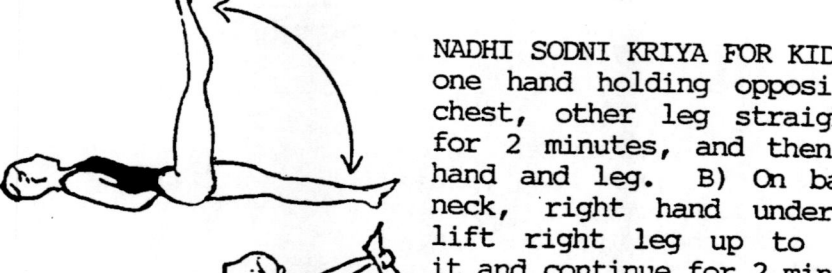

NADHI SODNI KRIYA FOR KIDNEYS: A) In ½ Bow Pose, one hand holding opposite leg, other hand on chest, other leg straight, do Breath of Fire for 2 minutes, and then repeat with alternate hand and leg. B) On back, left hand beneath neck, right hand under kidneys, inhale and lift right leg up to 90°, exhale and lower it and continue for 2 minutes. (NOTES)

Additional Exercises for the Liver & Colon

Liver & colon exercises are on 37, 42, 44, 45, 52, 56 & 62-75

WORKS ON THE LIVER: Stand with feet 18 inches apart and extend both arms up to exactly 60°, elbows straight. Powerfully twist the whole body from left to right as fast as possible for 5 mins. The 60° angle of the arms stimulates the liver area. (JOY - Set for Sciatic Nerve)

LIVER: Sit on heels, one hand on the knee and the other arm extended straight ahead and up to 60°. Move it in wide, stiff circles around the body. Reverse arms and repeat. (NOTES)

WORKS ON THE LIVER: In Easy Pose, interlace fingers behind the back in Venus Lock and swing the arms powerfully from left to right, powerfully twisting the body from side to side, rapidly for 3 minutes. (JOY - Set for Balancing the Brain)

FLUSHES TOXINS FROM THE LIVER: Stand with feet 2 feet apart, and extend the arms straight out in front, parallel to the ground, palms down. On "1", twist the upper torso to the right, on "2", squat in Crow Pose (arms still extended to the right), on "3" stand (arms still right), on "4" return to original position, on "5" twist left, squat on "6", back up on "7", original position on "8", and continue for 6 minutes. Squat all the way down and twist all the way around. This keeps knees flexible and flushes toxins from the liver. It is also good for the cardiovascular system. (K480 - "For Health & Openness")

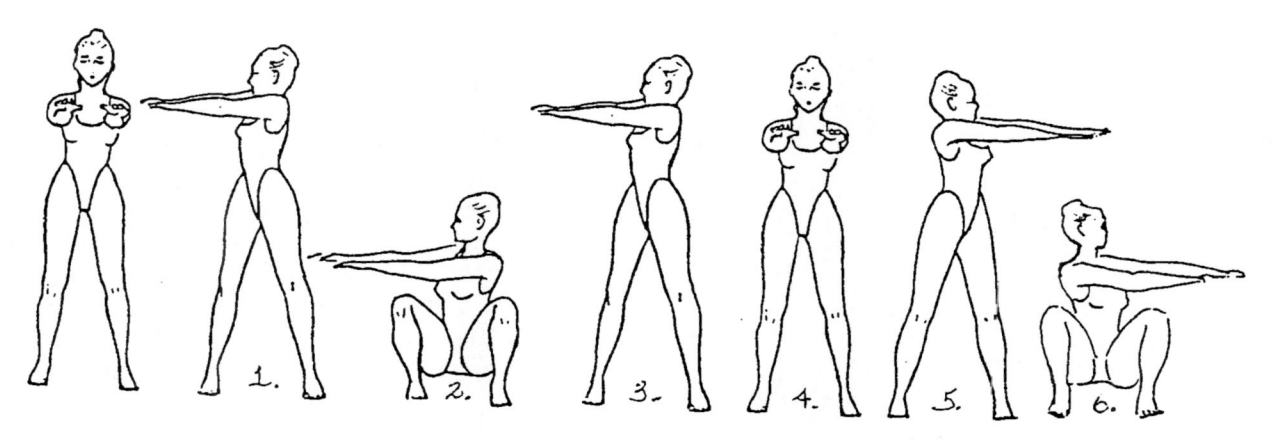

GOOD FOR THE LIVER: In Easy Pose, grind at the waist in a clockwise motion as though whirling a hula hoop for 3 minutes. Reverse directions for another 3 minutes. (MAIN - 5/1/77)

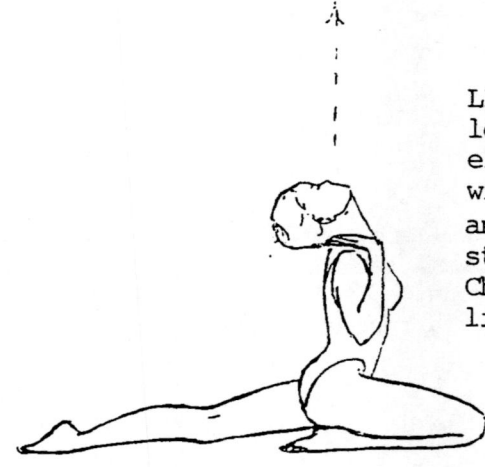

LIVER: Sit on the right heel and extend the left leg straight behind you. Bend the arms so that elbows press into the sides and hands are level with the jaws, palms forward and back at a 45° angle. Allow the head to fall back and fix gaze straight up. Hold steadfastly for $5\frac{1}{2}$ minutes. Change sides and repeat. Works directly on the liver. (BEADS)

WORKS ON LIVER, RELEASES ANGER: Sitting in Easy or Lotus Pose, interlace fingers in Venus Lock with index fingers extended, and stretch arms overhead, elbows straight. Inhale and stretch up with index fingers extended, arms overhead and elbows straight. Inhale and stretch up, exhale and stretch down bringing forehead to the left knee, buttocks remaining on the ground. Inhale up, exhale to right knee. Continue at moderate pace for 3 minutes. Works on the liver, releases anger and keeps you young. (JOY - Circulation Set)

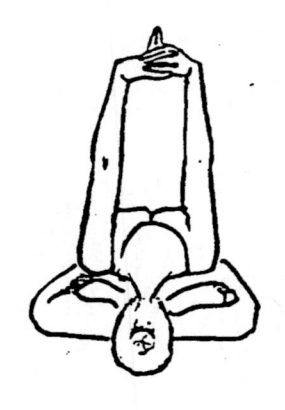

CORRECTS PROBLEMS OF THE COLON & LIVER. In Lotus or Easy Pose, clasp hands in Venus Lock, extending index fingers behind you. Bend forward raising arms as high as possible then come up. Bend forward to right knee (raising arms in back), then up, then bend to center and up, then to left knee and up and continue for 3 minutes. (YOG - Exercises for Body Cleansing and Disease Prevention)

WORKS ON COLON & LIVER: Sit with legs out in front and lock both hands under the left knee and rapidly begin to raise the leg all the way up and down, keeping knee straight. One lift takes 2 seconds. Continue powerfully for 1-2 minutes and then repeat on the opposite side. (JOY - Set for Sciatic Nerve)

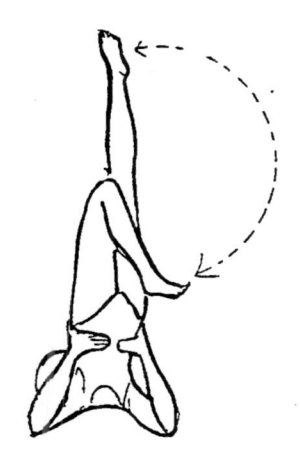

MASSAGES LIVER & COLON: In Shoulder Stand, pump alternate legs up and down for 1 minute. Eliminates problems with the liver, spleen or gall bladder, massages colon. (MAIN - 5/4/77)

CROW POSE FOR ELIMINATION: Squat down in Crow Pose and place palms down on the ground with the elbows outside the knees, keeping the head up. Chant your favorite mantra for 2 minutes. Crow Pose puts direct pressure on the colon - allow the pressure and don't worry. (NOTES)

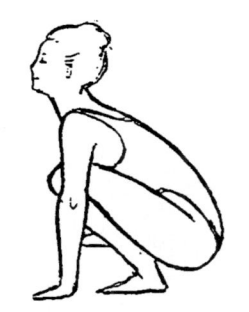

TO CLEANSE COLON: In Crow Pose, with feet 2' apart bend forward and touch the head to the floor 10 times. (NOTES)

FOR COLON AND GALL BLADDER: In Cobra Pose, cross ankles and kick buttocks, inhaling as the feet come up and exhaling as they go down. (NOTES)

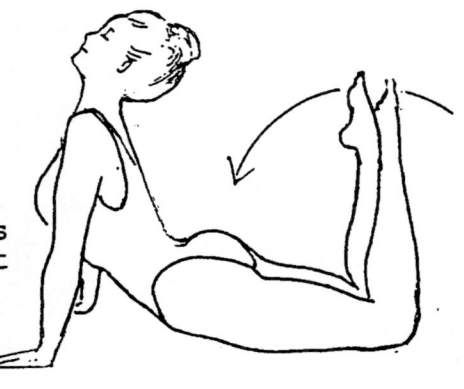

ACCUPRESSURE POINTS

THE SPINAL NERVES

cervical nerves (8)
1. Vertebral artery, eyes, throat, submandibular gland
2. Vertebral artery, larynx, eyes, sublingual gland
3. Heart, lungs, diaphragm, vertebral artery
4. Thyroid gland, diaphragm, vasomotor nerves, vertebral artery, trachea, esophagus
5. Thyroid gland, heart, diaphragm, vertebral artery, trachea, esophagus
6. Vertebral artery, trachea, esophagus, heart, lungs
7. Trachea, esophagus, eyes, lungs, heart
8. Eyes, lungs, trachea, bronchi, heart

thoracic nerves (12)
1. Eyes, ears, heart, lungs, pleura, vasomotor nerves, bronchi
2. Vasomotor nerves, intercostal nerves, pleura, heart, bronchi
3. Intercostal nerves, heart, lungs, pleura, liver, diaphragm, bronchi
4. Intercostal nerves, heart, lungs, pleura, diaphragm, trachea, mammary glands
5. Intercostal nerves, mammary glands, pleura, stomach, spleen, diaphragm, liver
6. Pleura, stomach, spleen, intercostal nerves, diaphragm, liver
7. Intercostal nerves, peritoneum, stomach, spleen, gallbladder, liver, pancreas
8. Intercostal nerves, peritoneum, stomach, spleen, bile duct, gallbladder, pancreas, suprarenal glands
9. Intercostal nerves, vasomotor nerves, suprarenal glands, pancreas, small intestine
10. Intercostal nerves, peritoneum, pancreas, spleen, bile duct, diaphragm, urinary tract, kidneys
11. Peritoneum, diaphragm, pancreas, kidneys, urinary tract, large intestine, small intestine
12. Peritoneum, diaphragm, kidneys, urinary tract, large intestine, small intestine, appendix

lumbar nerves (5)
1. Small intestine, appendix, uterus, ovaries, Fallopian tubes, testes, penis, bladder
2. Large intestine, small intestine, appendix, uterus, ovaries, testes, penis, ejaculatory duct
3. Uterus, ovaries, Fallopian tubes, prostate gland, ejaculatory duct, testes, penis, bladder
4. Rectum, anus, prostate gland, bladder, uterus, sigmoid colon
5. Bladder, prostate gland, rectum, testes, uterus, sigmoid colon

sacral nerves (5)
1. Bladder, anus, erection, emission, rectum, vagina, cervix of uterus
2. Bladder, anus, erection, emission, rectum, vagina, cervix of uterus
3. Bladder, anus, erection, emission, rectum, vagina, cervix of uterus
4. Bladder, anus, vagina, erection, emission, cervix of uterus
5. Bladder, anus, vagina, erection, emission, cervix of uterus

coccygeal nerve (1)
1. Anal area and coccyx perceptions

ON SPINE & BACK

Digestive System

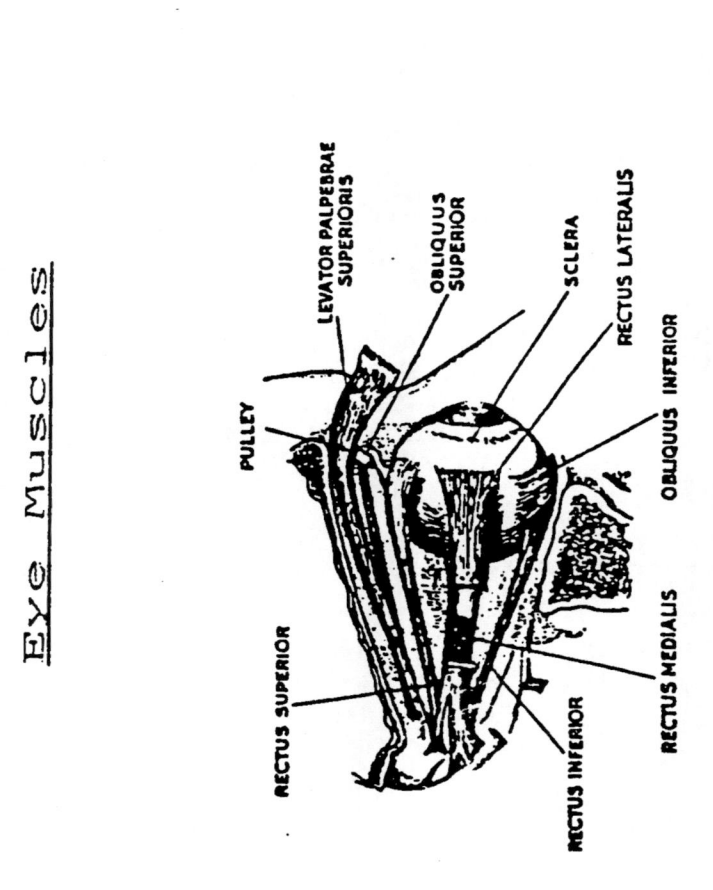

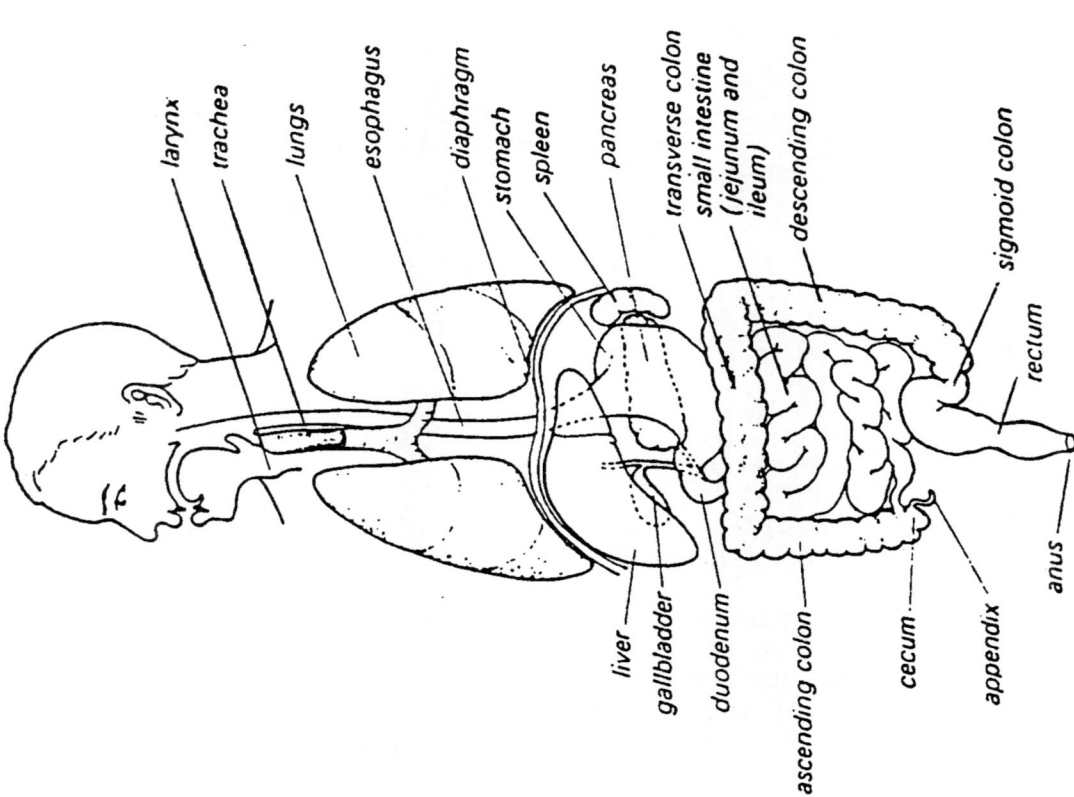

- larynx
- trachea
- lungs
- esophagus
- diaphragm
- stomach
- spleen
- pancreas
- transverse colon
- small intestine (jejunum and ileum)
- descending colon
- sigmoid colon
- rectum
- anus
- appendix
- cecum
- ascending colon
- duodenum
- gallbladder
- liver

Eye Muscles

- LEVATOR PALPEBRAE SUPERIORIS
- OBLIQUUS SUPERIOR
- SCLERA
- RECTUS LATERALIS
- OBLIQUUS INFERIOR
- RECTUS MEDIALIS
- RECTUS INFERIOR
- RECTUS SUPERIOR
- PULLEY

VEGETARIANISM: By eating animals you will not be God, try as you might. You are what you eat. If you want to eat meat, cut off your finger and feel the pain. God has provided all fruits and vegetables. An avacado can regenerate itself but a dead animal can't. Fear in the spiritual quest is due to the animal in you. The 4th vertebra is stiff with the animal in you.

SUGAR: The weakness of eating too much sugar is illustrated by the inablility to do Frog Pose - the circulation can't cater to the capillaries. Too much honey is equally bad.

Get your sugar from food. With this weak stamina you are unfit for action. Keep away from sugar! Also, too much protein is equally bad - leads to ureac acid and arthritis.

March 24, 1974

OVEREATING: It is a sin not to eat and it is a sin to overeat! Eat what you can digest. Take care of the physical self. Do a water fast if it is your habit to overeat and the digestive system needs a rest.

February 10, 1970

PROTEIN: Too much protein leads to uric acid and arthritis. LIVE LEAN, THIN AND SKINNY.

March 24, 1974

From Gururattan Kaur's Kitchen

GUIDELINES FOR STRESS REDUCING DIET

ELIMINATE PROCESSED & TOXIC FOODS

The first rule in a stress-reducing diet is to eliminate foods that over-stimulate, or take energy from the body, including food that is difficult to digest, and foods that are toxic. Read labels to avoid foods with the following ingredients.

1) <u>Caffeine</u>: In very concentrated doses, ccaffeine is actually a poison. Just pouring strong coffee on a car battery disolves the acids! Yet, we consume caffeine in every cup of coffee and tea, every cola drink, and every chocolate bar. Its habitual use causes problems for the nervous system - coordination, memory and perception. It puts stress on the adrenals and heart, raises cholesterol levels in the blood, irritates the stomach lining, and impedes digestion. It noticeably inhibits sleep, and by stressing the major muscle groups, makes it difficult to relax. It has not food value, and to all that, add, it is addictive. The lift is always followed by depression, as caffeine taxes the nerves and glands. Coffee addiction is complicated by its stimulating action on the colon, so that coffee is often unwittingly used as a laxative making it a compound addiction and even more difficult to break. However, cutting down slowly, to eventually eliminate it is not traumatic, and can be implemented by substituting Licorice-Sassafrass Tea (see recipes in appendix).

2) Hand in hand with caffeine addiction is <u>sugar addiction</u>, for sugar is another ingredient in colas, candy and some coffee and tea. It decays the teeth, and adversely affects the nerves, adrenal glands, the heart and muscles. Refined white sugar robs the body of B vitamins and disrupts the calcium/phosphorus balance causing nervousness and irritability. It is difficult to find packaged and processed foods in a grocery store without added sugar, and children today eat up to 20 times the sugar they consumed 50 years ago! Natural sugar, in moderation, as found in fruit and honey contains minerals and the B vitamins that are good for the nervous system. Fruit sweeteners can be substituted for refined sugar. Stevia or Sweet Leaf is a sweet tasting green herb that can be brewed with teas to sweeten them, and is without calories! It can be brewed very strong and stored in the refrigerator to sweeten other food. Licorice root and anise seeds added to teas and other food also sweeten without damage or calories.

3) <u>Salt</u> also overstimulates the adrenal glands, contributing to adrenal exhaustion, chronic fatigue and hypertension. Overuse also retains body fluids, adding pressure to the heart. Salt abusers set the stage for stomach ulcers, by

4) <u>Nicotine</u>, though not a food, damages the entire body, especially the lungs and heart. Smoking depletes vitamin C and iron so if you are trying to quit, add those to your diet.

5) <u>White Flour</u>, found in white bread, pastries, and other junk food, has been refined by removing all the bran and wheat germ, containing most of the vitamins! In the processing only a small part of the lost vitamins are

synthetically replaced. Refined, white flour is thought of as a major cause of colon cancer because of the missing fiber.

6) <u>Processed Foods</u>, including canned and frozen foods, lunch meats, hard cheeses and fryed foods are often indigestible, and without food value because of the heat and chemical processing.

7) <u>Chemical sweeteners and Preservatives</u> are difficult or impossbile to digest and some additives are actually poisenous.

8) <u>Red Meat</u> takes 72 hours to digest and putrefies in the stomach, which along with white flour, constitutes a major threat of colon cancer. The traumatic slaughter of livestock releases fear hormones that remain in the meat, and there is evidence that people become calmer by eliminating meat from the diet. Meat eating also exposes us to the growth stimulating hormones and pesticides in the animal's diet. (See <u>Diet for a Small Planet</u> by Frances Moore Lappe.)

SUBSTITUTE WHOLE, NATURAL FOOD

<u>Live Foods</u> are fresh, raw foods in their natural form like fruits and uncooked vegetables. As cooking kills many of the vitamins and enzymes necessary for digestion, it is important to include raw foods in the diet. Sprouts are a living food and easily integrated into a diet. They are simply and inexpensively grown at home and provide generous amounts of chemical free vitamins and enzymes, especially during the winter months when fresh produce is scarce. Alfalfa and mung beans are the most popular sprouts, but sunflower seeds, cabbage and radish sprouts add delicious zest to salads and sandwiches.

The ideal diet would include only <u>fresh organically grown food</u>, but without an year-round garden, this is difficult. Because of the pesticides and herbicides sprayed on the non-organic foods we often eat, it is necessary to wash them thoroughly, and soak them in soap or vinegar, if necessary, to reduce those toxins, and peel any food that has a wax coating (like shiney apples). The fresher the food the more vitamins it contains, so pick or buy food as close as possible to the time it is to be eaten.

<u>Fruits</u> are God's sweetest gift to man. They are beautiful, fragrant and delicious. They can be eaten, in a natural environment, without the labor of sowing, cultivating, harvesting or cooking. Trees and vines freely offer their fruit without harm to themselves. Except for bananas, they are agressive intestinal cleansers. A sane and spiritual diet includes plenty of fresh fruit, in season. Bananas soothe the mucous membranes and are easily digested when fully ripe. The scrapings from the inside of the peel contain as much vitamins and minerals as the rest of the banana, while the white part of orange peel contains rutin for the circulatory system, and bioflavinoids. Apricot seeds and seeds in apple core contain laetrile-like cancer-preventing elements, and papaya has valuable digestive enzymes. All yellow-orange fruit provide abundant vitamin A, as well as C. Dried fruit sometimes increase in food value. Raisons are iron rich and contain vitamin C (making it an excellent food for smokers), and only a small handful satisfies the appetite. It is best to drink water sometime after eating raisons or other dried fruits, seeds or nuts, to replace the evaporated water.

Whole Grains are high in protein, and carbohydrates in the unprocessed and natural state, containing the bran and the germ to reproduce itself. They are rich in vitamins, and the staple food of most of the world's populations.

Legumes like beans, lentils, peas and peanuts are high energy, protein packed foods, that, combined with whole grains offer balanced and ideal proteins for human consumption Most legumes provide fiber as well.

Nuts, especially almonds are another unearned gift of God (in the sense of requiring neither harm to the tree, nor man's labor to enjoy), and are high protein foods offering sustained energy. Almonds are known as a potency food for men in many cultures. As the skin is difficult to digest and adds no nutritional benefits, blanching is best - just soak them in hot water for a few minutes and the skin peels right off.

Seeds, like sunflower seeds, are packed with vitamin E and protein. Sesame seeds are a staple in many countries, and make a delicious spread, Tahini, as well as a candy, the scrumptious Halvah. Sunflower seeds are easily sprouted for more enzymes, and digestibility. (Simply cover with water and let stand overnight or 24 hours) and can be added to grain dishes for added flavor and protein.

As dairy products provide high quality protein and calcium for vegetarians they are staples in many diets. But many adults cannot digest milk products, and they are mucous forming. Raw milk is more digestible than pasteurized, and it retains the valuable enzymes. Raw goats milk is easier to digest than cows milk, less mucous forming, and it contains a high grade phosphorous that implements meditation and nourishes the brain! Cheese is a concentrated protein food but difficult to digest and constipating so it should be eaten in moderation. Yogurt and whey are aids to the digestive system.

Green vegetables are a must in a stress-free diet, because they strengthen the nervous system and cleanse the body. Besides steaming, they can be juiced or used raw in salads. Green, leafy vegetables, like spinach, watercress and various greens provide large quantities of vitamin A and the B complex, with calcium, magnesium, potassium, iron and copper.

Roots, providing carbohydrates and valuable vitamins, like carrots, beets, sweet potatoes, ginger and many others should be included in any diet.

Foods that promote elimination are very important because of the preponderance of refined and processed foods in our diets, and the common problem of constipation. Elimination is promoted by drinking plenty of water, and eating fresh ripe fruits, especially Black, Mission Figs, grapefruit, peaches, and apricots, raw green vegetables, bran, ground flax seeds, chlorophyll, wheat germ and millet. (Constipating foods are cheese and other dairy products, rice, processed and refined foods, starches and most junk food.)

Water! We need 8 glasses a day and more in dry climates. Stress can be reduced by drinking a big glass of water, and drinking water between meals can eliminate hunger caused by nervousness (when we are simply thirsty, but translate the feeling to hunger). The best time to drink water is upon arising in the morning, between meals and before going to bed at night, but neither water nor other beverages should be consumed with meals, be cause that dilutes the digestive juices. Most tap water contains toxic chemicals in addition to chlorine so it is advisable to drink purified water. The water-filters using carbon core filters installed in the kitchen are the most effective. Bottled water may not be of the highest quality, and boiling tap water simply concentrates the chemicals.

Less cooking retains the vitamins, particularly in vegetables. Steam and bake food rather than boil or fry it. (Vegetables steamed in a cooking parchment are best, for all the nutrients are then preserved.) Grains, of course must be cooked long enough to make them digestible.

Optimum food combining means eating only those foods that are easily digested together at the same meal. (See chart, "Food Combining for Best Digestion".) Each type of food requaires certain enzymes for digestion, and eating incompatible foods taxes the digestive system and may prevent some foods from being assimilated. In general the fewer items at a meal, the better.

Food Supplements: Though the ideal diet of organic, locally grown, fresh foods would supply all the nutrients we need, because of the time it takes to arrive at the market from the farm, and because of some harmful means of preserving food, and/or processing it, many vitamins and minerals are lost and supplements may be taken to ensure adequate nutrition. They should come from natural, rather than synthetic sources, and should not replace wholesome food! If you can't feel a difference the supplement is probvably useless. Just be sure to have enough vitamin C, B-Complex and calcium.

As with all things, test foods on yourself and see how you feel. Our needs and digestive tolerance changes from time to time, and in season. Eat those foods that give you energy, and make you feel and look good.

Today we eat for entertainment as much as to sustain our bodies. We have learned from families and social customs to thoughtlessly eat the wrong foods, or to overeat. It is very important to tune into our own bodies and discover which foods nourish us and which do not, and how much leaves us feeling comfortable, and how much is too much.

Food preparation should be undertaken in a positive, peaceful, happy frame of mind, while listening to beautiful music or perhaps chantting. Those who share our food will feel the energy that went into it.

Beaing grateful and peaceful just before meals, blessing the food, and eating slowly and calmly is crucial for good digestion as well as for the elimination of stress.

Meals should be pleasant and unhurried. While blessing the food, it is effective to see it healing and nourishing the body. Eat slowly chewing each bit well to partially digest it before swallowing, (saliva being an important digestive enzyme) because inadequate chewing contributes to indigestion and stress.

We are a nation of over-eaters. Even good, healthy food in excess depletes energy, over-taxes the digestive system, and makes us overweight. As a rule, we should eat only until the stomach is 3/4 full, and to give the digestive system a rest, not between meals.

We should eat only when hungry but before we are famished, so that meals are relaxed and pleasant. It is better not to eat after sunset and not for 2-3 hours before bed, for late eating disturbs sleep. Never eat when upset as a tense stomach causes indigestion.

Summary

ELIMINATE	SUBSTITUTE
Caffeine: Coffee, Black Tea, Colas Candy	Herbal Teas (take your own tea bag, and use a restaurant's or office's hot water. Stimulating teas are Peppermint, Ginger Tea, and Yogi Tea (see recipes). Calming teas are Camomile and sleepytime. Coffee substitutes are Pero, Bambu, Roast Aroma and Licorice-Sassafrass Tea (see recipes).
Sugar: Pastries, candy, junk food, most processed food.	Honey, molasses, barley malt, maple syrup, fruit sweeteners, stevia (sweet leaf or sweet herb), and fresh fruit.
Salt: Most processed foods.	Braggs Liquid Aminos (Tamari and Soy sauce, containing salt can be used in moderation.
Junk Food Snacks: Pastries, chips, pizza, salted nuts.	Fresh fruit, almonds and nuts, raw sunflower seeds, dried fruits like raisons, and cucumber, celery and carrot sticks
Processed Foods: Canned and frozen foods, and most packaged food.	Fresh vegetables and fruits, raw if possible.
Animal Protein: Red meat, poultry, fish, eggs.	Grains and legumes, unpasturized, unhomogenized dairy products, goats milk, cheese & yogurt, and nuts and seeds.
Animal Fats: Fryed food and butter and most junk food.	Tahini and nut butters in moderation, humus, ghee (clarified butter and cold-pressed vegetable oils.)

Food Combining for Best Digestion

PROTEINS
Nuts & Seeds
Legumes
(Beans, Peas, Peanuts)
Whole Grains
Meat, Fish, Poultry, Eggs *
Cheese, Yogurt, Milk

←—— Poor ——→

STARCHES
Irish & Sweet Potatoes, Yams
Pumpkins, Winter Squash,
Chestnuts
Grains
(Cereal, Bread, Rice)
Pastries

LOW & NON-STARCH VEGETABLES
Lettuce, Spinach, Watercress
Parsley, Cucumber, Artichoke
Green Beans, Asparagus, Onions
Scallions, Fresh Peas, Corn
Sprouted Seeds & Beans
Dandelion, Mustard, Turnip,
Beet, & Daikon Radish Greens
Chard, Collards, Kale
Cabbage, Cauliflower, Broccoli
Carrots, Beets, Radishes
Parsnips, Turnips, Rutabaga
Zuchini, Summer Squash

(Good ↑ to Proteins; Poor ↓ to Acid Fruits)
(Good ↑ to Starches; Poor ↓ to Sub-Acid Fruit)

ACID FRUITS
Oranges, Grapefruit
Lemon, Lime, Tangerine
Strawberries, Pineapple
Pomegranate, Kiwi, Tomatoes
Sour Apples & Sour Plums

←—— FAIR ——→

SUB-ACID FRUIT
Bananas, Dates, Sapote
Persimmons, Cherimoya
Dried Fruit
(Raisons, Figs, Dates
Apples, Papaya, etc.)

Poor ↘   ↙ FAIR

SWEET FRUITS
Apples, Apricots, Plums
Mango, Papaya, Melon
Peaches, Pears, Nectartines
Grapes, Berries, Cherries
Figs, Watermelon

FATS
May be combined with all foods
except protein & melon

ALSO
4 or fewer foods per meal.
Foods from 2, only, classifications
1 protein & one starch, only, per meal
Honey, Sugar, Syrup, & Molassus
ferment combined with other foods.
Beverages should be taken alone.

EXCEPTIONS
Nuts may be eaten with fruits.
Lettuce, Celery O.K. with fruits.
Avacados, Tomatoes O.K. with veggies.
Melons should be eaten alone.

*Not recommended - included for clarity

Gururattan's Guide to Grains & Legumes

The biggest challenge for vegetarians is to get enough protein without resorting to animal sources, or adding too many calories. Common substitutes for meat are nut butters and cheese, but both are difficult to digest, and if eaten in sufficient quantity, they tax the liver.

The best source of easily digestible protein for vegetarians are grain and legume combinations.

To avoid gas, cook beans with Komba or Wakame Seaweed, and/or add caraway seeds. Black beans cause very little gas. Beans should be soaked overnight before cooking.

A good seasoner and salt substitute, which adds supplementary protein to such meals is Braggs Liquid Aminos. It looks and tastes a little like soy suace, but contains a balanced combination of amino acids without any salt.

Sprouts can top grain dishes or combine with salads for added healthy protein.

Here is my simple formula for preparing main dishes. Modify it according to your tastes and creativity:

1. Rinse beans in hot and then cold water and soak them overnight. If they take longer than the grains to cook, begin them first. (Split peas and mung beans cook in less time than whole beans and peas.)

2. Before cooking grains, rinse them in hot and then cold water first. (All grains, seeds and beans should be rinsed to remove possible mold.)

3. Add ginger and onions.

4. Add vegetables in order of cooking time required.

5. Add seaweed or green vegetables last. Seaweed should be well rinsed and soaked until soft and any sand is removed.

6. Serve with a little olive, almond or sesame oil, Braggs and "Spike", or seasonings of choice. Fresh oil added to the cooked food adds a delicious flavor and is important in the diet.

To every 2 cups of water, add
1 cup of rinsed grains
$\frac{1}{4}$ - $\frac{1}{2}$ cup of soaked legumes
1-2 T chopped ginger
1 chopped onion
Vegetables of choice
Seaweed of choice
Seasoning of choice
Serve with a little olive oil or ghee, Braggs, Spike, or pepper, and top with sprouts or yogurt for added protein (optional).

Favorite beans include mung beans, black beans, adzuki beans, garbanzos and lentils. Favorite grains are millet (not-mucous forming), barley, brown, wild and basmati rice, and quinoa, a high protein grain from South America.

My favorite combinations are millet, together with barley and split yellow peas, carrots and seaweed. Tumeric can be added for color,

Millet and barley, adding a side dish of black beans or garbanzo beans with oil and Braggs,

Millet with tumeric, carrots and butternut squash and a side dish of beans,

Brown and wild rice with carrots, celery and red and green peppers (added at the end to keep their color and crunchiness), served with plain yogurt or tahini.

Mung Beans & Rice.

Recipes

MUNG BEANS & RICE

A balanced, protein meal that can substitute for meat, this dish gives you light, sustained energy.

To 1 gallon of filtered water, add
3 cups rinsed, de-stoned mung beans
4 cups rinsed white basmati rice
5-6 large chopped onions
2 cloves peeled, minced garlic
1 can tomato sauce (optional
1 tsp. tumeric
t tsp. coriander (seeds or ground)
½ tsp cumin (seeds or ground)

(For a hotter dish, double the above spices and add ½ tsp. cayenne. The mung beans can be soaked for a day or two and sprouted, which reduces cooking time to that of rice. In a jar, just cover beans with water, and rinse them twice a day, until tiny sprouts appear.)

Serve with Braggs (or tamari, soy sauce or salt), ghee or olive oil, and (optional) top with yogurt for added protein.

HUMUS

1. Rinse and soak 1 cup garbanzo beans for 12 hours, pouring off soaking water, and adding fresh to cook.

2. Cook beans, bringing them to a boil and then simmering until soft (over an hour). Drain, leaving a little water.

3. In food processor, blend

the cooked beans
½ cup sesame tahini
1 T "Spike"
1 T Soy Sauce, Tamari or Braggs
juice of 2-3 limes
1-2 cloves garlic (optional - elephant garlic is milder)
1 bunch parsley (optional).

Serve with whole-grain sprouted bread in sandwiches, or as a dip with wholesome chips.

CHEDDAR BEETS
A Yogi Bhajan recipe*

Arrange sliced, steamed beets on foil, add black pepper, bay leaves and seasoning to taste, top with cheddar cheese and broil until cheddar is red. Good enough for guests!

COTTAGE BEETS *

(Yogi Bhajan's recipe* with 1 or 2 additions)

To a pint of raw cottage cheese, add
1 medium to large grated beet
1 small to medium grated carrot
grated lemon rind & pepper to taste
OR lemon pepper to taste
a dash of olive oil

Combine and serve with salad or rice dish. This high protein dish is good for the liver and elimination, pleases the palate, and it is beautiful, too!

SPINACH-WATERCRESS SALAD

Wash thoroughly, remove stems and combine

1 bunch fresh spinach
1 bunch fresh water cress
3 or 4 chopped green onions
4 or 5 sliced fresh mushrooms
1 tsp. fresh or dried dill weed
1 clove pressed or minced garlic
Grated lemon peel, salt & pepper to taste OR lemon pepper (Gaylord Hauser), to season
Toss with enough olive oil to shine shine the leaves or with Tahini Salad Dressing.

This scrumptious, vitamin rich, selenium rich, nucleic acid rich salad is also a powerful intestinal cleanser.

TAHINI SALAD DRESSING

½ cup tahini
½ cup olive oil
juice of 3 limes
2 T vinegar
4 T honey
Italian spices
Spike, Braggs, Lemon Pepper to taste
¼ cup water (approximately, may be necessary)
1 bunch parsley
5 stalks celery

Blend until finely chopped.

BREAKFAST MUESLI

The night before, combine

½ cup rye flakes (or rolled oats)

1 tsp carraway (or anise) seeds

2 T raisons or dried dates
1 pt. plain yogurt or
2/3 cup raw goat's or cow milk

for each serving. Soak overnight and serve uncooked with sliced banana.

(Anise, fennel and carraway seeds eliminate mucous. Millet and rye are the least mucous-forming cereals)

EAT TO LIVE, don't live to eat! Energy is wasted in digestion.

January 21, 1970

EARTHY, RED NECTAR

Juice together

2-3 beets
2 large carrots
fresh ginger to taste.

Drink immediately. Delicious!

LICORICE SASSAFRAS TEA

In a pot of water, gently simmer

1 heaping T licorice root
1 heaping T Sassafras root
1 heaping T dried orange peel

for 20-30 minutes, adding water as necessary. Serve with raw milk (to cut astringency) and honey if desired.

This naturally sweet, root-beer flavored tea helps break sugar and coffee addictions. If you drink it without adding honey, you eliminate the craving for sweets (only for as long as you go without them). As it is hearty, and mildly stimulating to the colon, it can substitute for morning coffee. And it is good for the liver and colon.

GOLDEN MILK
(From Yogi Bhajan)*

Boil 1/8 tsp. turmeric in ¼ cup of water for 8 minutes to form a thick paste, adding more water if necessary. Meanwhile, bring 8 oz. of milk to a boil with 2 tbls. of raw almond oil. As soon as it boils, remove from heat and combine the 2 mixtures, adding honey to taste.

This is recommended for arthritis as well as for drug damage

YOGI TEA *

(Can be bought pre-packaged in health food stores, or made at home.)

5 quarts of water
1 T peppercorns
3 T cardamon pods, opened
½ T cloves
5 cinnamon sticks
1 medium chopped ginger root
1 black tea bag
honey to taste
raw milk

Bring water to a boil, add cloves and simmer 1-2 minutes, then add the other spices, simmering at least 45 minutes, then take off the heat, and allow to steep with a black tea bag (optional) for less than 2 minutes.

Strain and add half the amount of water and bring to a boil again. Store and serve with honey to taste, and equal parts of tea and milk, heating as needed.

This tea of Yogi Bhajan's is recommended for energy, cleansing and all-around good health. It is especially good for rebuilding the liver and the brain from damage due to drug use.

---

*NOTE: Recipes with astericks appear in The Ancient Art of Self-NUTRITION compiled by Siri Amir Singh Khalsa, D.C., a fascinating collection of Yogi Bhajan's recipes and recommendations for healing and healthy food. To order, write the Khalsa Clinic, 711 E. 37th Av., Eugene Oregon, 97405

Healing Foods & Herbs For Stress Related Problems

NERVES & STRESS

A diet to reduce stress is one meal a day of mung beans and rice for 28 days, which is also good for meditation and internal cleansing. Add yogurt, green vegetables, another meal of tabouli with lots of parsley and Yogi Tea. Shorter periods of a week or 10 days are beneficial, too. Celery and celery juice with parsley and cucumber are good too. Nature's tranquilizers are the amino acid L-Triptophane and the mineral Calcium, both found in milk. Other kitchen remedies include Caraway, Garlic, Basin, Rosemary (for headache), Tumeric, Nutmeg and Parsley.

<u>Sedative and muscle relaxing herbs</u> include Valerian, Skullcap, Chamomile, Catnip, Lobelia, Lady Slipper, Mugwort, Passion Flower, Hops, Lemon Balm, Wood Betony, Gota Kola, Kava Kava, Hawthorne, Blue Cohosh, Black Cohosh, Rasberry Leaves and Ru. Some of these herbs are toxic in large doses so investigate before use. Oriental herbs for relaxation include Yellow Chrysanthemum Tea, Bupleurum (Ch'ai hu), Eleuthero (Siberian Ginseng), Fu Ling (aka. Poria Cocos or Muk Sheng), Ginseng, (for overcoming fatigue), Jujube Date (Da T'Sao) and Dong Quai.**

KIDNEYS & ADRENALS

Drink lots of hot water upon arising (which also cures constipation and eyesight). Yogi Bhajan recommends a 3 day mono-diet of watermelon to cleanse and heal kidneys.

<u>Herbs for Adrenals and Kidneys</u> are Parsley, Marshmallow Root, Irish Moss, Dandelion and Usa Urvi. Oriental herbs are Fu Ling (or Poria), and Fo Ti (or Ho Shu Wu).**

FOR THE LIVER

Toxins like smoke, smog, aerosol sprays meat, food preservatives, alcohol and drugs can over-tax the liver making it sluggish or worse, with low bile production, constipation, jaundice, loss of energy and grave illness.

Yogi Bhajan advises eating plenty of raw, grated beets for immediate improvement in liver function. He also recommends:

Beet and banana fast of 40 days.

On 11th day of the new moon, steam beets and eat with beet greens, and nothing else on that day.

Eat beets and beet greens until you have red elimination and continue until they are no longer red.

Beet and carrot juice in moderation. *

Other foods mentioned by Yogiji are horseradish, mangos, watermelon, acidophilus, artichoke and daikon radish.*

Common sense bids limit fats, especially animal fats. Avoid alcohol, drugs (including asperin and penicillin and coffee.

Drink lots of pure water.

<u>Herbs for the liver</u> are Dandelion Root, Licorice Root, Sassafras Root, Wild Yam, Oregon Grape Root, Eyebright, Cascara, Mandrake, Camomile and Parsley Oriental herbs include Fo Ti, Peony, Chrysanthemum, Wild Ginger & Bupleurum.** Newly popular is Silymarin or Milk Thistle.

FOR THE EYES

Almonds, daikon radishes "on the 11th day of the new moon, eat Daikon Radishes grated with steamed beets and beet greens and nothing else"- and mangos. An "eye-juice drink" is 6 oz. carrots, 6 oz. celery, 2 oz. endive and 2 oz parsley blended together."*

Herbs for the eyes are Eyebright Tea, and Golden Seal which can be combined with Eyebright Tea in an eyewash.**

Raw potato peels can be applied to the eyes for a miracle refresher. Change them as they dry out, and try it at bedtime to wake up with clear, sparkling eyes.*

Common sense for the eyes includes curtailing TV viewing, especially color TV which is very hard on them. Keep the room well-lit and limit programs.

Sleep in total darkness, leaving neither lights nor TV on.

If you swim in heavily chlorinated pools, wear goggles.

If you wear eye makeup, remove it before retiring. (Bacteria collects and multiplies on mascara and eyeliner, so throw it out every few months, and buy new.

According to Dr. Bates, closing the eyes and envisioning a field of total blackness is a good relaxation exercise, (and a difficult one for many! How completely you can imagine a totally black field of inner perception, corresponds directly to the health of the eyes.) Begin with the image of a black object, like a black velvet jacket, and then expand the blackness to the limits of inner perception. Or, imagine entering a dark tunnel, and see only darkness for as long as possible.***

Dr. Bates also recommends warming the hands by rubbing them together, and then placing the palms over the eyes to relax them.***

FOR ELIMINATION

Eat baked apples just before going to bed to relieve constipation.*

Eat 3 bananas followed by the contents of 1 cardamon pod every hour until the bowels move.*

Live on steamed beets and beet greens for hemorrhoids and obesity for awhile.*

Papaya removes most intestinal disorders.*

To clean stomach and intestines, and for a laxative, finely chop orange peel and saute in olive oil adding tumeric and a little water.*

Eat mangos.*

Eat mung beans and rice.*

Drink lots of hot water upon arising to cure constipation.*

FOR ALCOHOLICS

Mono diet for 3 days of beets and Brewers Yeast.*

---

*From The Ancient Art of Self-Nutrition, (see recipes)

**From The Way of Herbs, by Michael Tierra, C.A., N.D. This book is a comprehensive account of uses of domestic and Oriental herbs.

***From Better Eyesight Without Glasses, by W. H. Bates, M.D., the famed authority on healing one's own eyes through exercise and relaxation.

Establishing a Personal Stress-Reduction Program

Using the techniques in this book can completely change your life for the better. But they must be practiced to work! The more you practice, the more quickly and effectively thew changes will occur.

For significant change, it is recommended that you do at least 30 minutes a day, divided into 2 convenient periods, each consisting of an 11 minute and a 5 minute exercise.

Determine how much time you will realistically be able and willing to devote, and then commit to that. If it is only 5 minutes a day that you are sure you will always perform, then start with that, adding more when you have extra time, but sticking to that minimum 5 minutes daily.

Make a schedule. Decide what needs attention most, and add the less important things later. For example, do the most important exercise on Monday, Wednesday and Friday, (sticking to the same meditation however) and on Tuesday, Thursday and Saturday choose others of less importance.

Groups and friendships are powerful incentives to practice, so if you can, share these exercises with a friend or two. The results and energy will multiply.

To be happy, relaxed and healthy (reasonable and universal goals!), be clear about what you want, and get committed to it. Become consistent in working to achieve your desires and goals. Then you will attain success.

A major part of the task has already been accomplished - you have decided to change your life, and you have acquired the means of doing it! Now, set out on paper your clear, specific goals for the immediate future, and a schedule of exercise and meditation to realize them. Add long term goals, and an overall plan of future exercises and meditations for their achievement.

DON'T JUST HANG AROUND: 'I owe Yogiji a debt!' Be great!!
October 14, 1969

SELF IMPROVEMENT: Discard the past, love the future, respect and understand others.
June 15, 1970

PURITY & GREATNESS of self are required to pass the barrier of the ages. Improve; don't waste a day! Project positivity - truth will prevail.
September 16, 1969

YOU MUST CATCH UP & PROCEED FURTHER THAN YOUR TEACHER, or you will hurt him.
May 7, 1973

18

FUNDAMENTALS OF KUNDALINI YOGA

Kundalini Yoga is an ancient art and science dealing with the alteration and expansion of consciousness, the awakening and raising of KUNDALINI ENERGY up the spine through energy centers called CHAKRAS, activating them. This is accomplished by the mixing and uniting of PRANA (Cosmic Energy) with APANA (eliminating energy) which generates pressure to force Kundalini to rise, by means of PRANAYAMA (breathing exercises), BHANDAS (body locks) in KRIYAS (exercise sets) using ASANAS (postures), MUDRAS (gestures), and MANTRAS (chanted words). Kundalini yoga sets and meditations also use visualization, projection and focussed attention to attain specific effects. This knowledge has been a guarded secret, handed down from Guru to selected students for centuries but thanks to Yogi Bhajan, it is now offered to the public.

Through the practice of Kundalini Yoga an individual can unite his consciousness with Cosmic Consciousness on a regular basis by carefully performing the exercises and meditations in specific sequence and combination. A student soon becomes adept at perceiving the movement of energy within and outside of his body, and consciously begins to direct its flow to stimulate and awaken the chakras, for healing himself and others, and clearly becomes a co-creator with God.

The science is said to be 70,000 years old. Tradition attributes it to the Hindu God Shiva instructing his wife, the Goddess Parvati. The teachings were then imparted only to the initiated in temples and monasteries in India, Nepal and Tibet. Kundalini yoga is closly related to Trantra, which also raises Kundalini energy (Shakti power) to achieve extraordinary consciousness. There are 3 forms of tantra: White Tantra, which is taught by Yogi Bhajan, uniting male and female energy in non-sexual union, Red Tantra which relies on sexual union, and Black Tantra, a form of shamanism.

Kundalini Yoga was brought to the West in 1969 by Yogi Bhajan, the only living Master of White Tantric Yoga on the planet. His followers have adapted the Sikh relition, and they wear the white clothing and turbans with uncut hair that signify purity. All Sikhs do not necessarily practice Kundalini Yoga, and Kundalini yoga devotees are by no means all Sikhs.

COMPONENTS OF KUNDALINI YOGA

KUNDALINI

An incredibly powerful storehouse of psychic energy symbolized as a coiled, sleeping serpent at the base of the spine ('Kundal' means 'curl'). Once awakened it uncoils and ascends through the spinal column (in the psychic channel, SUSHMANA) to the SAHASRARA (the masculine Crown Chakra) at the top of the head, and triggers a transcendent spiritual state. Repeated experiences produce enlightment.

PRANA & APANA

Prana is the basic life force of consciousness in the air we breathe and the food we eat, assimilated effortlessly, and Kundalini yoga practice enhances its absorption. Apana is the eliminating energy stored in the lower chakras. When it is raised and united with prana (by breath retention & body contractions or locks), psychic heat is generated which raises Kundalini through the chakras.

KRIYAS

A series of one or more exercises or postures in combination with pranayama, locks, chanting, visualization, projection, etc. in specific sequence designed to produce specific effects. Some of Yogi Bhajan's kriyas are centuries old. The total effect of a kriya is greater than the sum of its parts. 'Kriya' literally means 'work' or 'action'.

ASANAS

A pose or posture designed to stimulate glands, organs or body awareness, and to quiet the mind for meditation. Asanas often apply pressure on nerves or accupressure points, reflexing to the brain and body for certain effects. The most common meditation asanas are:

EASY POSE (or Sukasana): Cross the legs comfortably at the ankles or both feet on the floor, pressing the lower spine forward to keep the back straight.

PERFECT POSE (Or Siddhasana): Right heel presses against the perineum, sole against left thigh. Left heel is placed on top of the right heel and presses the body above the genitals with the toes tucked into the groove between the right calf and thigh. Knees should be on the ground with heels one directly above the other. This is the most comfortable asana for many and is believed to promote psychic power.

LOTUS (or Padmasana): Lift left foot onto upper right thigh, then place right foot on left thigh as close to the body as possible. This locked in posture is easier to do than it looks and it enhances deep meditation. The right leg is always on top.

ROCK POSE (or Vajrasana): Kneel and sit on heels (tops of feet on the ground) so that they press the nerves in the center of the buttocks. (It is named "Rock Pose" because its effect on the digestive system enables one to digest rocks.)

CELEBATE (or Hero Pose): With feet hip width apart, kneel and sit between the feet. This posture channels sexual energy.

If you sit in a chair, be sure that both feet are flat and evenly placed on the ground, and keep the spine straight.

MUDRAS

A gesture or position, usually of the hands, that locks and guides energy flow and reflexes to the brain. By curling, crossing, stretching and touching the fingers and hands, we can talk to the body and mind as each area of the hand reflexes to a certain part of the mind or body. Some commonly used mudras are:

(In each mudra, exert enough pressure to feel the flow of energy through the "nadis" (psychic channels) up the arms but not enough to whiten fingertips.)

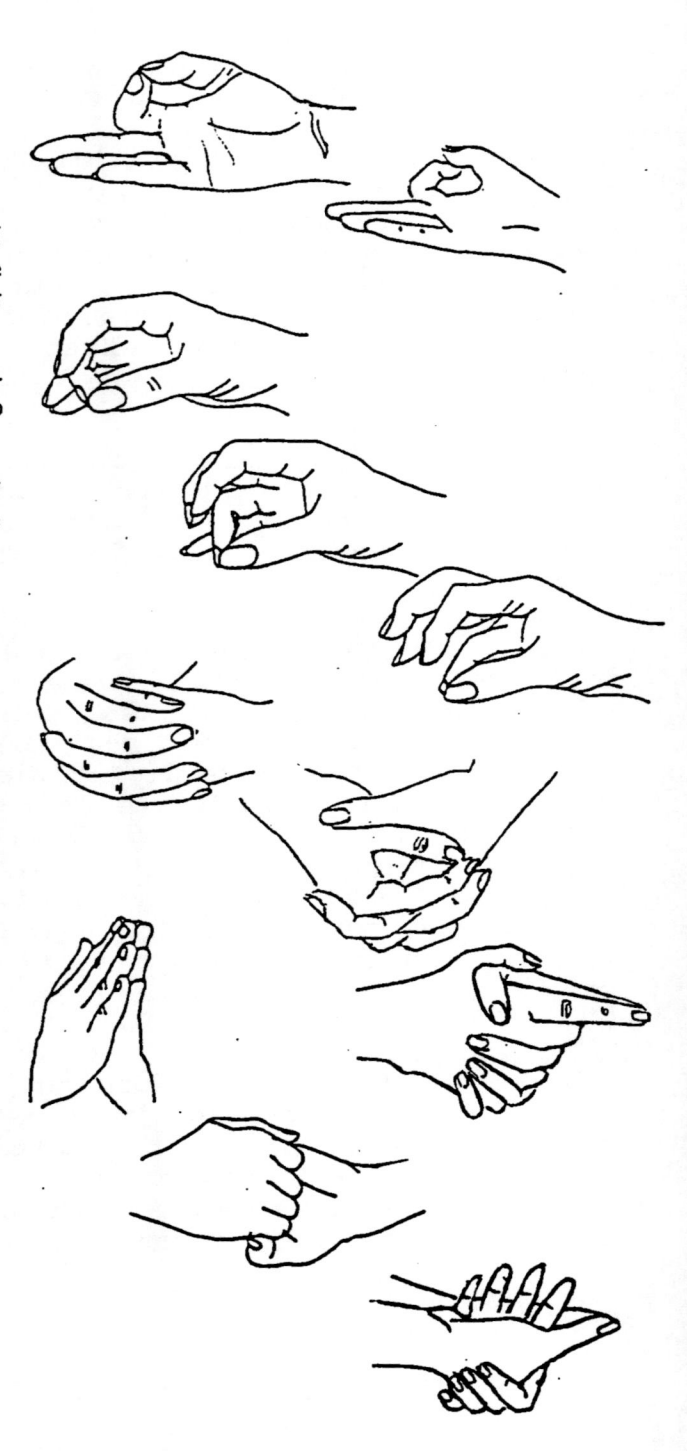

GUYAN MUDRA: The tip of the thumb touches the tip of the index finger, stimulating knowledge and ability. The index finger is symbolized by Jupiter, and the thumb represents the ego. Guyan Mudra imparts receptivity & calm.

ACTIVE GUYAN MUDRA: The first joint of the index finger is bent under the first joing of the thumb, imparting active knowledge.

SHUNI MUDRA: Tip of middle finger (symolized by Saturn) touches the tip of the thumb, giving patience.

SURYA or RAVI MUDRA: Tip of the ring finger (symbolized by Uranus or the Sun) touches the tip of the thumb, giving energy, health and intuition.

BUDDHI MUDRA: Tip of little finger (Mercury) touches tip of thumb for clear and intiuitive communication.

VENUS LOCK: Interlace fingers with left little finger on the bottom, with the right index finger on top for men and the left for women. The Venus mounds at the base of the thumbs are pressed together channeling sensuality and sexuality, and glandular balance, helping to focus and concentrate.

PRAYER MUDRA: Palms are pressed together, neutralizing and balancing yin & yang, for centering.

BEAR GRIP: Left palm faces out from body with thumb down, and right palm faces body, thumb up, and fingers are curled and hooked together to stimulate the heart and intensify concentration.

BUDDHA MUDRA: Right hand rests on left for men, left on right for women, palms up, thumbs tips touching each other in a receptive gesture.

BHANDAS

Body locks or muscular contractions applied for the retention and channeling of Prana. The principle ones are:

MULABHANDA: Mulbhand or Root Lock is the most frequently applied. It is the contraction of the anal sphincter, drawing it in and up (as if trying to hold back a bowel movement), then drawing up the sex organ (so that the urethral tract is contracted). Last, the navel point is drawn back towards the spine. This is applied with breath retention, either in or out, and unites the two major energy energy flows, prana and apana, generating psychic heat which triggers the release of Kundalini energy, and often ends an exercise.

UDDIYANA BHANDA: Diaphragm Lock is aplied by lifting the diaphragm high up into the throax and pulling the upper abdominal muscles back towards the spine, creating a cavity, and giving a gentle massage to the heart muscles. Stimulates the hypothalmic-pituitary-adrenal axis in the brain and develops the sense of compassion. Can give new youthfulness to the entire body. It is applied on the exhale. In Laya yoga, the rhythmic application of this lock achieves the highest effects of chanting.

JALANDHARA BHANDA: Neck Lock or Chin Lock is usied during all chanting meditations. The chin rests in the notch between the collar bones and the head stays level without tilting forward, straightening the cervical vertibrae, and allowing the free flow of prana to the brain. In practice, the chin is pulled straight backwards and slightly lowered. Prevents headaches and uncomfortable pressure in eyes, ears and heart during pranayama.

MAHABHANDA: The application of all 3 locks at once. When all the locks are applied, the nerves and glands are rejuvenated.

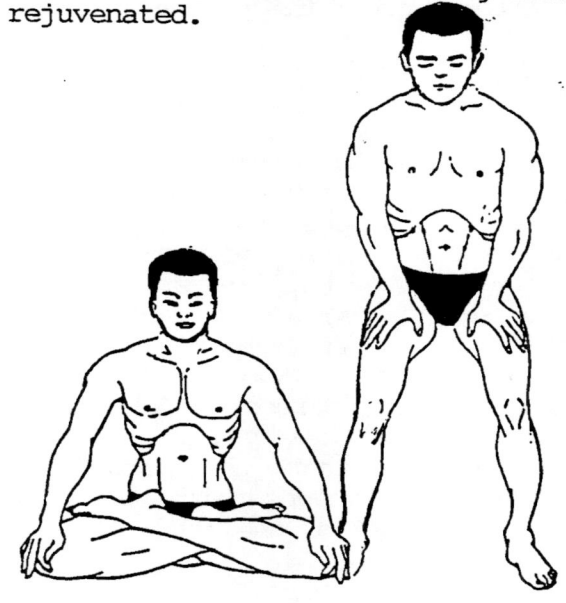

BHANDA EXERCISE

To fully understand & experience the Sit on heels and spread the knees wide apart, palms on thighs. (A) Apply Root Lock & relax it. (B) Apply Diaphram Lock & relax it. (C) Apply Neck Lock and relax it. Repeat in rhythmic alteration for 3-11 minutes, pulling locks on the exhale (the breath naturally goes out on the first 2 locks). PRACTICE ON AN EMPTY STOMACH. This will help to distinguish the locks and perceive energy movement along the spine.

CHAKRAS

In the body, centers of exchange between the psychic and physical dimensions. Like transformers they change subtle prana into physical energy flowing through a system of 'nadis' (psychic channels like the meridian system of Oriental medicine). Chakras are energy vortexes perceived as spinning discs of light ('chakra' means wheel) situated along the spine. Traditionally there are 7 of them and Yogi Bhajan designated the Electro-Magnetic Field (Aura) as the 8th. When the chakras are opened the particular talents of each are assimilated and consolidated into the character and behavior of the person.

ELECTRO-MAGNETIC FIELD: The psychic field of energy surrounding all beings, human or otherwise, through which we project ourselves to others and protect ourselves from danger. A strong aura insures physical health and success. One reason for wearing white is to help expand the aura. (To see auras, close your eyes and think of a famous guru, or a movie or rock star. Next to him, imagine an ordinary person. Beholding the two of them side by side, it is easy to perceive that the "star" has a brilliant, developed aura that clearly outshines that of the other.)

SAHASRARA: The 'Crown Chakra is located at the top of the head and is often pictured as a 1000 petaled lotus. This is the individual's superconsciousness and his link with God and Universal or Cosmic Consciousness & Infinity. It is associated with the Pineal Gland.

AJNA: The 3rd Eye or Brow Chakra is associated with the pituitary gland and it is the seat of intuitive awareness. Located between the eyebrows, it is the home of the "true self", and is pictured as a white light. (One's Guru can seat themselves there to provide guidance.)

VISHUDDHI: The 5th or Throat Chakra is associated with the Thyroid Gland and this is where poisens are purified, respiration is controlled and speech originates. It is perceived as a violet disc, and its proper function ensures truthful speech, a pure and clean body and mind, and some psychic faculties.

ANAHATA: The 4th or Heart Chakra is the seat of compassion, true love, free will and wish-fulfillment. 'Anahata' means 'unbeaten', (reminding us of 'stout hearts' & 'having heart'). It is associated with the Thymus Gland so its strength insures a strong immune system and a glittering aura. It is variously described as pink, red, golden, white, and sometimes as dark blue. To live in the Heart Chakra is to be a well-developed human being.

MANIPURA: The 3rd or Navel (Nabhi) Chakra is the center of power, energy and well-being. It is sometimes regarded as the 'Solar Chakra', and is known as the 'Delight Center', and the 'Jewel in the Lotus' - (Manipura' means 'jeweled lotus'). It is associated with the adrenal glands and is variously pictured as a spinning blue, grey or green disc of light. A strong navel chakra bestows character and physical vitality and power.

SVADISTHANA: The 2nd Chakra, at the sex organs, is the home of Kundalini. It is the seat of creative, sexual energy and is always pictured as a bright red-orange. In balance the person can channel powerful reproductive energy to use for other creativity

MULADHARA: The 1st or Root Chakra is the anal chakra. It is associated with the qualities of stability and security. When it is well functioning, the person is comfortable in physical existence. It is often pictured as a disc of red light.

Mantra

A mantra is a syllable, word or phrase in one of the sacred languages (like Sanscrit & Ghurmeki) and sometimes in English, which elevates or modifies consciousness through its meaning, the sound itself, rhythm, tone, and even the reflexology of the tongue on the palate. Mantra is "The Yoga of the Mind". Some of the most frequently used follow:

AD GURAY NAMEH, JUGAD GURAY NAMEH, SAT GURAY NAMEH, SIRI GURU DEVAY NAMEH is the Mangala Charn Mantra, and is chanted for protection. It surrounds the magnetic field with protective light, and means "I bow to the primal Guru (guiding consciousness who takes us to God-Realization), I bow to wisdom through the ages, I bow to True Wisdom, I bow to the great, unseen wisdom."

ADI SHAKTI, ADI SHAKTI, ADI SHAKTI, NAMO, NAMO, SARAB SHAKTI, SARAB SHAKTI, SARAB SHAKTI, NAMO NAMO, PRITHUM BHAGAWATI, PRITHUM BHAGAWATI, PRITHUM BHAGAWATI, NAMO NAMO, KUNDALINI, MATA SHAKTI MATA SHAKTI, NAMO, NAMO. The First Shakti Mantra tunes into the frequency of the Divine Mother, and to primal protective, generating energy. Chanting it eliminates fears and fulfills desires. Adi Shakti means the "Primal Power," Sarab Shakti means "All Power," and Prithum Bhagawati means "which creates through God."

AKAL, MAHA KAL means "Undying, Great death" is a powerful life-giving chant removing fear and relaxing the mind.

AP SAHAEE HOA SACHE DA SACHE DHOA, HAR, HAR, HAR means "The Lord Himself has become our protector, the Truest of True has taken care of us, God, God, God", or "The Lord HImself is my refuge, true is the support of the True Lord". Chanted for prosperity and protection.

ARDAS BAYE, AMAR DAS GURU, ARDAS BAYE, RAM DAS GURU, RAM DAS GURU, SUCHE SAHE guarantees by the grace of Guru Amar Das, who is hope for the hopeless, and Guru Ram Das, who is King of the Yogis and Bestower of Blessings, past, present and future, that the prayer will be answered, and that all one's needs are provided for, signed, sealed and delivered!

DHARTI HAI, AKASH HAI, GURU RAM DAS HAI. Dharti means "earth" and Akash is Ether, and Guru Ram Das is the venerated 4th Sikh Guru. This is the 1st Sodhung Mantra.

EK ONG KAR, SAT GUR PRASAD is the Magic Mantra so named for its power and sacredness. It is usually chanted in reverse (Ek Ong Kar Sat Gur Prasad, Sat Gur Prasad, Ek Ong Kar). Many pages are devoted to the ecplanation of this mantra and we are warned to chant it in reverence. It means, "There is one Creator - Truth revealed through Guru's grace".

EK ONG KAR, SAT NAM, KARTA PURKH, NIRBHAO, NIRVAIR, AKAL MOORT, AJUNI SAI BHANG, GUR PRASAD, JAP. AD SUCH, JUGAD SUCHIHE SUCH, NANAK HOSI BHEE SUCH is the Mul Mantra, the root of all mantras. It means, "The creator of all is On Truth is His Name. He does everything, fearless, without anger, undying, unborn, self-realized, realized thru Guru's Grace, Meditate: He was true in the beginning, true thru all the ages, true even now. Nanak shall ever be true."

EK ONG KAR, SAT NAM, SIRI WHA (HE) GURU is the Adi Shakti Mantra, and it is very powerful for awakening Kundalini and suspending the mind in bliss. Ek means "One, the essence of all," Ong is the primal vibration from which all creativity flows, Kar is "creation", Sat, "truth", Nam "name" Siri "great", Wha "ecstacy," and Guru is "wisdom". Taken together it means, "There is one Creator whose name is Truth. Great is the ecstacy of that Supreme Wisdom"!

GOBINDE, MUKUNDE, UDARE, APARE, HARING, KARING, NIRNAME, AKAME is the Guru Gaitri Mantra which means "Sustainer, liberator, enlightener, infinite, destroyer, creator, nameless, desireless". It brings stability to the hemispheres of the brain and works on the Heart Center to develop compassion, patience and tolerance, uniting one with the Infinite.

GURU GURU WAHE GURU, GURU RAM DAS GURU calls upon Guru Ram Das in praise of his spiritual guiding light and protective grace.

HAR means Creative Infinity, a name of God. HARA is another form. HARI is the active form of Creation.

HARI NAM, SAT NAM, HARI NAM, HARI. HARI NAM, SAT NAM, SAT NAM, HARI: The name of God is the True Name.

HUM DUM HAR HAR: This mantra opens the Heart Chakra and means "We the universe, God, God."

ONG means Creator - the Primal Vibration from which all creativity flows.

ONG NAMO, GURU DEV NAMO is the Adi Mantra that precedes Kundalini Yoga practice, tuning one in to the higher self. Ong is "Infinite Creative energy in manifestation and activity" ("Om" or Aum is God absolute and unmanifested) Namo is "reverent greetings", implying humility, Guru means "teacher or wisdom Dev means "Divine or of God" and Namo reaffirms humility and reverence. In all it means, "I call upon Divine Wisdom".

ONG SO HUNG is "Creator, I am Thou!" a heart-opening and empowering mantra.

PRANA, APANA, SUSHUMNA, HARI. HARI HAR HARI HAR, HARI HAR, HARI: Prana is the life force, Apana the eliminating force, and Sushumna is the Central channel for that force. This helps draw energy up the spine for healing. Hari and Har are names of God.

PRITVI HAI, AKASH HAI, GURU RAM DAS HAI (see "Dharti Hai") - Pritvi means earth - calling on the name of the venerated Guru Ram Das is very powerful

RA MA DA SA, SA SAY SO HUNG is the Siri Gaitri Mantra, and is chanted for healing. Ra is the sun, Ma is the Moon, Da is the earth, and Sa is Infinity. Say is the totality of Infinity, and So Hung is "I am Thou". "Ra Ma Da Sa" is the Earth Mantra. and "Sa Say So Hung" is the Ether Mantra.

SA TA NA MA is the Panj Shabad expressing the five primal sounds of the universe. "S" is Infinity, "T" is life, "N" means death and "M" is rebirth. (The 5th sound is "A".) This is one of the most frequently used mantras in Kundalini Yoga.

SAT NAM is the Seed Mantra or Bij Mantra and it is the most widely used in the practice of Kundalini Yoga. Sat is truth, Nam means identity, or to call on the truth, expressing the reality of existence. Chanting this mantra awakens the Soul, and more simply means "really" (Y.B.1/14/89)

SAT NARAYAN, WHA HE GURU, HARI NARAYAN SAT NAM: Narayan is the aspect of Infinity that relates to water, and Hari Narayan is Creative sustenance, which makes the one who chants it intuitively clear or healing. Sat Narayan is True Sustainer, Wahe Guru, indescribable Wisdom and Sat Nam, True Identity. This is the ancient Chotay Pad Mantra.

WAHE GURU is the Guru Mantra, the mantra of ecstacy. It is not translatable, but chanting it elevates the spirit.

WAHE GURU, WAHE GURU, WAHE GURU, WAHE JEEO: "The ecstacy of consciousness is my beloved."

PRAYAYAMA

Breathing to channel and direct the flow of prana and alter consciousness & physical state. The most frequent are

BREATH OF FIRE: This is a cleansing and energizing breath, powered by abdominal contractions. Pumping the abdomen forces air out of the lungs, which then re-inflate effortlessly. Breath of fire is fast, usually 2-3 breaths per second through the nose unless otherwise specified.

LONG DEEP BREATHING: This is calming and produces an automatic 'high' if done properly and slowly enough. Place the tongue on the roof of the mouth and inhale as slowly as possible, allowing only a thin stream of air to flow. When you can no longer inhale begin to exhale at the same slow, steady pace. Both inhale and exhale are through the nose. You will fill the lower portion of the lungs first, expanding the abdomen, then the middle, expanding the diaphram, and then the top, expanding the chest. If you can slow the breath down to 6 or fewer breaths per minute (5 seconds of inhale and 5 seconds of exhale), the pituitary is stimulated, automatically activating the 3rd Eye. If you can slow down to 4 or fewer breaths a minute ($7\frac{1}{2}$ second inhale and $7\frac{1}{2}$ second exhale), the Crown Chakra is activated by the Pineal Gland - Instant Cosmic Consciousness!

ALTERNATE NOSTRIL BREATHING: Breathing through the left nostril is tranquilizing and through the right nostril is energizing. There are many combinations of alternate nostril breathing for different purposes. See "Breathing to Change Nostrils at Will" to assert control over the nostrils.

SITALI PRANAYAM: Breathing through the mouth, through a trough made by the curled tongue cools the air and the body. It is used to lower fevers (or the body temperature on hot days) and daily practice is a perscription for good health.

WHISTLE BREATH: Inhaling and/or exhaling throughthe puckered mouth to produce a whistle has a profound effect on consciousness.

BREATH RETENTION: Holding the breath, either in or out is a powerful tool in creating Tapa or psychic heat, and is often used to stimulate Kundalini arousal, alter consciousness, and body chemistry. DIRECTIONS SHOULD BE CAREFULLY FOLLOWED.

MEDITATION

The stilling of the rational, reasoning, dualistic (I am I and everything isn't) egotistical mind to allow the neutral mind to focus awareness on inner reality beyond intellectual concepts, and on outer reality beyond physical, earthly objects. Meditation uses many techniques to achieve this purpose, and produces a calm, sensitive less emotional, alert, intuitive, effective, efficient and self-controlled personality and an enhanced sense of being and consciousness. Consistent meditation promotes inner peace, happiness and life in higher consciousness.

FOCUS OF ATTENTION, VISUALIZATION AND PROJECTION

Important components in the practice of Kundalini Yoga are focus, (we may be asked to gaze at the nose, focus on the spine, a chakra, the breath, a mantra, physical functions or on something outside of the body), visualzation (of energy movement, magnetic fields, thought forms, astral bodies, ether, light, color, etc.) and projections of consciousness out into the universe. These practices develop awareness of the mobility of consciousness, the ability to hold several things in the mind at once and to direct energy movements empowering our sense of dominion and potential impact on the world.

MEDITATION IS CLEANING HOUSE: When you meditate the entire garbage of the subconscious starts floating. Meditation is not pleasant. It cannot be pleasant, otherwise it is not meditation. Meditation is just cleaning the house.

When you sit and meditate, your mind goes berserk. It is a wrestling match. You fight with your own mind and you win.

August 26, 1988
Beads of Truth, Winter '88

KINDNESS TO SELF: Life must start with kindness and kindness MUST be to the self. Kindness to yourself starts at 3:00 am. Whosoever shall sit for $2\frac{1}{2}$ hours in the early morning shall have no problem. Guru Nanak vouches it, guarantees it, stands by it. And that is the secret.

August 26, 1988
Beads of Truth, Winter '88

THE DANCE OF SHIVA: People who know the Truth are many; people who practice Truth are few. The being has a divinity which constitutes the Self. It vibrates at a rate which depends on its connection with the Supreme Supply Line (God). We do not see it, we do not know it, we do not believe it, but the atoms (the protons electrons & neutrons) dance! Their existence is the Dance of Shiva.

Bibliography

Most of the sets and meditations are previously unpublished and many come from Yogi Bhajan's early classes. The dates are given whenever they are available.

Sources of the published sets are indicated in the Table of Contents by the abbreviations noted below.

The Ancient Art of Self-Nutrition, compiled by Siri Amir Singh Khalsa, D.C., Khalsa Clinic, 711 E. 37th Ave. Eugene, Oregon 97405 — SELFNUT

Beads of Truth, 3HO Foundation, Los Angeles, various issues. — BEADS

Healing Through Kundalini - Specific Applications, S.S. Vikram Kaur Khalsa and Dharm Darshan Kaur Khalsa, San Diego, 1987 — HEAL

Keeping Up with Kundalini Yoga, Kundalini Research Institute, (KRI), Pomona, Calif., 1980 — KEEP

Kundalini Maintanence Manual, KRI, 1981 — MAIN

Kundalini Meditation Manual, KRI, 1978 — MED

Kundalini Slim & Trim Exercises, KRI, 1978 — SLIM

Kundalini Yoga for the 80's, KRI, 1980 — Y480

Kundalini Yoga/Sadhana Guidelines, KRI, 1978 — SADA

Kundalini Yoga for Youth & Joy, 3HO Transcripts, Eugene, Oregon, 1983 — JOY

Kundalini Yoga Manual, KRI, 1976 — YOGA

Survival Kit, SS. Vikram Kaur Khalsa & Dharm Darshan Kaur Khalsa, San Diego, 1980 — SURV

Transitions to a Heart-Centered World, Gururattan Kaur Khalsa, PhD., and Ann Marie Maxwell, San Diego, 1988 — HEART

Student notes from early classes were taken by Mark Lamm and Michael Turner. More recent notes were taken by Gururattan Kaur Khalsa from Yogi Bhajan's classes and also those of MSS Gurucharan Singh Khalsa (Millis, Ma.) and the latter are indicated as follows. — NOTES / NOTES-GSK

NOTE: Music mentioned in sets may be obtained by ordering from Golden Temple Recordings, 1605 So. Robertson, Los Angeles, Ca. 90035

YOGI BHAJAN (Siri Singh Sahib Bhai Sahib Harbhajan Singh Khalsa Yogiji) is a true spiritual teacher of the Aquarian Age. He has selflessly shared, without profit motive or commercialization, the science of Kundalini Yoga, and openly taught the secrets of self-knowledge and discovery (that had been guarded for an elite few for thousands of years), to all who desired to learn.

Yogi Bhajan became a Master of Kundalini Yoga at sixteen, after becomming a master of Hatha Yoga. He is the only Mahan (great) Tantric Master on the planet and leads White Tantric Yoga courses, which cleanses the subconscious mind through the balancing of male and female polarities. He bears the title of Siri Singh Sahib, the Chief Religious and Administrative Authority for Sikh Dharma in the Western Hemisphere. In 1960,

In 1969, at age 39, he came to Los Angeles and began teaching yoga. He founded the Happy, Healthy, Holy Organization (3HO), which has expanded to over 150 centers teaching Kundalini Yoga throughout the world. He then founded the Grace of God Movement for the Women of the World, and Khalsa Women;'s Training Camp, both devoted to helping women realize their divinity, dignity and grace. He has received a BA and MA in Economics, and a Ph.D. in Psychology.

GURURATTAN KAUR KHALSA received her Doctorate in Political Science from the the Institute of International Studies in Geneva, Switzerland, and her Masters Degree in International Affairs from Johns Hopkins School of Advanced International Studies. She has taught international environmental and economic development studies, history and philosophy at MIT, Dartmouth College, New Hampshire College and U.S. International University in San Diego, and written a book and published several articles in international journals.

Dr. Khalsa has studied personal development philosophies for 18 years, and studied Kundalini Yoga with Yogi Bhajan for 12 years, and Hatha Yoga for 7. She currently teaches workshops on "The Art and Science of a Successful Woman", "Meditation for Modern Living", "Relax and Rejoice - Stress Reduction in 2-11 minutes", and "Merging - The New Age Relationship."

ANN MARIE MAXWELL RECEIVED HER Bachelor of Fine Arts from the University of California in Berkeley. She is an prize-winning artist, a prize winning writer, and danced professionally for 20 years in over 40 cities in the U.S.A. and Canada. She is the author of <u>The Secret Source of Beauty</u>, and has been a student of yoga for 30 years.

BOOKS BY GURU RATTANA, Ph.D.

The Power of Neutral — Soul Alchemy in Meditation
Explains how the mind works, offers practical ways to direct your meditation practice, and gives you the keys to open the door to your inner journey.

The Gift of Womanhood — Inner Mastery, Outer Mystery
Guru Rattana decodes woman's mysterious design and guides you to find your authentic identity as a sacred woman, using Kundalini Yoga techniques that awaken your soul.

The Inner Art of Love — Awaken Your Heart with Kundalini Yoga
Learn to use the sacred technology of Kundalini Yoga and Meditation to connect with your inner reality, awaken your heart, and become a conscious soul-directed human being.

Transitions to a Heart-Centered World
Offers the most comprehensive resource of the Kundalini Yoga sets and meditations of Yogi Bhajan relating to the empowerment of the lower chakras and opening your heart to unconditional love.
New! 2nd edition, revised and updated. Released March 2014!

Relax and Renew
Takes stress reduction to the level of holistic resolution. The techniques offered in this book, don't just cover up the symptoms, they help cure the problem!

Sexuality and Spirituality
Instead of avoiding sexuality, Yogi Bhajan taught us how to spiritualize sexual energy so that we can enjoy more depth and pleasure in sacred sexual union — a revolutionary concept!

Introduction to Kundalini Yoga
Explains the fundamentals and benefits of Kundalini Yoga and Meditation, and outlines what to expect from and how to begin your spiritual practice.

Your Life Is in Your Chakras
Guru Rattana assembles a unique collection of information, techniques, and teachings on how to develop the faculties and gifts residing in your chakras.

The Destiny of Women Is the Destiny of the World
An inspiring and invaluable handbook that offers every woman a way to elevate her consciousness, unleash her creativity, live her dream, and celebrate her womanhood.

How to Order

Guru Rattana's manuals and an extensive selection of Kundalini Yoga Books, DVDs, and CDs are available from the Yoga Technology Online Store, http://www.yogatech.com, which offers discounted prices and rapid order fulfillment. Special wholesale terms are available for teachers who sign up for our forum.

You can also view a sample streaming video, sign up for Guru Rattana Online Classes, discover a wealth of information about Kundalini Yoga, and read and subscribe to the Guru Rattana Blog.

God bless this world with peace!

Relax and Renew
Offering a Permanent and Successful Treatment for Stress

- ♥ Over 100 Yoga Sets & Meditations
- ♥ Relax & Release Stress in 2-11 mins.
- ♥ Repair Effects of Drug Abuse
- ♥ Get High, Legally & Healthily
- ♥ Rejuvenate Nerves, Liver, Eyes & Memory
- ♥ Energize, Tranquilize

Relax and Renew offers techniques that take stress reduction to the level of spiritual resolution. They don't just cover up the symptoms, they completely cure the problem!

Regular practice of even one of these powerful techniques will change your energy and introduce you to a new dimension of being. This manual even contains a section on quick techniques (2-11 minutes!) for busy, active, stressed-out people who do not have the time for the full scale practice of Kundalini Yoga.

"I want you to know how much the book means to me. After practicing the exercises for just a few weeks, I feel like a new person. It amazes me how much better we all could feel. Most people, esp. in this country, don't realize there is the potential to feel better spiritually as well as physically. I just want to thank you all SO much." - Tara

About the Author

Guru Rattana, Ph.D., (Gururattan Kaur Khalsa) is author of five classic Kundalini Yoga and Meditation manuals: *Transitions to a Heart-Centered World* (also in Spanish), *Relax and Renew, Sexuality and Spirituality, Introduction to Kundalini Yoga* & *Your Life is in Your Chakras*. Also her epic: *The Destiny of Women is the Destiny of the World*. She is President of Yoga Technology, LLC, and Director of Kundalini Rising Teacher Training. She lives in Coronado (San Diego) California.

Guru Rattana received her Doctorate in Political Science from the University of Geneva, Switzerland, and her MA from John Hopkins School of Advanced International Studies in Washington, D.C. and Bologna, Italy. She has worked for the United Nations Environment Program. She has taught International Environment and Development Studies at Dartmouth College, MIT, and New Hampshire College, and Philosophies of Life and History at U.S. International University (San Diego). She has been a lecturer at the Institute of Transpersonal Psychology (Palo Alto, CA) and taught Kundalini Yoga and Meditation at Stanford University Health Improvement Program.

For more information about Guru Rattana, her books, trainings, astrological newsletter - *New Millennium Being* - and Kundalini Yoga & Meditation, go to: http://www.yogatech.com

ISBN 978-1-888029-04-8